THE INDUSTRIAL REVOLUTION IN BRITAIN

Triumph or Disaster?

REVISED EDITION

REVISED EDITION
PROBLEMS IN EUROPEAN CIVILIZATION

THE
INDUSTRIAL REVOLUTION
IN BRITAIN
Triumph or Disaster?

EDITED WITH AN INTRODUCTION BY
Philip A. M. Taylor
UNIVERSITY OF HULL, ENGLAND

D. C. HEATH AND COMPANY
Lexington, Massachusetts

CONTENTS

INTRODUCTION   vii

GLOSSARY   xiii

THE CONFLICT OF OPINION   xiv

ARNOLD TOYNBEE
   The Classical Definition of the Industrial Revolution   1

JAMES PHILLIPS KAY
   Working-Class Conditions in the 1830s, seen in Manchester by
   a Social Reformer   6

ANDREW URE
   Working-Class Conditions in the 1830s, seen by an Enthusiast
   for the Factory System   11

THOMAS S. ASHTON
   Workers' Living Standards: an Early Modern Revision   17

ERIC J. HOBSBAWM
   Pessimism Re-Stated by a Modern Scholar   25

RONALD M. HARTWELL
   Improvement Defended   33

PAUL MANTOUX
   The Destruction of the Peasant Village   43

JONATHAN D. CHAMBERS AND GORDON E. MINGAY
   Enclosures Not Guilty   52

JOHN L. AND BARBARA HAMMOND
   The Rulers and the Masses   63

EDWARD P. THOMPSON
   Variety within the Working Class—and the Facts of Political
   Inequality   73

R. S. NEALE
   The Labourers of Bath   85

SIDNEY G. CHECKLAND
   Improvements Still Unachieved in the Later Nineteenth Century   95

PHYLLIS DEANE
   An Attempted Summing-Up   101

SUGGESTIONS FOR ADDITIONAL READING   111

INTRODUCTION

TEN years ago, it was still possible to combine, in a single volume of readings, two problems: the definition of "Industrial Revolution" and the effects of industrial change, whatever it was to be called, on the working-class standard of life. It is possible no longer. So many books and articles have been written that this new edition is concerned entirely with the Industrial Revolution's effects. Later, perhaps, another volume, prepared by another editor, will be devoted to problems of industrial growth.

Although a high proportion of the excerpts are necessarily new, there are two good reasons for retaining Toynbee's contribution. It includes a convenient summary of the facts of economic change. It expounds a judgment which was widely accepted for many years, both by researchers and popular writers: "The effects of the Industrial Revolution prove that free competition may produce wealth without producing well-being."

Modern scholars have made use of the writings of men who lived through the Industrial Revolution, but they have not found them in agreement about what they saw. Writing in the 1830's, James Kay, a physician, pointed out the physical separation of social classes in Lancashire, the neglect of civic institutions, the drudgery of industrial work, and the impossibility of satisfactory management of homes and children when most women worked in the mills. Although, in his opinion, factory workers' wages were adequate, he was sure that many workers in related occupations, handloom weavers for example, were in dire poverty. In the same decade, however, Andrew Ure was convinced that workers could be comfortable if only they would display more thrift, more self-restraint, more willingness to experiment with saner methods of preparing food. Industrial conflict certainly existed, but it was the workers' fault, though, no doubt, they were swayed by demagogues. Everyone should understand that improvement could come only through regular and honest work, leading to further industrial growth. Ure also tried to demonstrate that the more mechanised the industry, the higher were the wages paid, and the easier the conditions of work. He devoted many pages to refuting his contemporaries' attacks on child labour. He claimed never to have seen brutality towards factory children, who indeed were always cheerful and ready to play on leaving the mill. He put the matter more strongly. Their work itself resembled play: small tasks requiring no physical exertion, with much time doing nothing at all. Their leisure, it is true, was normally made up of fractions of a minute; but some were idle for as many as four minutes at a time.

Modern controversialists necessarily lack the advantages of personal observation, but they can use a great variety of statistical and documentary evidence.

Writing in the 1920's, J. H. Clapham protested mildly against pessimistic assumptions about working-class standards, pointed to the variety of conditions that prevailed, and insisted that, on the whole, improvement took place before the middle of the nineteenth century. J. L. Hammond, in a brief rejoinder, underlined the less tangible elements in the concept "standard of living." The controversy was then suspended for almost twenty years.

It was revived by T. S. Ashton, who had previously written specialised monographs rather than broad interpretations. His contribution was made in two forms. In the article here reprinted, Ashton examined successive types of evidence —population growth, trade expansion, statistics of wages and prices—which might throw light on the problem of living standards. He admitted that the years of war between Britain and France were bad for the workers, but argued that from 1821 some general improvement occurred. Very carefully he demonstrated how many were the fluctuations through time, and how great were the variations from place to place. He presented Lancashire figures he had discovered, and hoped that other researchers would find more of the same kind. One of the improvements he detected in the early nineteenth century was a change in the balance of occupations. A smaller proportion of British workers pursued the depressed callings of farm labourer and handloom weaver: more and more, engaged in factory employment, earned enough to leave them a surplus for newspapers, subscriptions to chapels and friendly societies, and even, to some extent, educating their children. It was unfortunate that, about the same time, Ashton developed his view in a more rhetorical form, in a little book on the Industrial Revolution, and in a contribution to Hayek's *Capitalism and the Historian*, a self-conscious defense of free-enterprise ideology. For some readers, the rather strident tone of this latter essay weakened the force of the cautious and scholarly work on which, in the author's view, it was firmly based.

What now looks like a rejoinder, though it was not expressed in exactly that way, appeared just too late to be included in my first edition. Hobsbawm pointed out the deterioration in mortality figures in the 1820's and 1830's, which indicated bad urban conditions. He suggested that considerable unemployment must have existed, affecting the validity of wage statistics. He suggested that the few available figures on food consumption pointed to a very low standard of living. Although evidence was seldom conclusive, he saw nothing to refute the pessimistic conclusions of so many firsthand observers. With population rising and distribution unequal, why should workers have benefited, in those early years, from the rise in gross national product? Much later in the nineteenth century, his own researches had shown, there existed a small "labour aristocracy," a large group in poverty, and nearly half the workers in between these extremes. Why should the early years of the century have seen anything better? Certainly, he thought, the onus of proof still rested on the optimists.

A spokesman for these optimists was not long in appearing. Hartwell stressed the overall improvement in the British gross national product per head. More workers, he argued, were coming to be employed in the better-paid jobs, while the prices of manufactured goods they used were at the same time falling fast. Several pieces of positive evidence suggested improved standards: food production at home rose faster than population; some workers could afford to deposit money in savings banks and building societies, and to organise cooperatives. He insisted that improvement in the 1840's was marked. He argued against the fallacy of a golden age for workers in the previous century. Standards in the Industrial Revolution were indeed low. They were not deteriorating, though, with the development of a public conscience, abuses were more often exposed.

So far, the controversy has referred to industrial workers. Even in the middle of the nineteenth century, however, agriculture employed far more people than any branch of manufacturing. As to these rural workers, the pessimists among historians have been represented by Mantoux and the Hammonds, and since the latters' book was so much concerned with one episode, the risings of 1830 in the southern counties, Mantoux's treatment is here preferred. British farming, Mantoux argued, saw technical improvement, due to the rise of the "business spirit," and this enabled industrial workers in new towns to be fed. But the dislocation of traditional routines led to widespread displacement of workers, who went into industry because cut off from their traditional occupations; and this process was effected under pressure from the greater landowners, who possessed political power.

The most recent survey of agricultural change starts from quite different assumptions. Agriculture is an economic activity, in which skilled management extracts returns from soil, livestock, implements, human labour, and the opportunities of the market. With few inventions and, down to the middle of the nineteenth century, a very imperfect spread of new techniques, improvement came mostly from a reorganisation of existing resources, and this meant enclosure, replacing open fields by consolidated farms under individual management. Chambers and Mingay insist that the Enclosure Commissioners were usually fair; that very small farmers gained from the rise in land values; that labourers, who lost customary rights, gained from the many jobs which the enclosures themselves produced. They argue, in this connection, that widespread rural poverty was to be found, not so much in the newly-enclosed Midlands as in the southern counties which had been enclosed long before. They insist that the workers' standard of living depended, not on the existence or absence of enclosure, but on the proximity of alternative work in industry. What matters, then, in these writers' opinion, is a series of economic conditions, not the phenomena of political power and of injustice between classes which obsessed earlier scholars since Toynbee.

From the controversy as thus far summarised, several questions begin to emerge. Much seems to depend on the distribution, between social groups, of a national income which certainly rose. There is little statistical evidence on this. Certainly it is not enough to say that workers "must" have had a share in the improvement. As for wages and prices, historians agree that the 1780's saw gains in wages and in the amount they would buy. They agree that the long war against the French wiped out these gains. They agree, more or less, that the 1840's saw the beginning of substantial improvement. Disagreement continues over the 1820's and 1830's: did those decades show a worsening of conditions, or did they contribute to a slight improvement? The question still remains, however, improvement for whom? It is not enough to say, for the country as a whole, nor even, for the working class as a whole, for that class was far from a single unit. Whose wages rose? Who had the steady jobs, secure in face of business cycles? Who, exactly, had a surplus to spend on comforts, amenities and new institutions? Even the concept "standard of living" permits debate. Is it enough to define it as real wages which, more or less, can be measured? Or is it, rather, a composite phenomenon, made up of real wages, working conditions, housing, and the urban environment as a whole? Does it include the character of family life, and even relations with other social classes? If it is anything like the latter, then many psychological factors enter.

Workers newly settled in towns, newly confronted with large-scale organisation, newly subjected to the discipline of factory work, could develop feelings about hardship and injustice, about change itself, which would affect their judgment of the monetary component of their standard of life. Moreover, is economic life a closed system, or are such facts as class relations and the distribution of power relevant to the organisation of farming and industry, and to the distribution of a nation's economic gains?

Scholars have thrown light on several of these problems; and many contributions have been made within the past ten years.

As so often in their writings, the Hammonds are concerned with the less material elements in the working-class standard of life. For them, the significant fact is that the new industrial development occurred when there was excessive worship of profit and a general disposition to regard workers as instruments. Hence, while poverty was not new, inequality in society was greater than ever, the sense of public responsibility among the rich unprecedentedly low, and a humane urban environment therefore impossible to attain. "The new factories," as they put it, "were like the pyramids, telling of man's enslavement rather than of his power."

Thompson's highly controversial book *The Making of the English Working Class* throws light in two directions that are relevant to our inquiry. Thompson insists that exploitation was a consequence of the way in which power was distributed, and that many workers in the early nineteenth century saw this even if some modern historians look away from it. Economic fluctuations which affected the workers did so "not directly, but through the refraction of a particular system of ownership and power which distributed the gains and losses with gross partiality." Later in his book, Thompson turns to the variety within the working class. He distinguishes between old elites of craftsmen, new elites of workers in iron, textiles and engineering, and the masses of unskilled men. He insists that, by the 1830's, the traditional artisan class was in collapse.

He is sure, too, that in the newer industries, the Industrial Revolution "first multiplied hand-workers . . . and then extinguished their livelihood with new machinery."

There was variety of place as well as of job, and it is with this that R. S. Neale is concerned. He studies labourers around Bath, employed by the Overseers of Highways, and from unusually full and continuous figures of their wages, and of retail prices in the city, he calculates their real wages. He concludes that by 1812 these were fifty percent lower than in 1780; that by the mid-1830's they were seventy percent higher than in 1812; and that, after a brief setback, they rose, by 1840, to twice the 1812 level. Neale also adopts the interesting concept of the "age cohort." A labourer starting work in the 1780's and continuing for thirty years would have experienced little but disaster. One starting in the 1790's would have worked long enough to see a significant recovery in standards. One starting work in the early 1800's would have seen first loss, then gain, then a further brief loss.

Checkland is not participating in the controversy; yet his study of the British economy down to the 1880's throws some light upon it. He shows the extreme squalor of unplanned cities, with improvement beginning under any satisfactory organisation only in the 1870's. Late in the century, the backlog of social evils was enormous; and throughout the Victorian age the standard of life of all workers but the "labour aristocracy" remained meagre in the extreme.*

Phyllis Deane attempts a judicious summing-up. Throughout, she tries to discover areas of agreement between scholars and to identify the areas of controversy that remain. She is convinced that the Industrial Revolution, and the French wars too, had several contradictory effects: the wars depressed real wages as a whole, but promoted full employment and caused some industries to grow. She points out the unsatisfactory nature of statistical evidence in those days. She sees the controversy narrowing to conditions in the 1820's and 1830's. In those decades, national income figures suggest substantial improvement, but distribution between social groups remains uncertain. Wage and price figures suggest somewhat higher real wages; but some unknowable part of the gain was nullified by unemployment. Very cautiously Miss Deane concludes that some very small improvement probably occurred.

Controversy about working-class living standards in the Industrial Revolution reflects in part uncertainties in the evidence. In part it reflects ideological presuppositions among modern writers. Very largely, however, it reflects a dilemma universal among historians: whether history should be written from outside, as it were, or from inside the subject. Whenever he can, the historian is no doubt under an obligation to attempt both, as, bound by his fragmentary evidence and his own imperfect imagination and skill, he goes about his impossible task of rethinking the thoughts and reliving the lives of dead men. All of them, however, are likely to work more in the one direction than the other.

It is a pronounced modern tendency to emphasise the business system, to analyse factors of growth, and to assume that, since in the long run all was justified by results, it is a calm understanding of technical development that is required. Such historians, in a sense, are studying a closed economic order: Ashton, for example, is prone to argue that it was politicians, with their erroneous laws and disturbing wars, who prevented the entrepreneurs from demonstrating more quickly the benefits of the new industrial system. Within the limits of imperfect data, such an approach answers some questions very well. Yet the limits must be emphasised. We know little of unemployment or underemployment. We know too little about working-class consumption: did most workers really use the manufactured goods whose prices demonstrably fell, or even consume the meat and other foodstuffs about which historians argue? We know remarkably

*My mother can remember a small Essex town, c. 1900, in which, after each harvest, farm workers went to a draper's shop for the family's outfit of clothes, and were treated to a glass of beer when they paid. Only from additional earnings was such an outlay possible.

little about the distribution of national income; and some modern conclusions are of the order of "it must have been," "can we doubt that," or "it is my guess."

Politicians, however, are, and were, as real as businessmen. In the era of the Industrial Revolution, power in Britain was concentrated in very few hands; and the working class neither participated in politics, save by occasional riots, nor had much opportunity for industrial bargaining. The rulers of Britain were ambitious, confident of their own title to rule, but fearful of economic competition and political contamination from abroad, fearful of working-class agitation and revolt, and resentful of the obstacles which workers' traditional attitudes put in the way of progress. The slogan "laissez-faire, laissez-passer," after all, means "Get out of my way, let me get on with the job"; and entrepreneurs were impatient of all restraints, derived from whatever source. From time to time, indeed, one is tempted to say that class hatred downward was even more acute than the more commonly discussed class hatred looking up the social scale.

What, above all, is lost in much of the modern technical approach is a sense of the reality of working-class life. Few modern scholars, living in affluent societies, can imagine life at the level of subsistence, with frugal diet, barren environment, and almost no leisure. About such things, indices have little to say, and even family budgets may be hard to interpret, though the "age-cohort" approach may be one useful way of looking at the changes of fortune in working-class families. What is needed may be a revival of interest in contemporary observers. Doubtless there was only one Mayhew in the nineteenth century, and doubtless London had features that were unique. But when I read his investigations into life in the capital, with its variety of petty trades called forth by industry (even the collecting of dog's dung) and the wretched living-standards which themselves called forth such trades as the selling of second-hand articles in minute quantities and at amazingly low prices, then, for my part, I long for more such intelligent observers, who will take me into the squalid lodgings, show me the scanty fare, furniture and dress, and allow me to hear the accents and rhythms of speech of the labouring poor.

GLOSSARY

Although no attempt is made to annotate all authors and books referred to by the scholars whose works are cited, nor to explain all factual details, it may be useful to define a few words, which might not be found, in any relevant form, in a dictionary.

CHARTISTS   Members of a working-class organisation, active in Britain between 1837 and 1848. Their political programme, embodied in Six Points, sought a more democratic House of Commons. Such a reformed legislature, they hoped, would inaugurate sweeping social reform.

COMMON (OR OPEN) FIELDS   Fields around villages in the Middle Ages and later, within which cultivators held land in small and scattered strips, undivided by fences or hedges. Property-holding was individual, but the planning of crops necessarily involved many decisions taken in common.

COMMONS (OR WASTE)   That portion of a village's land which was permanent natural pasture, on which villagers could graze livestock roughly in proportion to their arable holdings in the open fields.

CONSOLS   British government securities, bearing fairly low rates of interest but representing the safest possible investment. Sometimes referred to as gilt-edged securities.

COPYHOLDER   Villager who held his land "by copy of court roll," a tenure of late medieval origin, but very common down to the eighteenth century. Such a man was something less than an owner; but his rent was more or less fixed (not, like a lease, subject to periodic review), and tenure was hereditary, though a "fine" was payable to the lord at each succession of an heir.

DOMESTIC (OR PUTTING-OUT OR OUTWORK) SYSTEM   Form of industrial organisation in which people worked in their own homes, with hand operated machinery often owned by themselves. Their material was distributed to them, and their finished product collected, by a capitalist who was responsible for marketing. This man became in a sense an employer, but exerted no detailed supervision or discipline of the factory type.

FARMER   In British usage, a tenant not an owner, though he might hold a considerable acreage and be a prosperous man.

GUILD (in modern times, usually spelled GILD)   Medieval organisation of master workers in a single craft. Their aim was in part economic, to supervise workmanship and to restrict entry, but partly social, a primitive and local form of social security.

NEW POOR LAW   The Act of 1834, superseding the Speenhamland System which has spread widely from the 1790's. Boards of Guardians were elected by the more prosperous inhabitants of a district. They provided relief at home for sick and disabled people. The able-bodied poor, however, had to live in workhouses under conditions, including separation of the sexes, designed to be "less eligible" than any encountered in paid employment.

TRUCK   Payment of wages, not in cash but in orders on a shop owned by the employer, the TOMMY-SHOP. Only in the second half of the nineteenth century did successive laws drive the system out of existence.

YEOMEN   A colloquial rather than a technical expression. It usually meant a freeholder, owning land on a modest scale, of respectable status but not ranked as a gentleman. Such men could hold offices, below the rank of Justice of the Peace; and, if their holdings were worth forty shillings or more a year, they were entitled to vote in parliamentary elections in their counties.

THE CONFLICT OF OPINION

One contemporary thought:

> To condemn man to such severity of toil is, in some measure, to cultivate in him the habits of an animal.
>
> —JAMES KAY

Another retorted:

> In an establishment for spinning or weaving cotton, all the hard work is performed by the steam-engine. . . . The factory system, instead of being detrimental to the comfort of the labouring population, is its grand Palladium; for the more complicated and extensive the machinery required for any manufacture, the less risk is there of its agents being injured by the competition of foreign manufactures, and the greater inducement and ability has the mill-owner to keep up the wages of his work-people.
>
> —ANDREW URE

Many scholars are convinced that working-class living standards were deteriorating during the wars with France and for a generation afterwards:

> The classical view has been put in Sidney Webb's works: 'If the Chartists in 1837 had called for a comparison of their time with 1787, and had obtained a fair account of the actual social life of the working-man at the two periods, it is almost certain that they would have recorded a positive decline in the standard of life of large classes of the population.' This view has not been so far made untenable.
>
> —ERIC J. HOBSBAWM

Others admit the existence of poverty, but insist on the fact of improvement, and on the coming into being of a keener social conscience:

> The standard of living of the mass of the people of England was improving in the first half of the nineteenth century, slowly during the war, more quickly after 1815, and rapidly after 1840 . . . Evils that had long existed—child labour, for example—and had long been accepted as inevitable, were regarded as new ills to be remedied rather than as old ills to be endured.
>
> —RONALD M. HARTWELL

As for the rural masses:

> Industry was in fact the only refuge for thousands of men who found themselves cut off from their traditional occupations. The manufacturers were to offer them the living they could no longer earn on the land.
>
> —PAUL MANTOUX

But modern specialists disagree:

> Enclosure meant more food for the growing population, more land under cultivation and, on balance, more employment in the countryside; and enclosed farms provided the framework for the new advances of the nineteenth century.
>
> —JONATHAN D. CHAMBERS AND GORDON E. MINGAY

But perhaps more than material issues were at stake:

> In adapting the new power to the satisfaction of its wants England could not escape from the moral atmosphere of the slave trade: the atmosphere in which it was the fashion to think of men as things.
>
> —JOHN L. AND BARBARA HAMMOND

Arnold Toynbee

THE CLASSICAL DEFINITION OF THE INDUSTRIAL REVOLUTION

Toynbee's *Lectures on the Industrial Revolution* appeared after his death in 1883, at the age of thirty-one. The book derived its influence partly from its own merits as a pioneer summary, but largely from Toynbee's personality. Although he was no doctrinaire, and was a member of no organised movement, his deep interest in working-class conditions, his desire for greater lay influence in the Church of England, and his criticism of the dogmas of nineteenth-century economics, all made a deep impression on his contemporaries at Oxford, most of whom lived into the present century. The study of economic history, reforms in the Church, workers' education, and the famous settlement in the East End of London that bears his name, all owe something to Toynbee.

THE essence of the Industrial Revolution is the substitution of competition for the mediaeval regulations which had previously controlled the production and distribution of wealth. On this account it is not only one of the most important facts of English history, but Europe owes to it the growth of two great systems of thought—Economic Science, and its antithesis, Socialism. The development of Economic Science in England has four chief landmarks, each connected with the name of one of the four great English economists. The first is the publication of Adam Smith's *Wealth of Nations* in 1776, in which he investigated the causes of wealth and aimed at the substitution of industrial freedom for a system of restriction. The production of wealth, not the welfare of man, was what Adam Smith had primarily before his mind's eye; in his own words "the great object of the Political Economy of every country is to increase the riches and power of that country." His great book appeared on the eve of the Industrial Revolution. A second stage in the growth of the science is marked by Malthus's *Essay on Population,* published in 1798, which may be considered the product of that revolution, then already in full swing. Adam Smith had concentrated all his attention on a large production; Malthus directed his inquiries, not to the causes of wealth but to the causes of poverty, and found them in his theory of population. A third stage is marked by Ricardo's *Principles of Political Economy and Taxation,* which appeared in 1817, and in which Ricardo sought to ascertain the laws of the distribution of wealth. Adam Smith had shown how wealth could be produced under a system of industrial freedom, Ricardo showed how wealth is distributed under such a system, a problem which could not have occurred to any one before his time. The fourth stage is marked by John Stuart Mill's *Principles of Political Economy,* published in 1848. Mill himself asserted that "the chief merit of his treatise" was the distinction drawn between the laws of production and those of distribution, and the problem he tried to solve was, how wealth *ought to be* distributed. A great advance was made by Mill's attempt to show what was and what was not inevitable under a system of free competition. In it we see the influence which the rival system of Socialism was already beginning to exercise upon the economists.

From Arnold Toynbee, *Lectures on the Industrial Revolution* (Rivington, London, 1884), Lecture VIII, pp. 85–93. The same passage occupies pp. 64–73 in the 1927 reprint. Documenting footnotes in this and subsequent selections have been omitted.

The whole spirit of Mill's book is quite different from that of any economic works which had up to his time been written in England. Though a re-statement of Ricardo's system, it contained the admission that the distribution of wealth is the result of "particular social arrangements," and it recognised that competition alone is not a satisfactory basis of society.

Competition, heralded by Adam Smith, and taken for granted by Ricardo and Mill, is still the dominant idea of our time; though since the publication of the *Origin of Species*, we hear more of it under the name of the "struggle for existence." I wish here to notice the fallacies involved in the current arguments on this subject. In the first place it is assumed that all competition is a competition for existence. This is not true. There is a great difference between a struggle for mere existence and a struggle for a particular kind of existence. For instance, twelve men are struggling for employment in a trade where there is only room for eight; four are driven out of that trade, but they are not trampled out of existence. A good deal of competition merely decides what kind of work a man is to do; though of course when a man can only do one kind of work, it may easily become a struggle for bare life. It is next assumed that this struggle for existence is a law of nature, and that therefore all human interference with it is wrong. To that I answer that the whole meaning of civilisation is interference with this brute struggle. We intend to modify the violence of the fight, and to prevent the weak being trampled under foot.

Competition, no doubt, has its uses. Without competition no progress would be possible, for progress comes chiefly from without; it is external pressure which forces men to exert themselves. Socialists, however, maintain that this advantage is gained at the expense of an enormous waste of human life and labour, which might be avoided by regulation. But here we must distinguish between competition in production and competition in distribution, a difference recognised in modern legislation, which has widened the sphere of contract in the one direction, while it has narrowed it in the other. For the struggle of men to outvie one another in production is beneficial to the community; their struggle over the division of the joint produce is not. The stronger side will dictate its own terms; and as a matter of fact, in the early days of competition the capitalists used all their power to oppress the labourers, and drove down wages to starvation point. This kind of competition has to be checked; there is no historical instance of its having lasted long without being modified either by combination or legislation, or both. In England both remedies are in operation, the former through Trades-Unions, the latter through factory legislation. In the past other remedies were applied. It is this desire to prevent the evils of competition that affords the true explanation of the fixing of wages by Justices of the Peace, which seemed to Ricardo a remnant of the old system of tyranny in the interests of the strong. Competition, we have now learnt, is neither good nor evil in itself; it is a force which has to be studied and controlled; it may be compared to a stream whose strength and direction have to be observed, that embankments may be thrown up within which it may do its work harmlessly and beneficially. But at the period we are considering it came to be believed in as a gospel, and, the idea of necessity being superadded, economic laws deduced from the assumption of universal unrestricted competition were converted into practical precepts, from which it was regarded as little short of immoral to depart.

Coming to the facts of the Industrial Revolution, the first thing that strikes us is the far greater rapidity which marks the growth of population. Before 1751 the largest decennial increase, so far as we can calculate from our imperfect materials, was 3 per cent. For each of the next three decennial periods the increase was 6 per cent.; then between 1781 and 1791 it was 9 per cent.; between 1791 and 1801, 11 per cent.; between 1801 and 1811, 14 per cent.; between 1811 and 1821, 18 per cent. This is the highest figure ever reached in England, for since 1815 a vast emigration has been always tending to moderate it; between 1815 and 1880 over eight millions (including Irish) have left our shores. But for this our normal rate of increase would be 16 or 18 instead of 12 per cent. in every decade.

Next we notice the relative and positive decline in the agricultural population. In 1811 it constituted 35 per cent. of the whole population of Great Britain; in 1821, 33 per cent.; in 1831, 28 per cent. And at the same time its actual numbers have decreased. In 1831 there were 1,243,057 adult males employed in agriculture in Great Britain; in 1841 there were 1,207,989. In 1851 the whole number of persons engaged in agriculture in England was 2,084,153; in 1861 it was 2,010,454, and in 1871 it was 1,657,138. Contemporaneously with this change, the centre of density of population has shifted from the Midlands to the North; there are at the present day 458 persons to the square mile in the counties north of the Trent, as against 312 south of the Trent. And we have lastly to remark the change in the relative population of England and Ireland. Of the total population of the three kingdoms, Ireland had in 1821 32 per cent., in 1881 only 14.6 per cent.

An agrarian revolution plays as large a part in the great industrial change of the end of the eighteenth century as does the revolution in manufacturing industries, to which attention is more usually directed. Our next inquiry must therefore be: What were the agricultural changes which led to this noticeable decrease in the rural population? The three most effective causes were: the destruction of the common-field system of cultivation; the enclosure, on a large scale, of common and waste lands; and the consolidation of small farms into large. We have already seen that while between 1710 and 1760 some 300,000 acres were enclosed, between 1760 and 1843 nearly 7,000,000 under-went the same process. Closely connected with the enclosure system was the substitution of large for small farms. In the first half of the century Laurence, though approving of consolidation from an economic point of view, had thought that the odium attaching to an evicting landlord would operate as a strong check upon it. But these scruples had now disappeared. Eden in 1795 notices how constantly the change was effected, often accompanied by the conversion of arable to pasture; and relates how in a certain Dorsetshire village he found two farms where twenty years ago there had been thirty. The process went on uninterruptedly into the present century. Cobbett, writing in 1826, says: "In the parish of Burghclere one single farmer holds, under Lord Carnarvon, as one farm, the lands that those now living remember to have formed fourteen farms, bringing up in a respectable way fourteen families." The consolidation of farms reduced the number of farmers, while the enclosures drove the labourers off the land, as it became impossible for them to exist without their rights of pasturage for sheep and geese on common lands.

Severely, however, as these changes bore upon the rural population, they wrought, without doubt, distinct improvement from an agricultural point of view. They meant the substitution of scientific for unscientific culture. "It has been found," says Laurence, "by long experience, that common or open fields are great hindrances to the public good, and to the honest improvement which every one might make of his own." Enclosures brought an extension of arable cultivation and the tillage of inferior soils; and in small farms of 40 to 100 acres, where the land was exhausted by repeated corn crops, the farm buildings of clay and mud walls and three-fourths of the estate often saturated with water, consolidation into farms of 100 to 500 acres meant rotation of crops, leases of nineteen years, and good farm buildings. The period was one of great agricultural advance; the breed of cattle was improved, rotation of crops was generally introduced, the steam-plough was invented, agricultural societies were instituted. In one respect alone the change was injurious. In consequence of the high prices of corn which prevailed during the French war, some of the finest permanent pastures were broken up. Still, in spite of this, it was said in 1813 that during the previous ten years agricultural produce had increased by one-fourth, and this was an increase upon a great increase in the preceding generation.

Passing to manufactures, we find here the all-prominent fact to be the substitution of the factory for the domestic system, the consequence of the mechanical discoveries of the time. Four great inventions altered the character of the cotton manufacture; the spinny-jenny, patented by Hargreaves in 1770; the water-frame, invented by Arkwright the year before; Crompton's mule introduced in 1779, and the self-acting mule, first invented by Kelly in 1792, but not brought into use till Roberts improved it in 1825. None of these by themselves would have revolutionised the industry. But in 1769—the year in which Napoleon and Wellington were born—James Watt took out his patent for the steam-engine. Sixteen years later it was applied to the cotton manufacture. In 1785 Boulton and Watt made an engine for a cotton-mill at Papplewick in Notts, and in the same year Arkwright's patent expired. These two facts taken together mark the introduction of the factory system. But the most famous invention of all, and the most fatal to domestic industry, the power-loom, though also patented by Cartwright in 1785, did not come into use for several years, and till the power-loom was introduced the workman was hardly injured. At first, in fact, machinery raised the wages of spinners and weavers owing to the great prosperity it brought to the trade. In fifteen years the cotton trade trebled itself; from 1788 to 1803 has been called its "golden age"; for, before the power-loom but after the introduction of the mule and other mechanical improvements by which for the first time yarn sufficiently fine for muslin and a variety of other fabrics was spun, the demand became such that "old barns, cart-houses, out-buildings of all descriptions were repaired, windows broke through the old blank walls, and all fitted up for loom-shops; new weavers' cottages with loom-shops arose in every direction, every family bringing home weekly from 40 to 120 shillings per week." At a later date, the condition of the workman was very different. Meanwhile, the iron industry had been equally

revolutionised by the invention of smelting by pit-coal brought into use between 1740 and 1750, and by the application in 1788 of the steam-engine to blast furnaces. In the eight years which followed this later date, the amount of iron manufactured nearly doubled itself.

A further growth of the factory system took place independent of machinery, and owed its origin to the expansion of trade, an expansion which was itself due to the great advance made at this time in the means of communication. The canal system was being rapidly developed throughout the country. In 1777 the Grand Trunk canal, 96 miles in length, connecting the Trent and Mersey, was finished; Hull and Liverpool were connected by one canal while another connected them both with Bristol; and in 1792, the Grand Junction canal, 90 miles in length, made a water-way from London through Oxford to the chief midland towns. Some years afterwards, the roads were greatly improved under Telford and Macadam; between 1818 and 1829 more than a thousand additional miles of turnpike road were constructed; and the next year, 1830, saw the opening of the first railroad. These improved means of communication caused an extraordinary increase in commerce, and to secure a sufficient supply of goods it became the interest of the merchants to collect weavers around them in great numbers, to get looms together in a workshop, and to give out the warp themselves to the workpeople. To these latter this system meant a change from independence to dependence; at the beginning of the century the report of a committee asserts that the essential difference between the domestic and the factory system is, that in the latter the work is done "by persons who have no property in the goods they manufacture." Another direct consequence of this expansion of trade was the regular recurrence of periods of overproduction and of depression, a phenomenon quite unknown under the old system, and due to this new form of production on a large scale for a distant market.

These altered conditions in the production of wealth necessarily involved an equal revolution in its distribution. In agriculture the prominent fact is an enormous rise in rents. Up to 1795, though they had risen in some places, in others they had been stationary since the Revolution. But between 1790 and 1833, according to Porter, they at least doubled. In Scotland, the rental of land, which in 1795 had amounted to £2,000,000, had risen in 1815 to £5,278,685. A farm in Essex, which before 1793 had been rented at 10s. an acre, was let in 1812 at 50s., though, six years after, this had fallen again to 35s. In Berks and Wilts, farms which in 1790 were let at 14s., were let in 1810 at 70s., and in 1820 at 50s. Much of this rise, doubtless, was due to money invested in improvements—the first Lord Leicester is said to have expended £400,000 on his property—but it was far more largely the effect of the enclosure system, of the consolidation of farms, and of the high price of corn during the French war. Whatever may have been its causes, however, it represented a great social revolution, a change in the balance of political power and in the relative position of classes. The farmers shared in the prosperity of the landlords; for many of them held their farms under beneficial leases, and made large profits by them. In consequence, their character completely changed; they ceased to work and live with their labourers, and became a distinct class. The high prices of the war time thoroughly demoralised them, for their wealth then increased so fast, that they were at a loss what to do with it. Cobbett has described the change in their habits, the new food and furniture, the luxury and drinking, which were consequences of more money coming into their hands than they knew how to spend. Meanwhile, the effect of all these agrarian changes upon the condition of the labourer was an exactly opposite and most disastrous one. He felt all the burden of high prices, while his wages were steadily falling, and he had lost his common-rights. It is from this period, viz., the beginning of the present century, that the alienation between farmer and labourer may be dated.

Exactly analogous phenomena appeared in the manufacturing world. The new class of great capitalist employers made enormous fortunes, they took little or no part personally in the work of their factories, their hundreds of workmen were individually unknown to them; and as a consequence, the old relations between masters and men disappeared, and a "cash nexus" was substituted for the human tie. The workmen on their side resorted to combination, and Trades Unions began a fight which looked as if it were between mortal enemies rather than joint producers. The misery which came upon large sections of the working people at this epoch was often, though not always, due to a fall in wages, for, as I said above, in some industries they rose. But they suffered likewise from the conditions of labour under the factory system, from the rise of prices, especially from the high price of bread before the repeal of the corn-laws, and from those sudden fluctuations of trade, which, ever since production has been on a large scale, have exposed them to recurrent periods of bitter distress. The effects of the Industrial Revolution prove that free competition may produce wealth without producing well-being. We all know the horrors that ensued in England before it was restrained by legislation and combination.

James Phillips Kay

WORKING-CLASS CONDITIONS IN THE 1830s, SEEN IN MANCHESTER BY A SOCIAL REFORMER

Born in 1804, Kay took his M.D. at Edinburgh, published medical books, and was Secretary to the Manchester Board of Health during the cholera epidemic of 1832. He became an Assistant Poor Law Commissioner, then Secretary to the Education Committee of the Privy Council. On his marriage in 1842, he changed his name to Kay-Shuttleworth. He wrote extensively on educational topics and was a pioneer in the training of teachers. He died in 1877. In this short book, he does not doubt the effects of industrial and commercial growth in promoting prosperity and spreading civilization. He pleads for free trade, so that the benefits of the new developments may be widely diffused. He urges capitalists to interest themselves in the welfare of their workers, and especially in their education, so as to guarantee social peace. But he is acutely conscious of the hardships and squalor which surrounded the workers in Britain's greatest export industry in the new factory age.

THE township of Manchester chiefly consists of dense masses of houses, inhabited by the population engaged in the great manufactories of the cotton trade. Some of the central divisions are occupied by warehouses and shops, and a few streets by the dwellings of some of the more wealthy inhabitants; but the opulent merchants chiefly reside in the country, and even the superior servants of their establishments inhabit the suburban [sic] townships. Manchester, properly so called, is chiefly inhabited by shopkeepers and the labouring classes. Those districts where the poor dwell are of very recent origin. The rapid growth of the cotton manufacture has attracted hither operatives from every part of the kingdom, and Ireland has poured forth the most destitute of her hordes to supply the constantly increasing demand for labour. This immigration has been, in one important respect, a serious evil. The Irish have taught the labouring classes of this country a pernicious lesson. The system of cottier farming, the demoralisation and barbarism of the people, and the general use of the potato as the chief article of food, have encouraged the population in Ireland more rapidly than the available means of subsistence have increased. Debased alike by ignorance and pauperism, they have discovered, with the savage, what is the minimum of the means of life, upon which existence may be prolonged. They have taught this fatal secret to the population of this country. . . . Instructed in the fatal secret of subsisting on what is barely necessary to life, the labouring classes have ceased to entertain a laudable pride in furnishing their houses, and in multiplying the decent comforts which minister to happiness. What is superfluous to the mere exigencies of nature, is too often expended at the tavern; and for the provision of old age and infirmity, they too frequently trust either to charity, to the support of their children, or to the protection of the poor laws.

When the example is considered in connexion with the unremitting labour of the whole population engaged in the

From James Phillips Kay, *The Moral and Physical Condition of the Working Classes employed in the Cotton Manufacture in Manchester* (Ridgeway, London, 1832), pp. 6–12, 19, 25–7, 42–3, 49, 55–6, 71–2. A reprint has recently been published by Frank Cass Ltd. of London.

various branches of the cotton manufacture, our wonder will be less excited by their fatal demoralisation. Prolonged and exhausting labour, continued from day to day, and from year to year, is not calculated to develop the intellectual or moral faculties of man. The dull routine of a ceaseless drudgery, in which the same mechanical process is incessantly repeated, resembles the torment of Sisyphus—the toil, like the rock, recoils perpetually on the wearied operative. The mind gathers neither stores nor strength from the constant extension and retraction of the same muscles. The intellect slumbers in supine inertness; but the grosser parts of our nature attain a rank development. To condemn man to such severity of toil is, in some measure, to cultivate in him the habits of an animal. He becomes reckless. He disregards the distinguishing appetites and habits of his species. He neglects the comforts and delicacies of life. He lives in squalid wretchedness, on meagre food, and expends his superfluous gains on debauchery.

The population employed in the cotton factories rises at five o'clock in the morning, works in the mills from six till eight o'clock, and returns home for half an hour to forty minutes to breakfast. This meal generally consists of tea or coffee with a little bread. Oatmeal porridge is sometimes, but of late rarely used, and chiefly by the men; but the stimulus of tea is preferred, and especially by the women. The tea is almost always of a bad, and sometimes of a deleterious quality, the infusion is weak, and little or no milk is added. The operatives return to the mills and workshops until twelve o'clock, when an hour is allowed for dinner. Amongst those who obtain the lowest rates of wages this meal generally consists of boiled potatoes. The mess of potatoes is put into one large dish; melted lard and butter are poured upon them, and a few pieces of fried fat bacon are sometimes mingled with them, and but seldom a little meat. Those who obtain better wages, or families whose aggregate income is larger, add a greater proportion of animal food to this meal, at least three times a week; but the quantity consumed by the labouring population is not great. The family sits round the table, and each rapidly appropriates his portion on a plate, or, they all plunge their spoons into the dish, and with an animal eagerness satisfy the cravings of their appetite. At the expiration of the hour, they are all again employed in the workshops or mills, where they continue until seven o'clock or a later hour, when they generally again indulge in the use of tea, often mingled with spirits accompanied by a little bread. Oatmeal or potatoes are however taken by some a second time in the evening.

The comparatively innutritious qualities of these articles of diet are most evident. We are, however, by no means prepared to say that an individual living in a healthy atmosphere, and engaged in active employment in the open air, would not be able to continue protracted and severe labour, without any suffering, whilst nourished by this food. . . . But the population nourished on this aliment is crowded into one dense mass, in cottages separated by narrow, unpaved, and almost pestilential streets; in an atmosphere loaded with the smoke and exhalations of a large manufacturing city. The operatives are congregated in rooms and workshops during twelve hours in the day, in an enervating, heated atmosphere, which is frequently loaded with dust or filaments of cotton, and impure from constant respiration, or from other causes. They are engaged in an employment which absorbs their attention, and unremittingly employs their physical energies. They are drudges who watch the movements, and assist the operations, of a mighty material force, which toils with an energy ever unconscious of fatigue. The persevering labour of the operative must rival the mathematical precision, the incessant motion, and the exhaustless power of the machine.

Hence, besides the negative results—the total abstraction of every moral and intellectual stimulus—the absence of variety—banishment from the grateful air and the cheering influences of light, the physical energies are exhausted by incessant toil, and imperfect nutrition. Having been subjected to the prolonged labour of an animal—his physical energy wasted—his mind in supreme inaction—the artisan has neither moral dignity nor intellectual nor organic strength to resist the seductions of appetite. His wife and children, too frequently subjected to the same process, are unable to cheer his remaining moments of leisure. Domestic economy is neglected, domestic comforts are unknown. A meal of the coarsest food is prepared with heedless haste, and devoured with equal precipitation. Home has no other relation to him than that of shelter—few pleasures are there—it chiefly presents to him a scene of physical exhaustion, from which he is glad to escape. Himself impotent to all the distinguishing aims of his species, he sinks into sensual sloth, or revels in more degrading licentiousness. His house is ill-furnished, uncleanly, often ill ventilated, perhaps damp; his food, through want of forethought and domestic economy, is meagre and innutritious; he is debilitated and hypochondriacal, and falls the victim of dissipation.

These artisans are frequently subject to a disease, in which the sensibility of the stomach and bowels is morbidly excited; the alvine secretions are deranged, and the appetite impaired. Whilst this state continues, the patient loses flesh, his features are sharpened, the skin becomes pale, leaden coloured, or of the yellow hue which is observed in those who have suffered from the influence of tropical climates. The strength fails, all the capacities of physical enjoyment are destroyed, and the paroxysms of corporal suffering are aggravated by the horrors of a disordered imagination, till they lead to gloomy apprehension, to the deepest depression, and almost to despair. We cannot wonder that the wretched victim of this disease, invited by those haunts of misery and crime the gin shop and the tavern, as he passes to his daily labour, should endeavour to cheat his sufferings of a few moments, by the false excitement procured by ardent spirits; or that the exhausted artisan, driven by ennui and discomfort from his squalid home, should strive, in the delirious dreams of a continued debauch, to forget the remembrance of his reckless improvidence, of the destitution, hunger, and uninterrupted toil, which threaten to destroy the remaining energies of his enfeebled constitution. . . .

Some idea of the want of cleanliness prevalent in their habitations, may be obtained from the report of the number of houses requiring white-washing; but this column fails to indicate their gross neglect of order, and absolute filth. Much less can we obtain satisfactory statistical results concerning the want of furniture, especially of bedding, and of food, clothing, and fuel. In these respects, the habitations of the Irish are the most destitute. They can scarcely be said to be furnished. They contain one or two chairs, a mean table, the most scanty culinary apparatus, and one or two beds, loathsome with filth. A whole family is sometimes accommodated in a single bed, and sometimes a heap of filthy straw and a covering of old sacking hide them in one undistinguished heap, debased alike by penury, want of economy, and dissolute habits. Frequently, the inspectors found two or more families crowded into one small house, containing only two apartments, in one of which they slept, and another in which they ate; and often more than one family lived in a damp cellar, containing only one room, in whose pestilential atmosphere from twelve to sixteen persons were crowded. To these fertile sources of disease were sometimes added the keeping of pigs and other animals in the house, with other nuisances of the most revolting character. . . .

The houses of the poor . . . are too generally built back to back, having therefore only one outlet, no yard, no privy, and no receptacle for refuse. Consequently the narrow, unpaved streets, in which mud and water stagnate, become the common receptacle of offal and ordure. Often low, damp, ill ventilated cellars exist beneath the houses; an improvement on which system, consists in the erection of a stage over the first storey, by which access is obtained to the second, and the house is inhabited by two separate families. More than one disgraceful example of this might be enumerated. The streets . . . are generally unsewered, and the drainage is consequently superficial. The houses are often built with a total neglect of order, on a summit of natural irregularities of the surface, or on mounds left at the side of artificial excavations on the brick grounds, with which these parts of the town abound.

These districts are inhabited by a turbulent population, which, rendered reckless by dissipation and want—misled by the secret intrigues, and excited by the inflammatory harangues of demagogues, has frequently committed daring assaults on the liberty of the more peaceful portions of the working classes, and the most frightful devastations on the property of their masters. Machines have been broken, and factories gutted and burned at mid-day, and the riotous crowd has dispersed ere the insufficient body of police arrived at the scene of disturbance. . . . The police form, in fact, so weak a screen against the power of the mob, that popular violence is now, in almost every instance, controlled by the presence of a military force.

The wages obtained by operatives in the various branches of the cotton manufacture are, in general, such, as with the exercise of that economy without which wealth itself is wasted, would be sufficient to provide them with all the decent comforts of life—the average wage of all persons employed (young and old) being from nine to twelve shillings per week. Their means are consumed by vice and improvidence. But the wages of certain classes are exceedingly meagre. The introduction of the power-loom, though ultimately destined to be productive of the greatest general benefits, has, in the present restricted state of commerce, occasioned some temporary embarrassment, by diminishing the demand for certain kinds of labour, and, consequently, their price. The hand-loom weavers, existing in the state of transition, still continue a very extensive class, and though they labour fourteen hours and upwards daily, earn only from five to seven shillings per week. They consist chiefly of Irish, and are affected by all the causes of moral and physical depression which we have enumerated. Ill-fed, ill-clothed, half-sheltered and ignorant; working in close, damp cellars, or crowded, ill-ventilated workshops, it only remains that they should become, as is too frequently the case, demoralised and reckless, to render perfect the portraiture of savage life. . . .

With unfeigned regret, we are . . . constrained to add, that the standard of morality is exceedingly debased, and that religious observances are neglected amongst the operative population of Manchester. . . .

The children . . . are often neglected by their parents. The early age at which girls are admitted into the factories, prevents their acquiring much knowledge of domestic economy; and even supposing them to have had accidental opportunities of making this acquisition, the extent to which women are employed in the mills, does not, even after marriage, permit the general application of its principles. The infant is the victim of the system; it has not lived long, ere it is abandoned to the care of a hireling or neighbour, whilst its mother pursues her accustomed toil. Sometimes a little girl has care of the child, or even of two or three collected from neighbouring houses. Thus abandoned to one whose sympathies are not interested in its welfare, or whose time is too often also occupied in household drudgery, the child is ill-fed, dirty, ill-clothed, exposed to cold and neglect, and, in consequence, more than one-half of the offspring of the poor (as may be proved by the bills of mortality of the town) die before they have completed their fifth year. The strongest survive; but the same causes which destroy the weakest, impair the vigour of the more robust; and hence the children of our manufacturing population are proverbially pale and sallow, though not generally emaciated, nor the subjects of disease. We cannot subscribe to those exaggerated and unscientific accounts of the physical ailments to which they are liable, which have been lately revived with an eagerness and haste equally unfriendly to taste and truth; but we are convinced that the operation of these causes, continuing unchecked through successive generations, would tend to depress the health of the people; and that subsequent physical ills would accumulate in an unhappy progression.

The increase of the manufacturing establishments, and the consequent colonisation of the district, have been exceedingly more rapid than the growth of its civic institutions. The eager antagonisation of commercial enterprise, has absorbed the attention, and concentrated the energies, of every member of the community. In this strife, the remote influence of arrangements has sometimes been neglected, not from the want of humanity, but from the pressure of occupation, and the deficiency of time.

We dam up not only the well-spring of our own wealth and happiness, but that of other nations, when we refuse to barter the results of the ingenuity and perseverance of our artisans, for the products of the bounty of other climates, or the arts and genius of other people. Unrestricted commerce, on the other hand, would rapidly promote the advance of civilisation, by cultivating the physical and mental power of individuals and nations, to multiply the amount of natural products, and to create those artificial staple commodities, by the barter of which they acquire the riches of other regions. Every new invention in agriculture and manufactures—every improvement in the powers of transition, would enable its possessors, by the same amount of labour, to obtain a greater quantity of foreign products in exchange. The labour of man would be constantly to an indefinite extent diminished, whilst its reward would be, at the same time, perpetually increased.

Distrust of the capitalists has long been sown in the minds of the working classes—separation has succeeded to suspicion, and many causes have tended to widen the gulf over which the golden chain of charity seldom extends. We would not have this so. The contest, thus engendered, too often assumes an appalling aspect. Capital is but accumulated labour: their strife is unnatural.

Greed does not become the opulent; nor does turbulence the poor. The general combinations of workmen to protect the price of labour are ultimately destined to have a beneficial influence on trade, by the destruction of partial monopolies and petty oppressions, but in these contests the poisonous shafts of personal malice should not be launched; much less, should the struggle issue into a barbarous destruction of property, or in daring assaults on the liberty of the subject.

The tendency to these excesses would be much diminished, did a cordial sympathy unite the higher with the lower classes of society. The intelligence of the former should be the fountain whence this should flow. If the *results* of labour be solely regarded, in the connexion of the capitalist with those in his employ, the first step is taken towards treating them as a mere animal power necessary to the mechanical processes of manufacture. This is a heartless, if not a degrading association. The contract for the rewards of labour conducted on these principles issues in suspicion, if not in rancorous animosity.

The operative population constitutes one of the most important elements of society, and when numerically considered, the magnitude of its interests and the extent of its power assume such vast proportions, that the folly which neglects them is allied to madness. If the higher classes are unwilling to diffuse intelligence among the lower, those exist who are ever ready to take advantage of their ignorance; if they will not seek their confidence, others will excite their distrust; if they will not endeavour to promote domestic comfort, virtue, and knowledge among them, their misery, vice, and prejudice will prove volcanic elements, by whose explosive violence the structure of society may be destroyed.

Andrew Ure

WORKING-CLASS CONDITIONS IN THE 1830S, SEEN BY AN ENTHUSIAST

FOR THE FACTORY SYSTEM

Like Kay, a qualified physician, Ure lived from 1778 to 1857. He was Professor of Chemistry at Glasgow, and wrote widely on that subject. He interested himself in scientific education for working men. In addition to *The Philosophy of Manufactures,* he wrote a *Dictionary of Arts, Manufactures and Mines* (1839).

WHEN the wandering savage becomes a citizen, he renounces many of his dangerous pleasures in return for tranquillity and protection. He can no longer gratify at will a revengeful spirit upon his foes, nor seize with violence a neighbour's possessions. In like manner, when the handicraftsman exchanges hard work with fluctuating employment and pay, for continuous work of a lighter kind with steady wages, he must necessarily renounce his old prerogative of stopping when he pleases, because he would thereby throw the whole establishment into disorder. Of the amount of injury resulting from the violation of the rules of automatic labour he can hardly ever be the proper judge; just as mankind at large can never fully estimate the evils consequent upon an infraction of God's moral law. Yet the factory operative, little versant in the great operations of political economy, currency, and trade, and actuated too often by an invidious feeling towards the capitalist who animates his otherwise torpid talents, is easily persuaded by artful demagogues, that his sacrifice of time and skill is beyond the proportion of his recompense, or that fewer hours of industry would be an ample equivalent for his wages. This notion seems to have taken an early and inveterate hold of the factory mind, and to have been riveted from time to time by the leaders of those secret combinations, so readily formed among a peculiar class of men, concentrated in masses within a narrow range of country.

Instead of repining as they have done at the prosperity of their employers, and concerting odious measures to blast it, they should, on every principle of gratitude and self-interest, have rejoiced at the success resulting from their labours, and by regularity and skill have recommended themselves to monied men desirous of engaging in a profitable concern, and of procuring qualified hands to conduct it. Thus good workmen would have advanced their condition to that of overlookers, managers, and partners in new mills, and have increased at the same time the demand for their companions' labour in the market. It is only by an undisturbed progression of this kind that the rate of wages can be permanently raised or upheld. Had it not been for the violent collisions and interruptions resulting from erroneous views among the operatives, the factory system would have developed still more rapidly and beneficially for all concerned than it has, and would have exhibited still more frequently gratifying examples of skilful workmen becoming opulent proprietors. Every misunderstanding either repels capital altogether, or diverts it from flowing, for a time, in the channels of a trade liable to strikes.

From Andrew Ure, *The Philosophy of Manufactures, or, an Exposition of the Scientific, Moral, and Commercial Economy of the Factory System of Great Britain*, 3rd edition, P. L. Simmonds ed. (Bohn, London, 1861; the first edition was 1835), pp. 278–80, 300–1, 309–12, 328–30, 333–6, 349–50, 379–80, 385–8. A reprint has recently been published by Frank Cass Ltd. of London.

No master would wish to have any wayward children to work within the walls of his factory, who do not mind their business without beating, and he therefore usually fines and turns away any spinners who are known to maltreat their assistants. Hence, ill-usage of any kind is a very rare occurrence. I have visited many factories, both in Manchester and in the surrounding districts, during a period of several months, entering the spinning rooms, unexpectedly, and often alone, at different times of day, and I never saw a single instance of corporal chastisement inflicted on a child, nor indeed did I ever see children in ill-humour. They seemed to be always cheerful and alert, taking pleasure in the light play of their muscles—enjoying the mobility natural to their age. The scene of industry, far from exciting sad emotions in my mind, was always exhilarating. It was delightful to observe the nimbleness with which they pieced the broken ends, as the mule-carriage began to recede from the fixed roller-beam, and to see them at leisure, after a few seconds' exercise of their tiny fingers, to amuse themselves in any attitude they chose, till the stretch and winding-on were once more completed. The work of these lively elves seemed to resemble a sport, in which habit gave them a pleasing dexterity. Conscious of their skill, they were delighted to show it off to any stranger. As to exhaustion by the day's work, they evinced no trace of it on emerging from the mill in the evening; for they immediately began to skip about any neighbouring playground, and to commence their little amusements with the same alacrity as boys issuing from a school. It is moreover my firm conviction, that if children are not ill-used by bad parents or guardians, but receive in food and raiment the full benefit of what they earn, they would thrive better in our modern factories than if left alone in apartments too often ill-aired, damp and cold.

Of all the modern prejudices that exist with regard to factory labour, there is none more unfounded than that which ascribes to it excessive tedium and irksomeness above other occupations, owing to its being carried on in conjunction with the "unceasing motion of the steam-engine." In an establishment for spinning or weaving cotton, all the hard work is performed by the steam-engine, which leaves for the attendant no hard labour at all, and literally nothing to do in general; but at intervals to perform some delicate operation, such as joining the threads that break, taking the cops off the spindles, etc. And it is so far from being true that the work in a factory is incessant, because the motion of the steam-engine is incessant, that the labour is not incessant on that very account, because it is performed in conjunction with the steam-engine. Of all manufacturing employments, those are by far the most irksome and incessant in which steam-engines are not employed, as in lace-running and stocking-weaving; and the way to prevent an employment from being incessant is to introduce a steam-engine into it. These remarks apply more especially to the labour of children in factories. Three-fourths of all the children so employed are engaged in piecing at the mules. "When the carriages of these have receded a foot and a half or two feet from the rollers," says Mr. Tufnell, "nothing is to be done, not even attention is required from either spinner or piecer." Both of them stand idle for a time, and in fine-spinning especially, for three-quarters of a minute, or more. Consequently if a child remains at his business twelve hours daily, he has nine hours of inaction. And though he attends two mules, he still has six hours of non-exertion. Spinners sometimes dedicate these intervals to the perusal of books. The scavengers who, in Mr. Sadler's report, have been described as being "constantly in a state of grief, alway• in terror, and every moment they have to spare stretched all their length upon the floor in a state of perspiration," may be observed in cotton factories idle for *four* minutes at a time, or moving about in a sportive mood, utterly unconscious of the tragical scenes in which they were dramatised.

Occupations which are assisted by steam-engines require for the most part a higher, or at least a steadier, species of labour than those which are not; the exercise of the mind being then partially substituted for that of the muscles, constituting skilled labour, which is always paid more highly than unskilled. On this principle we can readily account for the comparatively high wages which the inmates of a cotton factory, whether children or adults, obtain. Batting cotton by hand for fine spinning seems by far the hardest work in a factory; it is performed wholly by women, without any assistance from the steam-engine, and is somewhat similar in effort to threshing corn; yet it does not bring those who are engaged in it more than 6s. 6d. weekly, while close by is the stretching-frame, which remunerates its tenters or superintendents, women, and even children fourteen years old, with double wages for far lighter labour. In power-loom weaving also, the wages are good, and the muscular effort is trifling, as those who tend it frequently exercise themselves by following the movements of the lay, and leaning on it with their arms. It is reckoned a very healthy occupation, as is shown by the appearance of the females engaged in it, in every well-regulated establishment in England and Scotland.

The more refined the labour in factories, it becomes generally the lighter and pleasanter. Thus the fine spinning is the least laborious in Manchester, owing to the slowness with which the machinery moves in forming fine threads. The mule for No. 30 or No. 40 makes in general three stretches in a minute, but the mule for higher numbers makes only one stretch in the same time. During at least three-fourths of this minute, the four, five, or more piecers, who attend the pair of mules of 460 spindles each, have absolutely nothing to do but are seen in an easy attitude, till the carriage begins to start for a new stretch, when they proceed immediately to mend the threads, which break, or are purposely broken on account of some unsightly knot. The piecing is soon over, as the carriage does not stop an instant in the frame, but forthwith resumes its spinning routine, and when it has again come out somewhat less than two feet, it places the rollers and roving beyond the reach of the hands of the piecers, and gives them another interval of repose. There is so little scavenger work required in fine spinning, on account of the small quantity of waste from the long-stapled cotton, that it is usually performed by one of the piecers. From the same cause there is hardly any dust to be seen in the air of the rooms.

Under what pretext, or with what face of pretension, operatives, whose labour is assisted by steam or water power, can lay claim to a peculiar privilege of exemption from more than ten hours' daily labour it is hard to conjecture. They compare their toil with that of the small class, comparatively, of artisans, such as carpenters, bricklayers, stone-masons, etc., who, they say, work only from six to six, with two one-hour intervals for meals: a class, however, in this material respect distinguished from most factory operatives, that their work is done entirely by muscular effort, and after serving a long appprenticeship with no little outlay. But what do the factory operatives think of the numerous class of domestic operatives, the stocking or frame-work knitters, the hand-loom weavers, the wool-combers, the lace-manufacturers, and a variety of others, who work, and very hardly too, from twelve to sixteen hours a day, to earn a bare subsistence; and this frequently from a very early age, and in a state of confinement irksome to the mind and injurious to the body? The consideration is also overlooked by these interested reasoners, that by reducing the hours of labour, and thereby the amount of subsistence derivable from the less objectionable occupations, they would cause a corresponding increase of competition for employment in the more objectionable ones, and thus inflict an injury on the whole labouring community, by wantonly renouncing the fair advantages of their own.

On the principle expounded above, the woollen manufacturers in the large mills pay much better wages to their workmen than the domestic manufacturers do to theirs.

The factory system, then, instead of being detrimental to the comfort of the labouring population, is its grand Palladium; for the more complicated and extensive the machinery required for any manufacture, the less risk is there of its agents being injured by the competition of foreign manufactures, and the greater inducement and ability has the mill-owner to keep up the wages of his work-people. The main reason why they are so high is, that they form a small part of the value of the manufactured article, so that if reduced too low by a sordid master, they would render his operatives less careful, and thereby injure the quality of their work more than could be compensated by his saving in wages. The less proportion wages bear to the value of the goods, the higher, generally speaking, is the recompense of labour. The prudent master of a fine spinning-mill is most reluctant to tamper with the earnings of his spinners, and never consents to reduce them till absolutely forced to do so by a want of remuneration for the capital and skill embarked in his business.

It deserves to be remembered, moreover, that hand-working is more or less discontinuous from the caprice of the operative, and never gives an average weekly or annual product at all comparable to that of a like machine equally driven by power. For this reason hand-weavers very seldom turn off in a week much more than one-half of what their loom could produce if kept continuously in action for twelve or fourteen hours a day, at the rate which the weaver in his working paroxysms impels it.

A gentleman in Manchester, one of the greatest warehousemen in the world, told me that 1,800 weavers, whom he employed in the surrounding districts, seldom brought him in more than 2,000 pieces a week, but he knew that they could fabricate 9,000, if they bestowed steady labour on their looms. One young woman in his employment, not long ago, produced by her own industry, upon a hand-loom, six pieces a week; for each of which she received 6s. 3d. This fact strongly confirms what Mr. Strutt told me concerning the discontinuous industry of handicraft people. Learning that the inhabitants of a village a few miles from Belper, occupied chiefly by stocking weavers, was in a distressed state from the depreciation of their wages, he invited a number of the most necessitous families to participate in the better wages and steadier employment of their great spinning-mills. Accordingly they came with troops of children, and were delighted to get installed in such comfortable quarters. After a few weeks, however, their irregular habits of work began to break out, proving both to their own conviction, and that of their patrons, their unfitness for power-going punctuality. They then renounced all further endeavours at learning the new business, and returned to their listless independence.

In hand-weaving . . . the depreciation of wages has been extraordinary. Annexed are the prices paid at different periods in Manchester for weaving a sixty reed 6/4 cambric, as taken in the month of March each year; the weaver paying threepence out of each shilling, for winding his warp, for brushes, paste, etc.

In 1795	39s. 6d.	1820	8s.
1800	25s.	1830	5s.
1810	15s.		

The following painful statements made to the Factory Commissioners will show in how abject a condition are our so-called independent handicraft labourers, compared with that of those much-lamented labourers who tend the power-driven machines of the factories. The former class needs all the sympathy which Mr. Sadler's faction so perniciously expended upon the latter.

A number of instances are adduced by Mr. Felkin as fair specimens of the situation of the plain full-wrought cotton-hose workmen in March 1833. They are taken indiscriminately from a very large population similarly employed; but all of them are sober and industrious persons. They fully justify the public appeal made at a meeting of framework knitters in September 1832, "that their average earnings are not more than 6s. 6d. a week." On this sum, a man, wife, and children have to be maintained. Many among them are therefore extremely wretched and destitute of the necessaries of life; some have neither blanket nor sheet, and sleep in a little straw. The embroidery of bobbin-net, also a nonfactory household work, painfully illustrates our position. No less than one hundred and fifty thousand females, chiefly of very youthful ages, get their livelihood from this employment in Great Britain. The work is wholly domestic; and though requiring more skill and harder labour than any other branch of the lace business, it is the worst paid. "Almost the youngest of them," says Mr. Power (and they begin at the age of nine or ten), "is able to speak with regret of a better state of earnings and a period of less necessity for constant labour. They begin early and work late, and during this long daily period their bodies are constantly bent over the frame upon which the lace is extended, the head being usually kept within five or six inches of the frame, the edge of which presses upon the lower part of the chest. One effect universally produced by this habit is short-sightedness, and often general weakness of the limbs; with consumptive tendency, distortion of the limbs, and general debility from the confinement and the posture."

Mr. T. Ashton's cotton-works are agreeably grouped together on a gentle declivity, which is traversed by a little tributary stream of the Mersey. This supplies the condensing power to his steam-engines, while their expansive force is furnished from rich coal-measures immediately under the factory lands. This is the motive-element which pervades and animates the region all around. The houses occupied by his work-people lie in streets, all built of stone, and are commodious; consisting each of at least four apartments in two stories, with a small back-yard and a mews lane. The rent for a good lodging, containing an improved kitchen-grate, with boiler and oven, is only £8 per annum, and good fuel may be had for 9s. a ton. I looked into several of the houses, and found them more richly furnished than any common work-people's dwellings which I had ever seen before. In one I saw a couple of sofas, with good chairs, an eight-day clock in a handsome mahogany case, several pictures in oil on the walls, freshly painted for the family, a representation of one of the younger daughters like a smart peasant girl carrying a basket on her arm, one of the Virgin and Child at Bethlehem, and another of Christ crowned with thorns, all creditable to the travelling artist. In another house I observed a neat wheel barometer, with its attached thermometer, suspended against the snow-white wall. In a third there was a piano, with a little girl learning to play upon it.

My notice was particularly attracted to a handsome house and shop, in one of the streets where Mr. Ashton's operatives dwell. On asking who occupied it, I learned it was a spinner, who having saved from his earnings £200, had embarked this capital in a retail business, now managed by his wife, a tidy-looking person, while the husband continued to pursue his profitable avocations in the mill.

The most recent, and perhaps most convincing, evidence regarding the healthiness of factory children is that given in the official report of Mr. Harrison, the Inspecting Surgeon appointed for the mills of Preston and its vicinity. There are 1,656 under 18 years of age, of whom 952 are employed in spinning-rooms, 468 in carding rooms, 128 at power-looms, and 108 in winding, skewering cops, etc. "I have made very particular inquiries respecting the health of every child whom I have examined, and I find that the average annual sickness of each child is not more than four days; at least, that not more than four days on an average are lost by each child in a year, in consequence of sickness. This includes disorders of every kind, for the most part induced by causes wholly unconnected with factory labour. I have been not a little surprised to find so little sickness which can fairly be attributed to mill work. I have met with very few children who have suffered from injuries occasioned by machinery; and the protection, especially in new factories, is so complete, that accidents will, I doubt not, speedily become rare. I have not met with a single instance out of the 1,656 children whom I have examined, of deformity, that is referable to factory labour. It must be admitted, that factory children do not present the same blooming robust appearance as is witnessed among children who labour in the open air, but I question if they are not more exempt from acute diseases, and do not, on the average, suffer less sickness than those who are regarded as having more healthy employments. The average age at which the children of this district enter the factories is ten years and two months; and the average age of all the young persons together is fourteen years."

I examined samples of bacon as sold in several respectable shops in Manchester, and found it to be much more rank than the average of the London shops. In this piquant state, it suits vitiated palates accustomed to the fiery impression of tobacco and gin. These three stimulants are too much used by that order of work-people in Manchester who receive the highest wages, and they are quite sufficient to account for many chronic maladies of the stomach, liver, or spleen, without tracing them to mere factory labour or confinement. Were a judicious plan of cookery and diet, combining abundance of vegetable matter with light animal food, introduced among them, as it is among the families of the work-people at Belper, Hyde, New Lanark, Catrine, etc., joined to abstinence from tobacco and alcohol, I am confident that the health of the Manchester spinners would surpass that of any class of operatives in the kingdom. . . . Hypochondriasis, from indulging too much the corrupt desires of the flesh and the spirit, is in fact the prevalent disease of the highest-paid operatives, a disease which may be aggravated by damp, but must seek its permanent cure in moral regimen. Nothing strikes the eye of the stranger more in Manches-

ter than the swarms of empirical practitioners of medicine. Nearly a dozen of them may be found clustered together in one of the main streets; all prepared with drastic pills and alternative potions to prey upon the credulous spinners. . . .

Since they can purchase their favourite bacon at fourpence or fivepence a pound, they need not nor do they actually content themselves with a sprinkling, for they swallow a substantial rasher. This consequently creates thirst, which must be quenched with tea at bagging-time, qualified with some ardent spirit to aid as they think the digestion of their dinner. . . . What is carried about for distribution in dwelling-houses by the milkmen is inferior even to the average London milk. The mill-owners of Manchester could, in my humble opinion, do nothing more conducive to the welfare of their operatives than to establish an extensive dairy, under the superintendence of one of their benevolent societies. . . . Were the workpeople to adopt also to *pot-au-feu* cookery of the French, they might live in the most comfortable manner upon their wages. I know two talented young men . . . who . . . practised the said system of diet for several years, by which small pieces of animal food are made to impart a relish to a large quantity of esculent and farinaceous vegetables of various kinds. . . . On this plan they ascertained that they could board themselves comfortably for 2s. 6d. each week. The most savoury and salubrious cookery requires the slowest fire. A sumptuous French dinner could be dressed with one-tenth of the fuel consumed by an English cook in broiling a few beef-steaks or mutton-chops.

Thomas S. Ashton

WORKERS' LIVING STANDARDS: AN EARLY MODERN REVISION

Ashton taught at Sheffield, Birmingham, and Manchester, and ended his academic career as Professor of Economic History in London, 1944–54. The publications named in "Suggestions for Additional Reading" demonstrate his mastery of the industrial history of England in the eighteenth century and the early nineteenth. The excerpt which follows is a sober and scholarly attempt to assess the difficulties of research into working-class living standards, though in the end Ashton delivers a cautiously optimistic judgment. I have omitted a section which deals with retail prices in Oldham and Manchester. Professor Ashton died in 1968.

WHAT happened to the standard of life of the British working classes in the late decades of the eighteenth and the early decades of the nineteenth centuries? Was the introduction of the factory system beneficial or harmful in its effect on the workers? These, though related, are distinct questions. For it is possible that employment in factories conduced to an increase of real wages but that the tendency was more than offset by other influences, such as the rapid increase of population, the immigration of Irishmen, the destruction of wealth by long years of warfare, ill-devised tariffs, and misconceived measures for the relief of distress. Let me confess at the start that I am of those who believe that, all in all, conditions of labour were becoming better, at least after 1820, and that the spread of the factory played a not inconsiderable part in the improvement.

There is, it must be admitted, weighty opinion to the contrary. Most of the economists who lived through the period of rapid economic changes took a somewhat gloomy view of the effect of these changes on the workers. "The increasing wealth of the nation," wrote Thomas Malthus in 1798, "has had little or no tendency to better the conditions of the labouring poor. They have not, I believe, a greater command of the necessaries and conveniences of life; and a much greater proportion of them, than at the period of the Revolution, is employed in manufactories and crowded together in close and unwholesome rooms." A couple of generations later J. R. McCulloch declared that "there seems, on the whole, little room for doubting that the factory system operates unfavourably on the bulk of those engaged in it." And, in 1848, John Stuart Mill wrote words that, if they gave some glimmer of hope, were nevertheless highly critical of the society from which the technological changes had sprung. "Hitherto," he said, "it is questionable if all the mechanical inventions yet made have lightened the day's toil of any human being. They have enabled a greater proportion to live the same life of drudgery and imprisonment and an increased number of manufacturers and others to make fortunes. They have increased the comforts of the middle classes. But they have not yet begun to effect those great changes in human destiny, which it is in their nature and

From Thomas S. Ashton, "The Standard of Life of the Workers in England, 1790–1830," *Journal of Economic History*, IX (1949), Supplement IX, pp. 19–33, 36–38. By permission of the author and of the editor of *Journal of Economic History*. It should be noted that the article has been reprinted in F. A. Hayek, *Capitalism and the Historians* (Routledge, Kegan Paul, London, 1954).

in their futurity to accomplish." Alongside the economists was a miscellany of poets, philosophers, and demagogues; parsons, deists, and infidels; conservatives, radicals, and revolutionaries— men differing widely one from another in fundamentals but united in their hatred of factories and in their belief that economic change had led to the degradation of labour.

In the opposing camp there were publicists whose opinions are no less worthy of respect and whose disinterestedness and zeal for reform can hardly be called in question—men like Sir Frederic Eden, John Wesley, George Chalmers, Patrick Colquhoun, John Rickman, and Edwin Chadwick. To offset the passage from Mill, let me quote two sentences from Chadwick, who surely knew as much as anyone else of the squalor and poverty of large numbers of town dwellers in the forties: "The fact is that, hitherto, in England, wages, or the means of obtaining the necessaries of life for the whole mass of the labouring community, have advanced, and the comforts within the reach of the labouring classes have increased with the late increase of population. . . . We have evidence of this advance even in many of the manufacturing districts now in a state of severe depression." (He wrote in 1842).

If a public opinion poll could have been taken, it is probable that adherents of the first group would have been found to outnumber those of the second. But this is not a matter to be settled by a show of hands. The romantic revival in literature, which coincided in time with the Industrial Revolution, tended to strengthen the despondency. Popular writers, like William Cobbett, pictured an earlier England peopled with merry peasants or sturdy beef-eating, beer-drinking yeomen, just as their predecessors of the age of Dryden had conjured up the vision of a Patagonia peopled with noble savages. But neither native pessimism nor unhistorical romanticism is sufficient in itself to explain the prevalence of the view that the condition of the workers had deteriorated. It is part of my thesis that those who held this view had their eyes on one section of the working classes only.

II

It may be well to begin by making a rapid survey of the economic and demographic landscape. In these early decades of the nineteenth century population was increasing rapidly. Whether it is good or ill that more human beings should experience the happiness and misery, the hopes and anxieties, the ambitions and frustrations of life, may be left for the philosopher or the theologian to determine. But the increase in numbers was the result not of a rise of the birth rate but of a fall of the death rate, and it might be thought that this was indicative of an improved quality of life. "Human comfort," said Rickman in his letter to Southey, "is to be estimated by human health, and that by the length of human life. . . . Since 1780 life has been prolonged by 5 to 4—and the poor form too large a portion of society to be excluded from this general effect; rather they are the main cause of it; for the upper classes had food and cleanliness abundant before." Such an argument was not easy to refute; but Gaskell tried to meet it by declaring roundly that there was no direct connection between mortality and well-being. The noble savage was invoked. In his case, it was asserted, life was "physical enjoyment" and disease "hasty death." For the worker in the manufacturing town, on the other hand, life was "one long disease" and death "the result of physical exhaustion."

If only he had known it, Gaskell might have answered Rickman with a flat denial. For it is now held by statisticians that the fall in the crude death rate was the result of a change in the age distribution of the population and that there was, in fact, no prolongation of the average life. (The deaths per thousand fell simply because population changes in the later eighteenth century had produced a society in which the number of young adults was abnormally high.) But even if the expectation of life was not raised, it may be urged that the fall of the death rate conduced in some measure to a higher standard of life. For the pomp and circumstances of death and burial swallowed up no small part of the annual income of the workers. When the percentage of deaths to population fell, the proportion of income devoted to the dead probably diminished and resources were thus freed to add to the comforts of the living.

The growth of population, and, in particular, the increase in the number of people of working age, might well have resulted in a fall of wages. But there took place simultaneously an increase in the supply of other factors of production. Estimates of the national income for this period are few and unreliable. But the statistics of output, expenditure, and consumption all suggest that over the period as a whole it was growing somewhat more rapidly than population. Is there any reason to believe that the proportion of this increased income that went to the workers diminished and that other classes obtained a larger share? This is a question to which no sure answer can be given; all that is possible is to estimate probabilities. In attempting this, it is important to distinguish between the period of the war, the period of deflation and readjustment, and the succeeding period of economic expansion.

During the war heavy government expenditure of an unproductive nature produced a high level of employment but a low standard of comfort. Difficulties of obtaining foodstuffs from abroad led to an extension of the margin of cultivation, and the profit of the farmer and the rent of the landowner increased. Wartime shortages of timber, bricks, glass, and other materials limited the construction of houses; high rates of interest and a burdensome property tax reduced the incentives to build. With a growing population and an increased proportion of people of marriageable age the demand for homes increased; urban rents, like agricultural rents, rose. The growth of the national debt led to an expansion of the number of bondholders. The high rates at which loans were floated swelled the income of the passive investor, and, since the tax system was highly regressive, the gain to the rentier was largely at the expense of the poor. Prices in general rose, and, though rates of wages also moved up, they did so more slowly. This, as Earl Hamilton has argued, put additional resources at the

disposal of the entrepreneur, and the tendency was reinforced by other institutional factors. The trader's or manufacturer's token, the "long pay," and the truck system had existed in earlier times. But it is probable that the shortage of coin, which became acute during the period of inflation, led to an extension of these and other devices, the effect of which was to shift purchasing power from the workers to their employers. During the war, then, there took place a whole series of transfers of income—to landlords, farmers, houseowners, bondholders, and entrepreneurs—and these almost certainly worsened the economic status of labour.

The five or six years that followed the peace brought little alleviation. The landlords obtained legislation that enabled them to perpetuate their windfall gains. House rents remained high. Rates of interest fell but slightly. And, though wage rates were less affected than profits, the reduction of government expenditure, the contraction of the currency, banking failures, and a general reluctance to embark on long-term investment reduced the level of activity. Any gains that may have come from the lag of wage rates behind falling prices were probably offset by high unemployment. It is difficult to believe that these years of deflation and civil tumult saw any marked improvement in the condition of the wage-earners.

After 1821, however, economic forces bore less harshly on labour. The gold standard had been restored. A larger quantity of silver and copper was available for the payment of wages. Reforms of the fiscal system were in train. A series of conversions reduced the burden of the national debt, and by 1824 the gilt-edge rate was down to its pre-war level of 3.3. Wartime scarcities had disappeared. A more ample supply of bricks and timber combined with cheap money to stimulate the building of factories and dwellings. By the early thirties rents (in the north at least) had fallen about 10 per cent, and, in spite of a number of disturbing reports on conditions in the towns, it is fairly clear that the standard of housing was improving. The fall of prices—less marked than in the years immediately after the war—now represented not depression but a reduction of real costs. All in all, the economic climate had become more genial; it was possible for the workers to look forward to better conditions of life and work.

III

So far attention has been directed only to forces internal to the economy. What of those that operated from outside? It has been suggested that over the greater part of this period the power of British exports to exchange for goods from abroad was diminishing and that the unfavourable movement of the net barter terms of trade must have resulted either in lower money incomes for those engaged in the export trades or in higher costs of imported goods. Hence, other things being equal, it must have led to a fall in the standard of life of the workers.

The defects of early British commercial statistics are well known. Since both imports and exports were officially measured by a scale of prices that had become stereotyped in the first half of the eighteenth century, the movements of the figures from year to year represent changes in the volume, and not in the value, of overseas trade. From 1798, it is true, there are annual figures of the value of exports, derived from the declarations of merchants; but until recently there have been no corresponding estimates of the values of imports for the years before 1854. Mr. Schlote and Mr. Imlah have now filled the gap.

From 1803 to 1834 the course of export prices was almost continuously downward. That of import prices was less consistent. From 1802 there were wide fluctuations with no marked trend, but from 1814 there was a descent— steep to 1821, less steep thereafter. The terms of trade moved strongly against Britain during the second phase of the war and less strongly, though markedly, against her from 1816 to the middle thirties. Before jumping, however, to the conclusion that here was a factor pressing heavily on British labour, it may be well to look at the composition of the price index for exports. It will be observed that the prices of cotton yarn and fabrics fell much more steeply than

those of the products of the linen, woollen, and iron industries. During the war manufactured cotton had taken the place of manufactured wool as the British staple export, and during the whole of the first half of the nineteenth century its lead over the other commodities lengthened. It was the fall in the price of cotton yarn and cotton cloth that was responsible for the adverse trend of the terms of trade; the prices of exports exclusive of cotton goods actually declined less steeply than those of imports.

The reason for this extraordinary fall is twofold. Instead of producing muslins, cambrics, and other goods of high quality for sale in Europe and the United States, the factories of Lancashire were increasingly concerned with cheap calicoes for Indian and Far Eastern markets; a large part of the fall in price is to be accounted for by a change in the nature of the product of the industry. The other reason was the cost-reducing effect of technical and economic progress. The new mills of the postwar years were driven by steam instead of by water; improvements were being made year after year in the mule and the spinning frame; the power loom was steadily taking the place of the less efficient hand loom; with falling rates of interest capital charges were reduced; and with innovations in transport and trade the expenses of moving and merchanting the goods were diminished. The fall of the prices of cotton yarn and fabrics was not, then, the result of any decline of foreign demand; it reflected a reduction of real costs. And, though the labour cost of a pound of yarn or a yard of calico fell in a spectacular manner, there was no corresponding drop in the earnings of labour. The downward trend of the terms of trade did not represent any worsening of the economic situation either for the nation as a whole or for that part of it that depended on wages.

Figures purporting to show changes in the terms of trade are of dubious value for long-period studies; it is only over short series of years, when the nature of the commodities entering into trade and the state of technique do not change very much, that any safe conclusion can be drawn from them. Even in the short run, indeed, it is far from clear that a downward movement of the index should be taken as a sign of adversity. The terms of trade moved sharply downward in 1809–10, 1812–15, 1817–18, and 1825—all periods when the volume of trade rose to a peak. They moved sharply upward in 1811, 1816, 1819, and 1826—all years of diminished or stagnant trade. The explanation is, of course, that the prices of British exports rose in times of prosperity and fell in times of depression less violently than those of imports, for the raw materials and foodstuffs Britain imported were inelastic in demand and supply. It would be absurd, however, to suppose that the welfare of the workers diminished when trade was active and increased when trade declined.

An apparatus that is concerned only with prices is clearly inadequate as a measure of changes in the benefits derived from international trade. Not only the cost of living but also the opportunities of earning determine the degree of well-being. Incomes earned by exports provide employment and generate other incomes. How far these incomes will go in the purchase of goods from abroad depends on the price of imports. In the light of such reasoning a colleague of mine, Mr. Dorrance, recently suggested that a better instrument for measuring the social effects of international trade may be obtained by dividing the indexes of the *values* of exports by those of the *prices* of imports. I have applied his formula to the trade statistics of the period, again making use of Mr. Imlah's figures. The index shows little change during the war. It rises sharply in 1815 but falls from 1816 to 1819. In these four years of low investment and unemployment forces operating from overseas added, it would seem, to the distress. But from 1820 there is a marked upward movement broken only by the slumps of 1825–26 and 1831. In the twenties and thirties incomes derived from overseas trade were increasing, and these incomes purchased more of the goods that came in from abroad. Commerce was exerting an increasingly beneficial influence on the economic life of Britain; and, in view of the fact that

the imports consisted largely of such things as tea, coffee, sugar, and the raw materials of industry, it is difficult to believe that the workers had no share in the gain.

IV

It is time to pass from speculation and to say something about such figures as we have relating to wages and the cost of living. The outstanding contribution to our knowledge of the first of these was made forty years ago or more by A. L. Bowley and G. H. Wood. It is based mainly on printed sources, but it is unlikely that further research will invalidate it in any serious way. Nevertheless, it is greatly to be hoped that it may be supplemented by data derived from the wages books which, in spite of bombing and paper salvage, still exist in many scattered factories up and down England. In the hands of careful students these records may be made to yield much information not only about rates of payment but also about actual earnings and sometimes about hours of work and the rents of working-class homes. Until the task is performed, it will continue to be impossible to speak with assurance on the topic on which, greatly daring, I have ventured in this paper.

For information about the cost of living we are dependent almost entirely on the work of American scholars. If some of the remarks that follow are critical, I would add that I am filled with shame that English economic historians have done so little in this field and with admiration for the tenacity and skill which American statisticians have brought to the task.

No single contribution to the study of the industrial revolution in England exceeds in importance that made by Norman J. Silberling, whose untimely death deprived both economic history and statistics of an outstanding exponent. His index number of wholesale prices must remain an indispensable tool for as long ahead as we need look. It is unfortunate that, in my opinion, the same cannot be said of that by-product of his labours, the annual cost-of-living index from 1799 to 1850. This, I need not remind you, is based on the prices of fifteen commodities selected because of their supposed significance to consumers. The prices, however, are chiefly those of the wholesale, not of the retail, market; the index is valid only on the assumption that retail prices moved in the same direction and at approximately the same time as wholesale prices and that the spread between the two remained fairly constant. Now it is true that the structure of retail prices seems to have been far less rigid than it is today. The shopkeeper had not yet fully assumed his function as a shock absorber between merchant and consumer, and the price of a loaf of bread or a pound of beef might double or halve within the course of a few months or even weeks. Several of the commodities used in the index are, however, not consumer's goods at all but merely the raw materials of these. My ancestors of the period did not nourish themselves by munching wheat and oats; they did not cover their nakedness with raw wool and cotton and flax; they were not shod, literally, with leather. According to Silberling, this elementary fact is of small account. "It is well known," he wrote, "in the case of cotton goods that prices adjusted themselves with fair alacrity to the price of raw cotton." When, however, the price relatives of the two are set side by side, we find, as most of us would expect, a considerably greater amplitude of fluctuation in the figures for raw cotton than in those for cotton fabrics. It is surely unrealistic to assume that the prices of food and clothing and footwear are faithfully reflected in those of the substances of which they were made. Also, the prices used by Silberling have been refined by the elimination of customs duties. In actual fact customs duties constituted a large proportion of the cost of nearly everything brought into the country—a proportion that, moreover (as Mr. Imlah has shown), increased steadily down to the 1840s.

Nor is this all. The man whose scheme of expenditure conformed to that drawn up by Silberling had many idiosyncrasies. He did not occupy a house, or at least he was not called upon to pay rent. He allowed himself only a moderate amount of bread and very little porridge,

and he never touched potatoes or strong drink. On the other hand, he got through quite considerable quantities of beef and mutton and showed a fondness for butter. Perhaps he was a diabetic. The ordinary Englishman of the eighteenth century would have been puzzled by him. For this ordinary Englishman (like his descendant of 1949) was a granivorous and not a carnivorous animal. His staple of diet was bread or, in the north of England, oatmeal; meat was for him a luxury to be taken once, or at most twice in the week. Silberling's creature who quenched his thirst only with tea and coffee (with sugar but without milk) would have seemed to him a poor sort of fish. For however abstemious the ordinary Englishman may have been in respect to meat and many other things, he took small beer with each main meal of the working day and ale, in no small measure, whenever he had occasion to celebrate.

The portrait that appears in the scholarly pages of Elizabeth Gilboy has somewhat different features. In her index, cereals have a weight of 50 per cent of the total, as against 32 per cent assigned to them by Silberling, and animal products are rightly given a lower status. But her prices are those that were paid by hospitals, schools, and government departments and not by individual workmen; they are contract and not truly retail prices. Moreover, they are mainly London prices. One of the outstanding features of English life was (and still is) its regional variety. The price of foodstuffs varied greatly from one part of the country to another, and it was not uncommon for something of a local famine to coincide with conditions of relative abundance at places only a hundred miles or so away. As improvements were made in transport by river, road, and canal, prices in the provinces tended to come into line with those of the metropolis. "All the sensible people," wrote Arthur Young in 1769, "attributed the dearness of their country to the turnpike roads; and reason speaks the truth of their opinion . . . make but a turnpike road through their country and all the cheapness vanishes at once." But even fifty or more years later there were many areas of England without turnpikes. In these areas the prices of foodstuffs might be either lower or higher than in London; they were certainly subject to wider fluctuations.

No one has done more than Mrs. Gilboy to make us aware of local variations in the price of labour. But she has not taken full account of the possibility of a similar variation of retail prices or of local peculiarities of diet. Oatmeal remained the staple food of the poor in the north, and rye bread the staple in the Midlands, long after wheaten bread had come into common use in London and the south. To apply contract prices derived from the metropolitan area, and a system of weights based on metropolitan habits, to the earnings of workers in the provinces is indeed a hazardous procedure. What someone has unkindly called Mrs. Gilboy's bricklayers dressed up as bluecoat boys would hardly have been recognized as brothers by the pitmen of Northumberland or the weavers of Lancashire or Somerset.

But, if the scheme of expenditure varied from place to place, it varied also from time to time. Rufus T. Tucker, whose gallant attempt to trace the course of real wages of London artisans over two centuries must excite admiration, shows himself alive to this difficulty. His solution is to abandon the use of a fixed yardstick. When some new commodity seems to become significant in the workers' budget, a place is found for it, and the weights attached to other things are adjusted. Mr. Tucker divided the figures in his index of wages (for our period of time the wages of four kinds of building labour at Greenwich and Chelsea) by his chain index of prices in order to determine "the ability of a typical, regularly employed London artisan to purchase commodities of the sort artisans customarily purchased."

This typical London artisan was no static figure. At first his consumption was limited to a few commodities, including some inferior grain stuffs. Later he spread his expenditure over a wider range of goods, some of which were relatively expensive ("the commodities of the sort artisans customarily purchased" had changed). One might have sup-posed that the wider choice now open to him was one element in a rising standard of living. But no. Mr. Colin Clark has used Tucker's figures to support his thesis that average real income fell "from a fairly high level in the seventeenth century to an Asiatic standard at the beginning of the nineteenth." That Asiatic standard, I may remark in passing, included tea and sugar and some other minor products of Asia hardly known to the London artisan of the seventeenth century. Would the man of the early nineteenth century really have welcomed a return to the diet of his great-great-grandfather? The reception he gave to some well-intentioned efforts to induce him to use rye instead of wheat in his bread hardly leaves one in doubt regarding the answer. Like the labourers of Nottinghamshire, he replied that he had lost his "rye teeth."

Mr. Tucker's artisan was peculiar in another respect. Whatever his income, he always spent one-sixth of it on rent or one-fifth on rent and services combined. This is a proportion far higher than I have been able to discover in other areas, but, no doubt, dwellings were dear in London. It is the fixity of habit that is peculiar. Mr. Tucker says that his index "attempts to measure the workman's ability to purchase housing." But, if it is true that the workman always spent a fixed proportion of his income on housing, would not the figures of wages alone serve as a measure of that ability? In fact, rents are perhaps the most difficult of all prices to draw into an index number. Few consumer goods are completely standardized. A loaf of bread at a given time and place may be a very different commodity from a loaf at another time and place. "The veal that is sold so cheap in some distant counties at present," wrote Malthus, "bears little other resemblance than the name, to that which is bought in London." But this variation of quality is especially marked in the case of houses. A cottage with a living room and a single bedroom is a different commodity from one with four rooms and an attached wash-house or loom shed. A cottage near a factory would usually produce a higher rent than one far distant; for the tenant of the first not only avoided a long walk to and from work but was also able, if he wished, to increase his income by working overtime without trenching unduly on the hours of sleep.

The truth is that it is not possible to compare the welfare of two groups of people separated widely in time and space. We cannot compare the satisfaction derived from a diet that includes bread, potatoes, tea, sugar, and meat with that derived from a diet consisting mainly of oatmeal, milk, cheese, and beer. In the early and middle decades of the eighteenth century only a narrow range of commodities competed for the surplus income of the workers. That is why (to the distress of the well-to-do observer) any easement of the position of the poor was taken out in the form of more drink and more leisure—or in "debauchery and idleness," as the sedate and leisured observer usually put it. Later in the century the range of commodities available widened, and after the French wars new opportunities of travel and education were opened up. No index number can possibly take full account of such matters.

I have made these criticisms and asked these questions in no carping spirit. My object is simply to point to the difficulties of measuring arithmetically changes in the standard of living. The pioneers, as so often happens, have attempted too much. We must restrict our ambitions, realize the limitations of our bag of tricks, and refrain from generalizations. We cannot measure changes in real wages by means of an index of wholesale or institutional prices. We cannot apply the price data of one area to the wage data of another. We cannot safely draw up a table to cover a long series of years during the course of which changes may have occurred not only in the nature and variety of the goods consumed but also in human needs and human wants. We require not a single index but many, each derived from retail prices, each confined to a short run of years, each relating to a single area, perhaps even to a single social or occupational group within an area.

Following a fall after the famine of 1800–1801, the upward movement of prices continued, to a peak in 1812. Thereafter food prices fell to about 1820 but rose again during the following decade. In 1831 the standard diet of the poor can hardly have cost much less than in 1791. If this was so, it must seem that any improvement in the standard of living must have come either from a rise in money wages or from a fall in the prices of things not included in this index. One of the striking features of domestic production was the wide variations in the prices offered for labour. In December, 1793, according to Rowbottom, the weavers of ginghams at Oldham received 10s. per end; in April, 1794, they were paid 19s. and in August of the same year 24s.4d. During the same period the price of weaving nankeens rose from 16s. to 26s. a piece. Generally, for reasons set forth by Adam Smith, the price of labour rose when the cost of provisions fell and years of dearth were usually years of low wages. In these circumstances the standard of life of the worker was subject to violent fluctuation. One of the merits of the factory system was that it offered, and required, regularity of employment and hence greater stability of consumption. During the period 1790–1830 factory production increased rapidly. A greater proportion of the people came to benefit from it both as producers and as consumers. The fall in the price of textiles reduced the price of clothing. Government contracts for uniforms and army boots called into being new industries, and after the war the products of these found a market among the better-paid artisans. Boots began to take the place of clogs, and hats replaced shawls, at least for wear on Sundays. Miscellaneous commodities, ranging from clocks to pocket handkerchiefs, began to enter into the scheme of expenditure, and after 1820 such things as tea and coffee and sugar fell in price substantially. The growth of trade-unions, friendly societies, savings banks, popular newspapers and pamphlets, schools, and nonconformist chapels—all give evidence of the existence of a large class raised well above the level of mere subsistence.

There were, however, masses of unskilled or poorly skilled workers—seasonally employed agricultural workers and hand-loom weavers in particular— whose incomes were almost wholly absorbed in paying for the bare necessaries of life, the prices of which, as we have seen, remained high. My guess would be that the number of those who were able to share in the benefits of economic progress was larger than the number of those who were shut out from those benefits and that it was steadily growing. But the existence of these two groups within the working class needs to be recognized. Perhaps the explanation of the division of opinion, to which I called attention at the beginning of this paper, rests on this. John Stuart Mill and his fellow-economists were thinking of the one group; Rickman and Chadwick had their eyes fixed on the other.

Eric J. Hobsbawm

PESSIMISM RE-STATED BY A MODERN SCHOLAR

Educated in Vienna, Berlin, London and Cambridge, Hobsbawm has been Reader in History in London University since 1959. He is a specialist in working-class history, in Britain (*Labouring Men,* 1964, reprints many of his articles) and in Europe (*Primitive Rebels,* 1959, deals especially with Spain and Italy). The present article is based on nineteenth-century writings, on evidence before parliamentary inquiries, and on reports of Boards of Health. In it, he argues that a country starting industrialisation with an unequal distribution of income and an inefficient use of capital is unlikely to confer rapid gains upon the masses. He insists that, even much later in the nineteenth century, only a small proportion of the working class received substantial gains from the industrial system. He shows, as does Ashton, how unreliable are many of the statistical indices. He then sets forth, in the excerpt that follows, the solid evidence which, he thinks, supports the "pessimistic" view. A technical appendix on food consumption is omitted.

WE may consider three types of evidence in favour of the pessimistic view; those bearing on (a) mortality and health, (b) unemployment and (c) consumption. In view of the weaknesses of wage and price-data, it is best not to consider them here; in any case actual consumption figures shed a more reliable light on real wages. However, we know too little about the actual structure of the population to isolate the movements of working-class indices from the rest of the "labouring poor" and of other classes. But this would be troublesome only if the indices showed a fairly marked rise, which they do not. Since the "labouring poor" clearly formed the majority of the population, a general index showing stability or deterioration is hardly compatible with a significant improvement in their situation, though it does not exclude improvement among a minority of them.

A. SOCIAL INDICES

Our best indices are mortality rates (average expectation of life, infantile, TB mortality, etc.), morbidity rates and anthropometric data. Unfortunately in Britain we lack any reliable anthropometric data such as the French, and any index of health such as the percentage

From Eric J. Hobsbawm, "The British Standard of Living, 1790–1850," *Economic History Review,* Second Series, X (August 1957), pp. 51–61. By permission of the author and of the Editor, *Economic History Review.* It should be noted that the article has been reprinted in Hobsbawm's *Labouring Men* (Weidenfeld and Nicolson, London, 1964) of rejected recruits. Nor have we any useful morbidity figures. The Friendly Societies, whose actuarial advisers made some useful calculations about sickness rates, cannot be regarded as representative samples, since it is agreed that they included mainly the more prosperous or stably-employed workers; and in any case, as Farr (1839) demonstrates, there is little enough evidence from them before that date. It is possible that work on hospital records may allow us to find out more about sickness trends, but too little is available at present for judgment.

We must therefore rely on mortality rates. These have their limitations, though it has been plausibly argued that even the crudest of them—general mortality below the age of 50—is a sensitive indicator of living standards. Still, a high or rising mortality rate, a low expectation of life, are not to be neglected. We need not be too much troubled by the known imperfections of the figures, at any rate where trends emerge over periods of time. In any case, the worst imperfection, the fact that births are less completely registered than deaths— thus swelling earlier figures for infant mortality—helps to correct a pessimistic bias. For as registration improves, recorded mortality rates also drop automatically on paper, though in fact they may change much less in reality.

The general movement of mortality rates is fairly well known. On theoretical grounds, such as those discussed by McKeown and Brown, it is almost inconceivable that there was not a real fall in mortality rates due to improvements in living standards at the beginning of industrialisation, at least for a while. General mortality rates fell markedly from the 1780s to the 1810s and thereafter rose until the 1840s. This "coincided with a change in the age-distribution favourable to a low death-rate, namely an increase in the proportion of those in healthy middle life." The figures therefore understate the real rise in mortality rates, assuming the same age-composition throughout the period. The rise is said to have been due chiefly to higher infantile and youth mortality, especially in the towns, but figures for Glasgow

1821-35 suggest that there it was due primarily to a marked increase in the mortality of men of working age, greatest in the age-group from 30 to 60. Social conditions are the accepted explanation for this. Edmonds, who discusses the Glasgow figures, observed (1835) that "this is just what might be expected to occur, on the supposition of the rising adult population possessing a lower degree of vitality than their immediate predecessors." On the other hand we must not forget that mortality rates did not improve drastically until very much later—say, until the 1870s or 1880s— and may therefore be less relevant to the movement of living standards than is sometimes supposed. (Alternatively, that living standards improved much more slowly after the 1840s than is often supposed). Nevertheless, the rise in mortality rates in the period 1811–41 is clearly of *some* weight for the pessimistic case, all the more as modern work, especially the studies of Holland during and after World War II, tend to link such rates much more directly to the amount of income and food consumption than to other social conditions.

B. UNEMPLOYMENT

There is room for much further work on this subject, whose neglect is rather inexplicable. Here I merely wish to draw attention to some scattered pieces of information which support a pessimistic rather than a rosy view.

Little as we know about the period before the middle 1840s, most students would agree that the real sense of improvement among the labouring classes thereafter was due less to a rise in wage-rates, which often remained surprisingly stable for years, or to an improvement in social conditions, but to the upgrading of labourers from very poorly to less poorly paid jobs, and above all to a decline in unemployment or a greater regularity of employment. In fact, unemployment in the earlier period had been heavy. Let us consider certain components and aspects of it.

We may first consider *pauperism*, the permanent core of poverty, fluctuating relatively little with cyclical changes—

even in 1840–2. The trends of pauperism are difficult to determine, owing to the fundamental changes brought about by the New Poor Law, but its extent is sufficiently indicated by the fact that in the early 1840s something like 10 per cent of the total population were probably paupers. They were not necessarily worse off than the rest, for Tufnell, in the Second Annual Report of the Poor Law Commissioners, estimated that farm-labourers ate less than paupers; perhaps 30 per cent less in crude weight of foodstuffs. This was also the case in depressed towns.

As to the impact of *cyclical slumps*, we have evidence for the worst of these, that of 1841–2. Ashworth's survey of Bolton may be summarised as follows.

TABLE I: UNEMPLOYMENT IN BOLTON 1842

Source: H. Ashworth, "Statistics of the Present Depression of Trade in Bolton," *Journ. Stat. Soc.* V (1842), 74.

Trade	Total employed in 1836	Total employed whole or part-time in 1842	Percentage unemployed
Mills	8124	3063 (full time)	60
Ironworkers	2110	1325 (short time)	36
Carpenters	150	24	84
Bricklayers	120	16	87
Stonemasons	150	50	66
Tailors	500	250	50
Shoemakers	80	40	50

It will be seen that unemployment of ironworkers in this industrial centre was higher than the national average for the Iron-founders' Union, which was then about 15 per cent.

We are, as it happens, quite well informed about unemployment in this depression. In the Vauxhall Ward of Liverpool a little over 25 per cent of smiths and engineers were unemployed, in Dundee somewhat over 50 per cent of the mechanics and the shipbuilders. Slightly under 50 per cent of the Liverpool shoe-makers, over half the Liverpool tailors, two-thirds of the London tailors were unemployed, only 5 out of 160 Dundee tailors were in full work. Three-quarters of the plasterers, well over half the bricklayers in Liverpool, almost five sixths of the masons, three-quarters of the carpenters, slaters, plumbers, etc., in Dundee had no work. Neither had half the "labourers" and almost three-quarters of the women workers in the Liverpool ward. The following table summarises various contemporary enquiries.

TABLE II: UNEMPLOYMENT IN SOME TOWNS, 1841–2

Town	Fit for work	Fully Employed	Partly Employed	Unemployed
Liverpool, Vauxhall	4814	1841	595	2378
Stockport	8215	1204	2866	4145
Colne	4923	964	1604	2355
Bury	3982	1107	—	—
Oldham	19500	9500	5000 (half-time)	5000
Accrington (textiles)	3738	1389	1622	727
Wigan	4109	981	2572	1563

This list could be prolonged.

Such figures mean little, unless we remember what they implied for the standard of living. Clitheroe (normal population, 6700, normal employment in the five main factories, 2500) had 2300 paupers in 1842; the Brontes' Haworth (population 2400), 308. Twenty per cent of the population of Nottingham was on the Poor Law, 33 per cent of that of Paisley on charity. Fifteen to twenty per cent of the population of Leeds had an income of less than *one shilling* per head per week; over one-third of the families in the Vauxhall Ward of Liverpool had an income of less than five shillings a week, indeed most of them had no visible income at all. In this ward total earnings had halved since 1835, meat consumption had halved, bread consumption had remained stable, oatmeal consumption had doubled, potato consumption risen more than a third, and similarly dramatic declines in purchases—40 per cent in Manchester —are reported in all the towns investigated by the Anti-Corn Law League. No discussion which overlooks the massive waves of destitution which swamped large sections of the labouring poor in every depression, can claim to be realistic.

Vagrancy provides another little-used index of unemployment, since out-of-work labourers tended to tramp in search of jobs. The actual amount of vagrancy was large enough to have appalled the Tudor administrators who were troubled with sturdy beggars. The only full "census" of vagrants, that undertaken in 1847–51 by the police of the Derwent division of Cumberland, recorded 42,386 in 1847, (*excluding* Poor Law vagrants), 42,000 in 1848 (*including* them) and—as proof of the cyclical nature of this aspect of unemployment—rapidly declining numbers in subsequent years: 33,500, 24,000, 18,000. Allowing for those who used neither common lodging houses nor the Poor Law, but probably not allowing for the "tramping artisans" who were catered for by their unions, we may well have had something like 1000 tramps a week passing up and down this highway during a slump. Whether the estimates that 13,000 vagrants of all kinds passed through Preston in 1832 indicates incomplete information or a rise in unemployment between 1832 and 1847–51, is an open question.

It is, however, clear that vagrancy tended to increase from the Napoleonic wars until the early 1830s, largely because of "commercial fluctuations," partly because of the increase in Irish vagrants—that is to say, Irish-born unemployed rather than seasonal harvesters. The following Table III illustrates this trend.

TABLE III: VAGRANCY TRENDS 1803–1834

	Great North Road Vagrants with passes all*	Irish***		Irish vagrants passed out of Middlesex***	Berks**	Wilts***
1803	569 (Royston)					
1807–28	540					
1811–12	1014	1811	7	1811	1464	301	80
1815–16	2894	1816	58	1816	1974	690	121
1820	7000			1821	4583	1850	1148
		1826	331	1826	3307	2044	1811
		1831	1751	1831	9281	5428	4510

*V. C. H. Cambridgeshire, II, 103–4.
**Report of R. C. on Poor Law, App. E, Parl. Papers 1834, XXXVIII, 249–50.
***Same source. Includes Scots paupers.

Unemployment indices such as these may bear directly on the argument between optimists and pessimists, as in the case of the building trade, where the optimistic view (Clapham) based on "real wages" clashes particularly sharply with the pessimistic view (Postgate), based also on literary evidence. There is no debate about the relatively good wages of building artisans. However, Shannon's brick index shows that output, and hence also employment, in the industry fluctuated in the following manner. Periods of rapid expansion (e.g. 1800–4) are followed by periods of slower expansion (e.g. 1805–14) and these in turn by slumps (e.g. 1815–19). Both the latter phases create unemployment, for in an industry geared to expansion—and which, haphazardly recruited under private enterprise, tends to produce an excess labour force anyway—even a slowing of expansion will throw marginal workers out of jobs. In an era of pioneer industrialisation under private enterprise this effect will be all the greater, because workers are not yet accustomed to a fluctuating and blind economy. Thus builders in pre-industrial places are accustomed to a labour force whose size is fairly well adjusted to the "normal" amount of repair and replacement, and perhaps to a gradual expansion of demand by known consumers.

Now we know for a fact that builders, including artisans, tended to become exceptionally militant in the early 1830s. There is also some literary evidence about poverty and destitution among them. Clapham's argument cannot explain the first or admit the second, but Shannon's index explains both, for it suggests a short, sharp building boom in 1820–4, followed by a slowing expansion in 1825–9 and a marked slump in 1830–4. Nothing is more plausible than that, by the early thirties, there should be both poverty and discontent. This example shows very clearly how dangerous it is to rely on what purports to be statistical evidence, while neglecting equally relevant quantitative factors, which happen not always to be as easily traced as in the building trade.

Nor is the force of such arguments confined to builders. They apply to all manner of other crafts (including their attached labourers and dependents) which made the transition from the pre-industrial to the industrial rhythm of economic movement. The London furniture-makers whose plight Mayhew describes, and whose decline is shown by the collapse of their unions and collective agreements in our period, are a case in point. Local studies would no doubt reveal similar cases elsewhere, perhaps among the Sheffield metal operatives, after the collapse of their "golden age" in the 1810s and 1820s. It is too often forgotten that something like "technological" unemployment was not confined purely to those workers who were actually replaced by new machines. It could affect almost all pre-industrial industries and trades surviving into the machine age; that is, as Clapham has

shown, a great many. Doubtless the general expansion of the early industrial period (say 1780–1811) tended to diminish unemployment except during crises; doubtless the decades of difficulty and adjustment after the wars tended to make the problem more acute. From the later 1840s, the working classes began to adjust themselves to life under a new set of economic rules, recognised and—insofar as "political economy" and union policy could do so—counteracted. But it is highly probable that the period 1811–42 saw abnormal problems and abnormal unemployment, such as is not revealed by the general "real wage" indices.

Whether further study can give us more adequate figures about unemployment in the first half of the century is a matter for debate. It will certainly be unable to measure adequately the occasional, seasonal or intermittent unemployment and the permanent bulk of underemployment, though no estimate of real wages is worth much which neglects this. An estimate for Leeds may be quoted. It almost certainly underestimates the case, even if we assume that Leeds builders worked a much longer season than the 6–7 months of eighteenth-century London builders, but at any rate it indicates the deductions from theoretical wage-rates which might have to be made (Table IV). The mass of unskilled and, by definition, casual trades are not comprised in this or any other practicable list [see Table IV on page 30].

These notes on unemployment are sufficient to throw doubt upon the less critical statements of the optimistic view, but not to establish any alternative view. They may perhaps serve to remind us how much work there is still to be done in this field.

C. CONSUMPTION FIGURES

As Britain was not a bureaucratic state, we lack official national data, except for wholly imported articles. Nevertheless, we can get a good deal more information than has hitherto been brought into the discussion. This shows that, from the later 1790s until the early 1840s, there is no evidence of any major rise in the per capita consumption of

TABLE IV: AVERAGE UNEMPLOYMENT
PER YEAR, AND WEEKLY WAGES
CORRECTED FOR THIS. LEEDS, 1838

Source: "Condition of the Town of Leeds
and its Inhabitants," *Journ. Stat. Soc.*, II
(1839), 422.

Trades working 12 months	Weekly wages	Weekly corrected wages
Clothdrawers	24/6	24/6
Smiths	19/–	19/–
Millwrights	26/–	26/–
Plane Makers	21/–	21/–
Gunsmiths	25/–	25/–
Mechanics	24/–	24/–
Ironmoulders	25/–	25/–
Turners	22/–	22/–
Worsted Piecers	4/6	4/6
Preparers	6/6	6/6
Trades working 11 months		
Tailors	16/–	14/8
Joiners	19/6	17/11
Saddlers	21/–	19/3
Curriers	20/–	19/1
Brassfounders	25/–	24/1
Coopers	20/–	19/1
Printers	21/–	19/3
Trades working 10 months		
Shoemakers	14/–	11/8
Plumbers	23/–	19/2
Woolsorters	21/–	17/6
Woodturners	17/–	14/2
Masons	22/–	18/4
Weavers	13/–	10/10
Hatters	24/–	20/–
Woolcombers	14/–	11/8
Wheelwrights	18/–	15/–
Trades working 9 months		
Painters	20/–	15/–
Clothpressers	20/–	15/–
Slubbers	24/–	18/–
Plasterers	18/–	13/6
Bricklayers	23/–	17/3
Woollen Piecers	5/–	3/9
Woollen Fillers	6/–	4/6
Dyers	22/–	16/6
Woodsawyers	20/–	15/–

several foodstuffs, and in some instances evidence of a temporary fall
which had not yet been completely made
good by the middle 1840s. If the case for
deterioration in this period can be established firmly, I suggest that it will be
done on the basis of consumption data.

Tea, sugar and tobacco, being wholly
imported, furnish national consumption
figures which may be divided by the estimated population to give a crude index
of per capita consumption. However, we
note that Clapham, though an optimist
and aware of the figures, wisely refused
to use them as an argument in his favour
since absolute per capita consumption
in this period was low, and such increases as occurred were disappointingly
small. Indeed, the contrast between the
curve before and after the middle 1840s
when it begins to rise sharply, is one of
the strongest arguments on the pessimistic side. All three series show a slowly
rising trend and after the 1840s a much
sharper rise, though tobacco consumption fell (probably owing to increased
duties) in the 1810s. The tobacco series
includes Irish consumption after the
middle 1820s and is thus difficult to use.
The tea series is also hard to interpret,
since it reflects not merely the capacity
to buy, but also the secular trend to
abandon older beverages for a new one.
The significance of tea-drinking was
much debated by contemporaries, who
were far from considering it an automatic sign of improved living standards. At
all events it only shows four periods of
decline—1815–16, 1818–19, a dramat-
ically sharp fall in 1836–7 after a sharp
rise, and a slighter fall in 1839–40. Tea
seems to have been immune to the
slumps of 1826 and, more surprisingly,
1841–2, which makes it suspect as an
index of living-standards. Tobacco does
not reflect the slump of 1836–7, but
does reflect the others, though not
much. Anyway, this article shows virtually stable consumption. Sugar is the
most sensitive indicator though—owing
to various outside factors—it does not
always reflect trade-cycle movements. It
shows the slumps of 1839–40 and 1841–
2 well. Broadly speaking there is no
tendency for sugar consumption to rise
above the Napoleonic peak until well
into the 1840s. There is a sharp post-war
decline, a sharp rise to rather lower levels after 1818, a slow rise—almost a
plateau—until 1831, and then an
equally slow decline or stagnation until
1843 or 44. Tea, sugar and tobacco indicate no marked rise in the standards
of living, but beyond this little can be
deduced from the crude series.

The case of *meat* is different. Here we possess at least two indices, the Smithfield figures for London for the entire period, and the yield of the excise on hides and skins for the period up to 1825. The Smithfield figures show that, while London's population index rose from 100 in 1801 to 202 in 1841, the number of beef cattle slaughtered rose only to 146, of sheep to 176 in the same period. The following Table V gives the figures by decades.

TABLE V: DECENNIAL PERCENTAGE INCREASE IN LONDON POPULATION, BEEF AND SHEEP AT SMITHFIELD 1801–51

Date Population	Animals Average	Index			Decennial increase		
		Population	Beef	Sheep	Population	Beef	Sheep
1801	1800–4	100	100	100			
1811	1810–12	119	105	119	+19	+5	+19
1821	1819–22	144	113	135	+25	+8	+16
1831	1830–4	173	127	152	+29	+14	+17
1841	1840–3	203	146	176	+30	+19	+24
1851	1850–2*	246	198	193	+43	+42	+17

*The choice of base-dates for the animals cannot be rigid. Thus 1800–4 is chosen, because say 1800–2 would give abnormally high figures, thus understating the rise in the following decade. For sheep 1840–2 has been taken as a base-date, because the exceptionally high figure for 1843 would overstate the decennial rise. The choice of different dates would change the results slightly, but not substantially.

It will be seen that the increase in beef lagged behind that in population in all decades until the 1840s. Mutton also lagged—though less—except in the first decade. On the whole a per capita decline in London meat consumption up to the 1840s is thus almost certain.

The Excise on hides and leather yields somewhat cruder figures. The following table summarises what little we can get from them.

TABLE VI: YIELD OF EXCISE ON HIDES AND SKINS IN LONDON AND REST OF COUNTRY

1801 (1800–1 for Excise) = 100

Date	Population	Country yield	London yield
1801	100	100	100
1811	114.5	122	107
1821	136	106*	113*
1825	150	135	150

*This is probably understated.

Without going further into the somewhat complex discussion of the sources, it seems clear that the figures do not indicate a major rise in per capita meat consumption.

About *cereals* and *potatoes,* the staple of the poor man's diet, we can also find out some things. The fundamental fact is that, as contemporaries already knew, wheat production and imports did not keep pace with the growth of population so that the amount of wheat available per capita fell steadily from the late eighteenth century until the 1850s, the amount of potatoes available rising at about the same rate. It follows that, whatever the literary evidence, somebody *must* during this period have shifted away from wheat; presumably to potatoes. The simplest view would be that the major change from brown to white bread had already taken place by, say, the 1790s, and that the drift from wheat took place thereafter; but this would not explain the almost certain later drift from brown to white bread in the North and West. But this may have been "paid for" by a decline in per capita consumption elsewhere. This is technically possible. The mean consumption of bread-stuffs among farm labourers in 1862 was about 14½ lb. per week. Twelve counties consumed less than this —from 10¼ to 11¾ lb., six more than 13 lb., fourteen about the average. Where per capita consumption varied so widely —between 10¼ and 14¼, not to mention the 18¾ of Anglesey, there is scope for both an earlier decline in per capita consumption in some places and for considerable "compensation" between counties. However it is not my purpose to suggest explanations. All we can say is, that a rise in the per capita consumption of white bread in this period at *nobody's* expense is out of the question. Wheat consumption may have fallen with or without additional potato consumption, or some areas may have seen it rise at the expense of others (with or without a rise in potatoes).

We have no general statistics about the consumption of other common foodstuffs. It is difficult to see anything but a decline of *milk,* because cow-keeping must have declined with urbanisation (though it probably continued in towns on a larger scale than is sometimes admitted) and because of the decline of the traditional rural diet which relied heavily on "white meats." It survived longer in the North and West. Even in 1862 some fortunate groups of poor workers stuck to it, doubtless much to their benefit: the Macclesfield silk weavers consumed 41.5 fluid oz. per head per week, as against the 11 oz. of the Coventry weavers, the 7.6 oz. of the Spitalfields weavers, and the 1.6 oz. of Bethnal Green. But all the evidence points to a decline in milk consumption. Not so with *butter,* which was evidently—and naturally, since bread formed so large a part of the labourer's diet—considered a greater necessity than meat. In Dukinfield and Manchester (1836) outlays on it were comparable to those on meat, and comparison with 1841 shows that they were rather inelastic. The few comparable budgets from Eden show a similar pattern of expenditure, though perhaps a rather smaller outlay on butter than on meat. The poor man thus ate butter; only the destitute man might be unable to. It is not impossible that butter consumption rose during urbanisation, for other things to spread on bread—e.g. lard or dripping—must have been harder to come by when people kept fewer pigs and meat-consumption was low and erratic. *Cheese* consumption seems to have declined, for many urban workers seem not to have had it or to have developed the fashion of substituting it for meat. In Dukinfield and Manchester they spent much less on cheese than on butter, and the 1862 farm-labourers ate much more of it, even allowing for their slightly better position, than the "urban poor." *Eggs*

seem to have been of small importance. Per capita consumption can hardly have risen.

The evidence is thus not at all favourable to the "optimistic" view. Though it does not necessarily or firmly establish the "pessimistic" one, it rather points towards it. The growth of *adulteration* slightly strengthens the pessimistic case. Even if we assume that late eighteenth-century shopkeepers were no less dishonest than nineteenth-century ones, it must have affected more people, since a greater number and proportion had to rely on them. The *Lancet* enquiry in the 1850s brings the following points out very clearly: (i) all bread tested in two separate samples was adulterated; (ii) over half of oatmeal was adulterated; (iii) *all* but the highest-quality teas were invariably adulterated; (iv) a little under half the milk and (v) *all* butter was watered. Over half the jam and preserves included deleterious matter, but this may have been due simply to bad production. The only commodity of common use not largely adulterated was sugar, almost 90 per cent of which seems to have been straight, though often filthy.

The discussion of food consumption thus throws considerable doubt on the optimistic view. However, it should be pointed out that this does *not* mean that early nineteenth-century Britons had an "Asiatic" standard of living. This is nonsense, and such loose statements have caused much confusion. Britain was almost certainly better fed than all but the most prosperous peasant areas, or the more comfortable classes, in continental countries; but then it had been so, as Drummond and Wilbraham pointed out, long before the Industrial Revolution. The point at issue is not whether we fell as low as other countries, but whether, by our own standards, we improved or deteriorated, and in either case, how much.

It is not the purpose of this paper to discuss the evolution of living standards in the eighteenth century, since the major discussion of living standards has been about the period between the end of the Napoleonic Wars and "some unspecified date between the end of Chartism and the Great Exhibition." It is altogether likely that living standards improved over much of the eighteenth century. It is not improbable that, sometime soon after the onset of the Industrial Revolution . . . which is perhaps better placed in the 1780s than in the 1760s—they ceased to improve and declined. Perhaps the middle 1790s, the period of Speenhamland and shortage, mark the turning-point. At the other end, the middle 1840s certainly mark a turning-point.

We may therefore sum up as follows.

The classical view has been put in Sidney Webb's words: "If the Chartists in 1837 had called for a comparison of their time with 1787, and had obtained a fair account of the actual social life of the working-man at the two periods, it is almost certain that they would have recorded a positive decline in the standard of life of large classes of the population." This view has not been so far made untenable. It may be that further evidence will discredit it; but it will have to be vastly stronger evidence than has so far been adduced.

Ronald M. Hartwell

IMPROVEMENT DEFENDED

Hartwell's first book was on Australian economic history: *The Economic Development of Van Diemen's Land, 1820–1850* (1954). He is now Fellow of Nuffield College, and Reader in Recent Social and Economic History, at Oxford, and is one of the editors of *Economic History Review*. In this article, some of Hartwell's sources resemble Hobsbawm's. Many, however, are nineteenth-century commentaries or modern monographs, which serve either as sources of statistics or as starting-points for economic analysis. Some of the more technical portions of this analysis have been omitted in my editing; and I have also reduced the detail on food consumption.

THIS article argues for an upward trend in living standards during the Industrial Revolution; in section II, from an examination of national income and other aggregate statistics that have survived (or can be calculated or guessed with some certainty), from wage-price data, and from analogy; in section III, from an analysis of consumption figures; and in section IV, from the evidence of vital statistics, from a comparison with eighteenth century living standards, and from details of the expansion after 1800 of social and economic opportunities. Briefly the argument is that, since average per capita income increased, since there was no trend in distribution against the workers, since (after 1815) prices fell while money wages remained constant, since per capita consumption of food and other consumer goods increased, and since government increasingly intervened in economic life to protect or raise living standards, then the real wages of the majority of English workers were rising in the years 1800 to 1850.

II

Economic growth implies an increase in per capita national income, and, if distribution leaves labour with at least the same relative share of the increasing product, an increase in the average

From Ronald M. Hartwell, "The Rising Standard of Living in England, 1800–1850," *Economic History Review*, Second Series, XIII (April, 1961), pp. 397–416. By permission of the author and of the Editor, *Economic History Review*.

standard of living. Generally, as the historical analyses of economic development have shown, an increase in per capita income has been accompanied by a more equal income distribution. In Britain, contemporary estimates of the national income between 1800 and 1850 indicate that average real income doubled in this period, and, although the upward trend was uneven, with stagnation during the war and a possible small decline in the thirties, average per capita income had already increased fifty per cent by 1830. No juggling of the figures could suggest deterioration, but the estimates are inadequate both in their methods of compilation and in their statistical bases, so that they can be used only as an indication of trend, and not as a measure of change. This probable increase, of uncertain size, in per capita income becomes more plausible, however, when three other phenomena are taken into account: the increase in the output of manufacturing industry relative to the increase in population; the increasing and substantial proportion of manufacturing income in the national income; and the increasing and substantial proportion of the total working population employed in manufacturing industry. According to W. Hoffmann, the rate of growth of industrial output between 1782 and 1855 was 3 to 4 per cent per annum (except during the war years when the rate was about 2 per cent); over the same period the annual rate of growth of population varied from 1.2 to 1.5 per cent, with the highest rate between 1811 and 1831, and a declining rate thereafter. This, however, would have been of little significance if industrial output was so small a part of national income that changes in it could not have affected the average standard of life. But the contribution of manufacturing industry to the national income increased from about one fifth in 1770, to one quarter in 1812, to one third in 1831. Census figures for 1841 and 1851 show that about one third of the occupied population of England and Wales was engaged in manufacturing industry and that the 1851 proportion was not exceeded until 1951. In 1850, M. Mulhall estimated, manufacturing industry provided £269 millions (about 40 per cent) of a British national income of £690 millions. It is probable, therefore, that by 1830 manufacturing had a similar role as income producer as it has had since 1850, and that the growth of manufacturing output substantially affected living standards.

In the England of the Industrial Revolution, the rate of saving was necessarily low in a society where average incomes were still not much above subsistence, and where the capital market was imperfect; and the replacement of men by machines, of wind and water by steam power, and of the home by the factory, marked an increase in productivity that was often spectacular. But whereas the productivity of much new industrial equipment was high, its cost was often low. Thus the comparatively low capital output ratio was not incompatible with rising real incomes. By 1800 improvements in techniques and management were already making capital more fruitful, and it is certain that over the whole period the rate of growth of output depended as much on the rate of technical progress as on the rate of capital accumulation, on the quality as much as on the quantity of investment.

The employment effect, however, was also potentially large. Many of the new machines required less labour per unit of output, so that, theoretically, the consequent labour displacement could have been large enough to have prevented real wages from rising. On the other hand, because the new machines generally reduced costs, including the cost of goods consumed by the workers, there was at the same time a tendency for real wages to rise. It is because of this tendency, J. R. Hicks has suggested, that capital accumulation in the nineteenth century was so favourable to the standard of living. Moreover, money wages were stable between 1820 and 1850, a period of falling prices, indicating that there was insufficient competition from underemployed and unemployed labour to pull down wages. In spite of pockets of technological underemployment, the displacement of labour by machinery did not result in a decline of average real wages. And the existence of groups of wage-earners whose real wages were stable or declining—industrial groups like the handloom weavers or national groups like the Irish—bias the averages downwards and disguise the gains in the growing sectors of the economy. Indeed, to some extent, the displacement of labour was theoretical: the new machines required less labour per unit of output than did old plant making the same products; but much new plant was an addition to total plant, not a displacement of existing plant, and when this was so, the net effect on the total demand for labour was an absolute increase. Thus, for example, railways did gradually displace canals, but the displacement effect on canal labour was insignificant compared with the massive requirements for railway construction and maintenance. There was in this period a continually rising demand for industrial labour, a demand that caused a differential between agricultural and industrial wages, and a consequent continuous migration towards the industrial areas. As a spokesman of the agricultural labourers declared bitterly, "it is well known that in the great trading towns, such as Manchester, Sheffield, Birmingham, etc., four days work in a week amply supply the dissolute and the drunken."

But factories have to be administered, and machines have to be tended, and even the best equipment is of little value without able entrepreneurs and skilled labourers. The industrial revolution was as much a revolution in industrial organisation as in technology. Entrepreneurs increasingly centralised production into factories, worked out the problems of factory management, accounting, financing, merchanting and labour-relations. Not the least problem was to change craft and agricultural labourers into factory workers, with their different skills, different rhythm of work, different incentives, different social attitudes, and different way of life. The necessary transformation was certainly painful, but it was gradually achieved without political revolution, and with labour increasing its opportunities, its industrial skill and its bargaining strength. The quantitative effect of such changes on output cannot be measured accurately, but they certainly tended to increase productivity.

Study of the long-term trends in the wage-share of the national income show that since about 1860, that share has remained almost constant. If this stability had a longer history, the wage bill would have been increasing proportionately with the national income from some earlier date, possibly from the beginning of the industrial revolution. It is not unlikely, however, that the share of wages was less in 1780–1800 than in 1860, and thus, that wages were rising between those dates more quickly than national income. That this was probable is indicated by the continuous increase over the period of those employed in manufacturing industry. Agricultural wages lagged behind industrial wages, and as more workers transferred to higher productivity occupations, average real wages increased. Census figures show that the percentage proportions of agricultural to all families in 1811 and 1831 were 35.2 and 28.2, and that the percentage proportions of adult males employed in agriculture to all male workers in 1831, 1841 and 1851 were 31.7, 25.7 and 21.1. Further confirmation is provided by the increasing proportion over these years of total population engaged in commerce, finance and the professions, "a fairly precise measurement of the degree of economic advancement." Occupational statistics before 1841, except in broad categories, are not very helpful, but other evidence shows that there were large increases in the numbers employed in services—in transport, commerce and finance, in government, and in the professions—between 1780 and 1850. Between 1841 and 1851 the census figures show an increase in services, excluding domestic service, of from 9.1 to 12.2 per cent of the population, or, as corrected by C. Booth, of from 14.0 to 16.5 per cent. At the same time the proportion of gainfully occupied in the population increased, as the under-employed labour of the predominantly agricultural economy of pre-industrial Britain was gradually absorbed into fuller employment in industry and services. Thus, for example, the much publicised and criti- cised employment of women and chil- dren, though common in the farms and domestic industries of pre-industrial rev- olution England, was certainly more productive and generally more humane during the industrial revolution.

The workers' standard of living is af- fected by the redistribution of income by government, especially through taxa- tion and expenditure on social welfare. The tax structure between 1800 and 1850 was certainly regressive, although there was income tax during the war (the heaviest of the century) and again after 1842 when it yielded £5 millions annually. Government revenue came mainly from indirect taxation, of which customs revenue provided an increasing proportion until 1840, and thereafter a stable one. The reduction of tariffs after 1824, and especially after 1840, gave general benefit by lowering the price of many goods of common consumption and by encouraging the demand for goods which hitherto had been consid- ered luxuries. Other taxation, also mainly indirect, was reduced after the war, and remained relatively stable at £3–4 millions between 1825 and 1856. Total government revenue also declined after 1815 both absolutely (until 1843) and as a proportion of national income, and in terms of average per capita con- tributions. On the expenditure side, the national debt service was the largest and most regressive item, but its incidence remained stable in money terms, vary- ing from £33.9 to £28.1 millions be- tween 1815 and 1845, so that it was a decreasing proportion of national in- come even though in real terms its inci- dence increased in the period of falling prices. The civil and pensions list, to which *The Black Book* gave so much publicity, was a small item and it de- creased absolutely. "Social services" cost from £2 to £5 millions, increasing after 1830, but the benefit to the worker must have been very small. Much more impor- tant was the expenditure for the relief and maintenance of the poor through the poor and county rates, which in- creased to £7.9 millions in 1818, var- ied from £5.7 to £7.0 millions from 1818 to 1832, fell to £4.0 millions in

1834, and increased to £6.2 millions in 1848. All that can be said in summary about these collections and disburse- ments of government is that there was no marked trend, although there was a reduction in the average contributions, and an increase in the average receipts, of the labouring poor. In another way, however, government action was impor- tant. Government legislation which in- volved private expenditure in improving the condition of the working classes was considerable. Such legislation in- cluded protective acts like the factory and truck acts, enabling acts such as the legislation for savings banks and friendly societies, and acts of general benefit such as those improving munici- pal government. Under such legislation, for example, hours of work were reduced in factories and limits were set to the age at which children were allowed to work, women and children were excluded from mines, some educational facilities were enforced for factory children, and the provision of water and the disposal of sewage by municipal authorities were facilitated. Such legislation, J. M. Lud- low and L. Jones declared, secured "the primary elements of health, safety and well-being" for the people at large, and enabled them "to become a better fed, better clothed, better housed, more healthy, more orderly, more saving, more industrious, more self-reliant, bet- ter educated population." There is no doubt that humanitarian and legislative pressure increased the social-overhead cost of industry, directly benefiting the workers, and driving out of business those employers at the margin whose in- efficiency had previously been protected by the exploitation of labour.

III

Evidence of the condition of the work- ing class during the industrial revolu- tion can be found also in the statistics of savings, wages and consumption. After the establishment of savings banks in 1817 deposits increased to £14.3 mil- lions by 1829, and to almost £30 mil- lions by 1850, when the number of de- positors totalled 1,112,999. "The £30 millions of deposits in 1847 were pre- dominantly the savings of wage-earners, among whom domestic servants and artisans occupied the most prominent places." Friendly and Benefit Societies, of which there were 20,000 in 1858 with a membership of about two millions, had also accumulated £9 millions. Other societies catering for working-class savings, such as Building and Land Societies (after 1816) and Co-operative Societies (after 1844), did not advance with such rapidity, although their foundation in this period is evidence of the increased ability of the working class to save.

A large and long economic expansion like the industrial revolution was possible only with a large expansion of the market, with the creation or discovery of increasing and accessible markets with consumers willing and able to buy the expanding output of goods and services. For a shorter period, however, it is relevant, in an inquiry into living standards, to know how much of the increased production went into savings and investment rather than into consumption, and how much went abroad without immediate repayment in other goods. But, whatever the amount of savings and exports in the short run, in the long run capital accumulation would have increased productivity, and sales abroad would have resulted in increased imports. In any case neither capital accumulation nor exports, nor the two together, could have completely absorbed the increase in production in this period: capital accumulation was not so large as to make exorbitant demands on current output; and exports, as a proportion of national income, increased from 12 per cent in 1820 to 15 per cent in 1850 (retained imports meantime increasing from 12 to 18 per cent), while the balance of merchandise trade became increasingly *unfavourable* (averaging £8.66 millions in 1816–20, about 3 per cent of national income, and £26.8 millions in 1846–50, about 5 per cent of national income). There was, however, the period of the war, when much production went either into unproductive war effort at home, or into loans and subsidies for allies abroad. As G. W. Daniels has pointed out, "the increased power of production, instead of improving the material welfare of the community, had to be devoted to the prosecution of the war." The failure of living standards to rise much before 1815 was due, therefore, not to industrialisation, but to war.

The extension of the market was made possible more by reduced prices than by increased money wages. While money wages after the war remained relatively constant, the prices of manufactured and agricultural goods declined. The goods of the industrial and agricultural revolutions tended to be cheap and plentiful, for the new entrepreneurs were fully aware that great expansion of production was possible only by supplying goods suitable for mass markets. If only manufactured goods had fallen in price, however, the gain in real wages to a working class that spent a high proportion of its income on food and fuel would not have been large. But food prices also declined after 1815, along with the prices of most other consumer goods. R. S. Tucker's index of consumer goods prices—for food, fuel and light, and clothing, the most important items in working class budgets—shows a downward trend from 1813–15 to 1845, as also does Miss E. B. Schumpeter's index for 22 articles of food and drink, and nine articles of fuel, light and clothing. Money wages, in contrast, rose slightly less than prices during the war, and remained stable, or fell less than prices after the war, as the wages indices that have been compiled for this period show. The facts that aggregate money national income increased substantially, money wages remained stable, and prices of key foodstuffs remained stable or fell, suggest clearly that food supplies at least kept pace with population. When other commodities are taken into consideration, the implication is clear: an increase in real wages, at least after 1815, which it would be irresponsible to deny, and which, indeed, has been confirmed by the industrial histories of the period.

Although consumption statistics before 1850 are inadequate and unreliable, they do indicate modest though fluctuating increases in the consumption of most foodstuffs and other consumption goods. M. G. Mulhall, for example, has reckoned that between 1811 and 1850 the per capita consumption of meat, sugar, tea, beer and eggs increased, while that of wheat decreased somewhat between 1830 and 1850, increasing thereafter. Import statistics are the most accurate of the measures of consumption in this period, and these show important long-term gains in a wide range of commodities; for example, in tea, "from about 1815 there is a secular rise, notably accelerated in the last decade of the period"; in tobacco, also a "persistent upward trend"; and in sugar, "the trend movement is upward." By 1840, to take one source of imports, steamships were pouring into England an almost daily stream of Irish livestock, poultry, meat and eggs. During "the hungry forties" there were increases in the average per capita consumption of a number of imported foodstuffs: butter, cocoa, cheese, coffee, rice, sugar, tea, tobacco, currants. For this reason Peel, in his election letter to the electors of Tamworth in July 1847, noting the large increase in the import of non-essential foodstuffs between 1841 and 1846, declared: "Can there be a doubt that if the consumption of articles of a second necessity has been thus advancing, the consumption of articles of first necessity, of meat and of bread for instance, has been making at least an equally rapid progress?" Certainly, when P. L. Simmonds considered national eating habits in the 1850s he concluded "how much better an Englishman is fed than anyone else in the world."

There are, unfortunately, no adequate statistics for bread and meat consumption. The main statistical uncertainties in the case of bread are the acreage and the yield of cereal crops, especially wheat. There is no convincing evidence for Dr. Hobsbawm's statement that "The fundamental fact is that, as contemporaries already knew, wheat production and imports did not keep pace with the growth of population so that the amount of wheat available per capita fell steadily from the late eighteenth century until the 1850s, the amount of potatoes available rising at about the same rate." On the contrary, as T. Tooke, G. R. Porter, J. R. McCulloch and even

J. S. Mill pointed out, agricultural output increased faster than population. When F. M. Eden wrote in 1797, barley, oat and rye breads were common, especially in the north; when McCulloch discussed bread in his commercial dictionary in 1859 he commented on the disappearance of barley and oat breads, the inconsiderable use of rye bread, and the universal consumption in towns and villages, and almost everywhere in the country, of wheat bread. Such a substitution in a rapidly growing population—and one usually associated with increasing living standards—would not have been possible without a large increase in the home production of wheat, for it cannot be accounted for by the increase in imports. In the century of the agricultural revolution, however, this is not surprising: between 1760 and 1864 the common fields and wastes of England were enclosed, increasing both the area of, and yield from, arable. Even without other improvements, enclosure generally increased yields substantially. Wheat and bread prices certainly support the view that there was no long-term shortage of wheat and flour. Wheat prices fell sharply after 1815 and were relatively stable, though with a discernible downward trend, after 1822, the yearly average reaching 70s. only on one occasion, 1839, before 1850, and the price in 1835, 39s. 4d., being the lowest for half a century. The price of bread was also relatively stable in these years; for example, the London four lb. loaf fluctuated from 6.8d. to 11.5d. between 1820 and 1850, but with a range of 6.8d. to 10.5d. in all but seven years, and with decade averages of 9.7d., 9.1d. and 9.3d.

Far less is known about potato consumption than wheat consumption, although R. N. Salaman reckoned that per capita daily consumption in England and Wales increased from 0.4 to 0.6 lbs. between 1795 and 1838. The theory that this increase was not a net addition to total diet, associated after 1815 with the increasing use of allotments by the working class, but a necessary substitute of an inferior vegetable for wheat bread, is based on the doubtful assumptions that bread consumption was declining, and that the potato was an inferior food. Prejudice against the potato stemmed partly from dislike of the Irish, and certainly the half million Irish in England in 1850 help to explain the increasing popularity of the root. But increasing consumption was due also to the simple facts that people liked potatoes and that they were good food, as Adam Smith demonstrated. Moreover the potato was but one of many vegetables and fruits whose consumption was increasing. Vegetables, that in 1800 had only been grown casually, like water-cress, were by 1850 commercialized; fruits that were not imported at all, or in very small quantities in 1800, were regularly imported by the 1830s—for example, cherries and apples—and in large quantities by 1850. In London, Covent Garden was rebuilt in 1827, and by 1850 there were in addition five other important markets supplying the metropolis with fruit and vegetables. By 1850 every large town had its market gardens and orchards, and for London, the largest and richest market, the movement was well under way which by 1870 had almost filled the Thames Valley with fruit trees and vegetable crops.

"Next to the Habeas Corpus and the Freedom of the Press," Charles Dickens wrote, "there are few things that the English people have a greater respect for and livelier faith in than beef." In the first fifty years of the nineteenth century, the English working class came to expect meat as a part of the normal diet. Above all other foods, wheat bread and meat were to them the criteria of increasing living standards and superiority over foreigners. "Until the 'Roast beef of old England' shall cease to be one of the institutions of the country—one of the characteristics whereby foreigners believe, at any rate, that they may judge us as a nation—butchers' meat will continue to be (with the exception of bread) the chief article in our commissariat," G. Dodd declared in 1856. The fifty years before had been a period of widespread livestock improvement. For example, the story of the English sheep in this period was one of substituting mutton for wool as the main criterion of breeding, a substitution firmly based on economic incentives; the flock owners were turning away from the ancient breeds to larger, stronger and quickly-maturing breeds like the New Leicester and the Southdown. As with sheep, so with cattle and pigs.

The only detailed statistics of meat consumption, however, are for London, based on killings at Smithfield, where, between 1800 and 1850, the slaughter of cattle increased 91 per cent and sheep 92 per cent while London population meantime increased 173 per cent. But these figures ignore any increase in carcass weight, and, also, the supply from other markets. Smithfield killings cannot be accepted as a reliable index for London meat consumption—as E. J. Hobsbawm does—for there were other fast growing markets—Newgate, Leadenhall, Farringdon and Whitechapel—in addition to a number of smaller markets, all of which were largely dependent on country-killed meat and on imported "preserved" meats, like bacon and salt pork. Even in the mid-eighteenth century, when London was smaller and Smithfield relatively more important, perhaps only two-thirds of the fresh meat for London went through Smithfield, "because the London butchers bought at the country markets and at fairs in Cambridge, Northampton and Norfolk as well as bringing carcases in." In the nineteenth century the limitations of Smithfield and the growth of London led inevitably to the development of other sources of supply, other markets that increased in size more rapidly than Smithfield. Newgate had 13 principal salesmen in 1810, and by 1850, 200, who were handling half as many sheep, three-quarters as many cattle, and more calves and pigs than Smithfield; in 1850, 800 tons of country-killed meat arrived there weekly, mainly by railway. In the same year Pool estimated that the yearly sales at Newgate and Leadenhall amounted to 76,500 tons. Certainly the railways much increased the supply of country-killed meat to London, but well before their time increasing quantities had been transported in waggons and carts. At the same time the import of bacon, ham and salt pork increased. Little wonder, therefore, that McCulloch concluded that "the . . . extraordinary increase in the supply of butchers' meat" was evidence of "a very signal improvement . . . in the condition of the population, in respect of food." Nor, of course, was the increased supply confined to London. As a farmer noted significantly in 1836, the fat stock of Gloucestershire and Cumberland were then going, not to London as before, but increasingly to Birmingham, Liverpool and the other industrial towns. Increased supply was reflected in prices, with steady prices generally from 1819 to 1841, and fluctuating prices in the forties.

Another important food whose consumption was increasing at this time was fish. We know that "a large proportion of the Fish caught upon the English coast was supplied by hand carriage to the London and Inland Markets," and, also, that the supply of fish increased after the abolition of the salt tax in 1825, and, after 1830, with technical innovations in fishing that increased yields, particularly the development of deep-sea trawling and of drift fishing; with improvements in the handling of fish, for example, the use of fast cutters, walled steamers and the railways, and the increasing use of ice; and with the discovery of new fishing waters, for example, the Great Silver Pitt, south of the Dogger, in 1837. By 1840 ice and fast transport were enabling trawlers to fish farther north, and were opening up new markets in the inland towns. The kipper was invented in 1843. By 1850 steamship and railway combined to transport catches quickly to the centres of consumption all over England: steamships linked the Channel, North and German Seas to the English ports; railways linked the ports to the internal towns and London. In season, herrings alone were arriving in London from Yarmouth at the rate of 160 tons an evening, and even the humble periwinkle, Simmonds estimated, was consumed at the rate of 76,000 baskets (or 1,900 tons) annually.

The conclusion from consumption figures is unquestionably that the amount and variety of food consumed increased between 1800 and 1850. Even an uncritical reading of those entertaining and informative volumes of G. R. Dodd (*The Food of London*) and H. Mayhew (*London Labour and the London Poor*), and of the article "The Commissariat of London" in the *Quarterly Review* (1854), will reveal the size, range and quality of London's food supplies. By 1850, using the admittedly rough calculations of Dodd, McCulloch, Mayhew, Poole, Mulhall and Levi, the Londoner was consuming each week 5 oz. of butter, 30 oz. of meat, 56 oz. of potatoes, and 16 oz. of fruit, compared with an English consumption today of 5 oz. of butter, 35 oz. of meat, 51 oz. of potatoes, and 32 oz. of fruit. Even allowing for contemporary exaggeration and enthusiasm, the consumption of *basic* foods in 1850 London was not wildly inferior to that of modern England.

IV

What conclusion follows from the evidence so far presented? Surely, since the indices point in the same direction, even though the change cannot be measured with accuracy, that the standard of living of the mass of the people of England was improving in the first half of the nineteenth century, slowly during the war, more quickly after 1815, and rapidly after 1840. And, if expectation of life depends partly on living standards, the increase in average life over these years is further proof of increased well-being. As Macaulay argued, "that the lives of men should become longer while their bodily condition during life is becoming worse, is utterly incredible." The expectation of life at birth in 1840–50 was higher than in 1770–80; by the 1840s infantile mortality rates had been reduced from "the terrifying levels of the eighteenth century," and "the death rate for ages 0–4 . . . was very low, at least for a highly urbanised country at that time." McKeown and Brown have shown that medical improvements could have had little effect on life expectation before 1850, and suggest that it was an improvement in the economic and social environment that lengthened life. People lived longer because they were better nourished and sheltered, and cleaner, and thus were less vulnerable to infectious and other diseases (like consumption) that were particularly susceptible to improved living standards. Factory conditions also improved. R. Baker, one of the early factory inspectors, in a paper to the Social Science Association at Bradford in 1859, declared of the years 1822 to 1856 that "all the diseases which were specific to factory labour in 1822 have as nearly as possible disappeared," and, quoting a Dr. Smith of Leeds, referred particularly to "the wonderful change in the condition of the female part of the population. . . . So striking a difference in twenty-five years I could not have believed, had I not marked and seen it with my own eyes."

But increasing life expectation and increasing consumption are no measures of ultimate well-being, and to say that the standard of living for most workers was rising, is *not* to say that it was high, *nor* is it to affirm that it was rising fast, *nor* that there was no dire poverty, and cyclical fluctuations and technological unemployment of a most distressing character. It is as foolish to ignore the sufferings of this period as to deny the wealth and opportunities created by the new industry. Moreover little understanding comes from trying to attribute blame for the suffering that did exist. The discomfort of the period was due in large part to an inability to handle new problems or old problems enormously magnified; problems of increasing population, of urbanisation, of factory conditions, of fluctuating trade and employment. And the tensions of the period arose naturally from the rapidly changing social and economic relationships. As the Hammonds point out: "When . . . society is passing through changes that destroy the life of custom, the statesman who seeks . . . to command man's will and not merely his deeds and services has a specially difficult task, for these changes bring into men's minds the dreaded questions that have been sleeping beneath the surface of habit." On the easier practical problems, to take an example, municipal authorities did not have the knowledge, and usually not the adequate authority, to deal with the various problems of sanitation in rapidly growing cities.

Such problems required study, experiment and experience, as well as a change of attitudes, before they could be solved, so that it was ignorance rather than avarice that was often the cause of misery. In any case, much of the ill that has been attributed solely to the industrial revolution existed also in the pre-industrial age. "Appalling as was the state of things revealed by the nineteenth-century reports (1840–45) on the sanitary state of towns it can hardly be doubted that the state of London was far worse in the eighteenth century." And by 1854 London was "the healthiest metropolis in Europe."

Thus much misunderstanding has arisen because of assumptions—mainly misconceptions—about England before the Industrial Revolution; assumptions, for example, that rural life was naturally better than town life, that working for oneself was better and more secure than working for an employer, that child and female labour was something new, that the domestic system (even though it often involved a house crammed with industrial equipment) was preferable to the factory system, that slums and food adulteration were peculiar products of industrialisation, and so on; in other words, the perennial myth of the golden age, the belief that since conditions were bad, and since one did not approve of them, they could not have been worse, and, indeed, must once have been better! But, as Alfred Marshall pointed out: "Popular history underrates the hardships of the people before the age of factories."

Rural life was just as appalling as urban life: on the estates of the Marquis of Ailesbury much later cottage conditions exhibited "a violation of all decency," "altogether filthy and disgusting," with, in extreme cases, 12 persons in one room and "depravity which the towns could scarcely have rivalled." Insecurity, as T. S. Ashton has demonstrated, was as much a characteristic of the eighteenth as of the nineteenth century, with regular cycles of trade complicated by harvest failures for which there was no adequate redress. In any case, already before the industrial revolution, large numbers of employees worked as wage-labourers for clothiers, ironmongers, hosiers, and the government. "In the textile trades, in particular, there must have been thousands of workers who never set eyes on their employer. The notion that the coming of the factories meant a 'depersonalisation' of relations is the reverse of the truth." Again, in the eighteenth century the domestic system and agriculture (the largest employer before the coming of the factories) depended heavily on the labour of women and children.

Similarly, food adulteration, which Dr. Hobsbawm seems to think was suddenly discovered in the 1850s, was well known to Smollett in 1771, when he complained that: "The bread I eat in London, is a deleterious paste, mixed up with chalk, alum, and bone-ashes; insipid to the taste and destructive to the constitution." "I need not dwell upon the pallid contaminated mash, which they call strawberries; soiled and tossed by greasy paws through twenty baskets crusted with dirt; and then presented with the worst milk, thickened with the worst flour, into a bad likeness of cream." "The milk . . . the produce of faded cabbage-leaves and sour draff, lowered with hot water, frothed with bruised snails, carried through the streets in open pails." Likewise with morals, it cannot be assumed that the moral standards of the working class had deteriorated, or, indeed, that they were worse than those of their betters. The Webbs were certainly shocked by the morals of the eighteenth century where they discovered "a horrifying mass of sensual and sordid delinquency" and "private licentiousness." Moreover, the evidence about morals is, to say the least, ambiguous; and, in any case, immorality in the slums was no worse, in quantity or kind, than immorality in high society.

But if misery was not a new phenomenon, the range and possibility of opportunities for workmen were new. As A. Toynbee admitted: "The artisan's horizon became indistinct; there was no visible limit to subsistence." Economy and society were in process of rapid change, and the opportunities for wealth and social advancement were greater than they had ever been before. The result was the increasing self-respect of the poor that so pleased Francis Place and the young Edwin Chadwick. One might well ask, however, as did the Hammonds, "Why did this age with all its improvements create such violent discontent?" But discontent is not merely a simple product of living standards. The vision of an age of plenty, stimulated by the obvious productivity of new machines that seemed to compete with labour, roused both anger and ambition. The breaking-up of the old social relationships was a liberating and stimulating experience that made possible, for the first time, an effective working class movement. And although the standard of living was rising, it was not rising quickly, and the individual was aware only that his wages were meagre and not sufficient to satisfy his wants and needs. As A. L. Bowley has pointed out: "The idea of progress is largely psychological and certainly relative; people are apt to measure their progress not from a forgotten position in the past, but towards an ideal, which, like the horizon, continually recedes. The present generation is not interested in the earlier needs and successes of its progenitors, but in its own distresses and frustration considered in the light of the presumed possibility of universal comfort or riches." Discontent, even disorder, were indeed understandable, and both, like suffering, it must be remembered, were also characteristic of the previous age. But the disorder of the forties was far less violent and destructive than the Gordon Riots, and this restraint was due, not only to better police, but "to the fact that the English industrial working class was on the whole better housed, better fed, better educated, and far less degraded than in preceding years." And the important thing about suffering during the Industrial Revolution was that it brought with it its own solution: increasing productivity in industry and agriculture, and, in society, faith that social conditions should and could be improved, and that economic progress was inevitable. "Amidst the varied reflections which the nineteenth century is in the habit of making on its condition and prospects," wrote J. A. Froude later in the century, "there is one common opinion in which all parties coincide—that we live in an era of progress . . . in every department of life—in its business and in its pleasures, in its beliefs and in its theories, in its material developments and in its spiritual convictions—we thank God that we are not like our fathers. And while we admit their merits, making allowance for their disadvantages, we do not blind ourselves in mistaken modesty to our own immeasurable superiority." The new attitude to social problems that emerged with the industrial revolution was that ills should be identified, examined, analysed, publicised and remedied, either by voluntary or legislative action. Thus evils that had long existed —child labour, for example—and had long been accepted as inevitable, were regarded as new ills to be remedied rather than as old ills to be endured. It was during the industrial revolution, moreover, and largely because of the economic opportunities it afforded to working class women, that there was the beginning of the most important and most beneficial of all the social revolutions of the last two centuries, the emancipation of women.

Paul Mantoux

THE DESTRUCTION OF THE PEASANT VILLAGE

Mantoux lived from 1877 to 1956. For a short time, he was Professor of French in London. Later, he was interpreter at the Paris Peace Conference, 1919, then Director of the Political Section of the League of Nations Secretariat. He ended his active career as professor in Paris. *The Industrial Revolution* is his only major work. It treats the early eighteenth-century economic system, commercial expansion, agriculture, inventions and industrial organisation, working conditions, and government policy. It may still be the best survey of the entire subject, even though far less rigorous in its economic techniques than more modern works. The present excerpt comes from the chapter entitled "Redistribution of the Land."

THERE was one obstacle in the way of the new methods. It was the existence of the open fields. For the greater part, those "unenclosed fields" were very badly cultivated: the arable lands, in spite of fallow years, were exhausted by the monotonous alternation of the same crops—the pastures, left to themselves, were overgrown with heather and gorse. How could it have been otherwise? Each farmer was tied down to the common rules. The system of crop rotation adopted for the whole parish was only suitable for some of the lands, and the other lands suffered thereby. The cattle and sheep fed on weeds, and their promiscuous mixing together was the cause of murrains. As for improvements, any man who attempted them would have ruined himself. He could not drain his fields without the consent and concurrence of his many neighbours. Each plot was contained within fixed limits and was too narrow to admit of cross-harrowing, as recommended by Jethro Tull. Before a farmer could choose his own

From Paul Mantoux, *The Industrial Revolution of the Eighteenth Century* (1906: English translation, Cape, London, 1928), Part I, chapter 3, pp. 168–80, 181–90. A more recent reprint exists (Cape, London, 1961) and a paperback of this (Methuen, London, 1964). In this last, the pages are 163–85; text and footnotes are unchanged; but there is an additional bibliography selected from the writings of the intervening half-century. By permission of Mme. Mathilde Mantoux, the translator, and Jonathan Cape Ltd. and The Macmillan Company.

time for sowing, the custom of allowing the open field to be used as a common grazing ground for several months in every year had first to be abolished. No such thing could be contemplated as growing an unwonted crop, or sowing clover where there had been rye or barley. To all these disadvantages should be added the extraordinary complication of the system, and the endless quarrels and law-suits that were its inevitable consequence. In the olden days, when farming had been a traditional calling, an accepted inheritance that supported a man year in year out, such a state of things could be put up with. But to the modern farmer, who looks upon agriculture as a business undertaking and reckons up exactly his expense and profits, the compulsory waste on the one hand, and, on the other, the sheer impossibility of doing anything whatever to increase the produce, are simply intolerable. The open-field system was doomed, therefore, to disappear.

Between the sixteenth and seventeenth century enclosures and those of the eighteenth century, there was an essential difference. The former had been opposed by the King's administration, the latter, on the contrary, met with assistance and encouragement from Parliament. Under the Tudors and Stuarts, enclosure was either the result of sheer spoliation, or of a mutual agreement between all the landowners of a parish. But the mighty had means at their disposal to suppress any opposition: "Unwilling commoners are threatened with the risks of long and expensive lawsuits; in other cases they are subject to persecution by the great proprietors who ditch in their own demesne and force them to go a long way round to their own land, or maliciously breed rabbits and keep geese on adjoining ground, to the detriment of their crops." Once enrolled in Chancery, the agreements could be enforced without any further formality. In the eighteenth century, the method was further improved. Whenever it was found impossible to obtain the necessary assent for concluding a *deed of mutual agreement,* the legal authorities could step in. All the Acts of Enclosure on the Statute Book, without exception, are evidence of so many cases when the unanimous consent of the landowners could not be secured. But no legal action could be taken unless there was a request for it. Here we shall see on whose initiative and for whose profit the enclosures were made.

The great landowners were the first to undertake a methodical exploitation of their estates according to the precepts of the new agricultural science. They were the men who bore most impatiently the obligations laid on them by the open-field system. And they, in almost every case, initiated the petition to Parliament for a Bill of Enclosure. As a rule, they began by holding a conference and choosing an attorney who was to be in charge of the legal side of the proceedings. The next step was to call a general meeting of all the landowners. In that meeting, the decision was not reached by a majority of individual votes: the importance of each voter was proportionate to the acreage of his land. For the petition to be considered in order, the number of signatories was of small account: but they must represent four-fifths of the lands to be enclosed. Those who owned the last fifth were often fairly numerous, sometimes they were the majority. Some petitions bore two or three names only, some could be found bearing but a single name. True, they were important, impressive names, accompanied by titles which recommended them to the considerate attention of Parliament. If the consent of some small landowner was indispensable, he was asked for it in such a manner that he could scarcely refuse. The local grandees—the lord of the manor, the vicar, the country squires—laid the request before him in tones which, we may surmise, resembled a command rather than an entreaty. If the man resisted, he was threatened, and he gave his signature even though he might withdraw it later. But very few occasions arose for taking such action; the villagers scarcely dared show their discontent: what they feared above all things was to "appear against their superiors."

Once the petition was duly signed, it was brought before Parliament. Then began a series of expensive proceedings of which the wealthier landowners bore the cost. Parliament was all for them: did not their own mandatories, their friends and relatives, sit in the House? The heads of the ancient nobility in the House of Lords, as also the many country squires in the House of Commons, were the representatives of the great landed interests. It often happened that the Bill was drafted at once, without any preliminary inquiry. When an inquiry was ordered, its conclusions were almost invariably identical with the desires of the petitioners. Counter-petitions had results in one case only, namely when they too originated in the possessing and ruling classes. The claims of the lord of the manor, who would suffer no curtailment of his former rights, those of the vicar, who wanted compensation for his tithes, had every chance of being received favourably. Where a single man owned one-fifth of the acreage to be enclosed, his opposition was enough to put an end to the proceedings. Thus, what the great landowners had done, could be undone by the great landowners alone.

What happened after the Bill of Enclosure had been passed? Although it was as a rule a lengthy document, burdened with complicated clauses, it did no more than prescribe the general conditions of the operation: on the spot only, and in the presence of the parties concerned, could points of detail be settled. A considerable and most delicate task remained then to be fulfilled. It consisted in actually finding out what was the state of every property, measuring all the plots of land that went to make it up, reckoning the income it brought in, as well as the relative value of the rights of common enjoyed by each owner. It was necessary to consider the whole territory of the parish, the common field together with the open field, to cut it into portions equivalent to the scattered properties for which they were to be substituted; to grant compensation, if the case arose, to direct and supervise the setting up of the fences that were now to divide one man's land from his neighbours'; to see that undertakings in the common interest prescribed by the Act, such as roadmaking or mending, drainage, irrigation, were duly carried out. In fact, all this was tantamout to a revolution throughout the parish—the land being, so to speak, seized and dealt out again among the land-owners in an entirely new manner, which, however, was to leave untouched the former rights of each of them. To ensure that this division should be carried out equitably, that errors and arbitrary measures should be avoided, what minute care, what a fine sense of valuation, and also what impartiality, what detachment from private interest, would have been required!

That very important and delicate task was entrusted to commissioners, to the number of three, five or seven. As far as the enclosure was concerned, they exercised unrestricted authority. In the words of Arthur Young, "they are a sort of despotic monarch, into whose hands the property of the parish is invested, to re-cast and re-distribute it at their pleasure." For a long time, there was no appeal from their decisions. It is most interesting, therefore, to know who these commissioners were, what social class they came from, by whom they were appointed. In theory, they held their authority from Parliament: their names were in the Act of Enclosure. But, since Parliament took no interest in and had no knowledge of the local questions that the commissioners were to settle, they were in fact nominated by the petitioners: which means that their appointment, even as all the previous proceedings, was in the hands of the great landowners. Here once more, the same characters played the foremost parts: "the lord of the soil, the rector and a few of the principal commoners monopolize and distribute the appointments." They chose men devoted to them, unless they preferred to sit on the Commission themselves. The unlimited authority of the commissioners was no other than their own. It is not very surprising that they should have used it to their own advantage.

The abuse was so plain that the most determined supporters of enclosures, and those least likely to oppose the interests of the great landowners, denounced it emphatically. In 1770, Arthur Young put forward a request, that the commissioners be elected in a meeting of all the landowners, and be made responsible to the county magistrates. But his protest did not secure attention, and not until 1801—when a general Bill was enacted for the purpose of settling once and for all the clauses common to all Acts of Enclosure—were any steps taken to prevent the inflicting of grievous wrongs. It was forbidden to appoint as commissioners the lord of the manor, his stewards, bailiffs or agents either in his service, or having left it less than three years before, or "any proprietor or person immediately interested in such moors, common or waste lands, half-year lands or uninclosed lands, intended to be . . . inclosed." Henceforward, the commissioners were under the obligation of giving a hearing to all complaints and mentioning them in their reports. Any person with a grievance had a right to appeal from the commissioners' decision to the Quarter Sessions. This belated legislation is evidence of spoliations that had been committed and had remained unpunished for a century.

The small man, whose field was not a capital to him, but a bare means of living, could but look on helplessly while those changes took place, and his right to his land, together with the very conditions of his existence, were in question. He could not prevent the commissioners reserving the best lands for richer men. He was constrained to accept the lot assigned for him, even though he might not consider it an equivalent of his former property. He lost his rights on the common, which was now to be divided. A portion of that common land was indeed allotted to him; but its size was in proportion to the number of animals he used to graze on the lord's waste. Thus, once more, he that had most, received most. Once in possession of his new land, the yeoman had to fence it round, and this cost him both labour and money. He had to pay his share of the expense incurred in carrying out the Act —and those expenses were often very heavy. He could not fail to be left poorer than before, if not actually burdened with debt.

As for the cottager who was traditionally allowed to live on the common, gather his firewood there, and perhaps keep a milch-cow, all that he considered as his possession was taken away from him at a blow. Nor had he any right to complain, for after all, the common was the property of other men. The possessing classes were unanimous in thinking that "the argument of robbing the poor was fallacious. *They had no legal title to the common land.*" This was so, no doubt, but they had until then enjoyed the advantages of a *de facto* situation, sanctioned by long tradition. Some writers have maintained that these advantages amounted to very little and that their loss could not seriously injure the cottagers. The law, however, seems to have recognized the grievous wrong inflicted on them: an Act of Parliament, passed in 1757, directed the commissioners for enclosures to pay into the hands of the Poor Law authorities certain compensations "to be applied towards the relief of the poor in the parish or township where . . . wastes, woods and pastures had been enclosed." This implied a recognition of the fact that the dividing up of the common was the cause of hardships. A further step was sometimes taken to alleviate them: a piece of ground was kept undivided for the use of the poorer inhabitants of the parish, the landless cottagers, or else they were awarded small lots whereon to graze their wretched flocks. But such compensation was seldom granted, and was in any case illusory: the lots were so very small and inadequate that the cottagers seized the first opportunity to dispose of them and make a little money. Nor had they long to wait.

For, after the enclosure had been made, the shares allotted, the fences set up around each piece of land, all was not yet over. The great landowners had not yet reaped all the profit they expected from the operation. After consolidating their estates, they sought to increase them, and, when nothing remained to be taken, they were prepared to buy. Some wished to add to their ploughed fields and meadows; others wanted to enlarge their parks or their hunting grounds; others yet, in a few cases, would "buy cottages near their mansions, for no other purpose than to shut them up, and to let them decay, because they did not like to have the poor for their neighbours." And besides those who were already landowners, others—merchants, bankers, and later, manufacturers—longed to rank with them. The moment was a favourable one. The redistribution of property had caused a wavering among the class that was most closely, most devotedly attached to the soil. The honest, hard-working, but short-sighted yeoman, a follower of the beaten track, was bewildered by the changes around him, and felt a coming danger in the formidable competition of the great farms run on modern methods. Whether he became discouraged or chose to seek his fortunes elsewhere, he was tempted by the rich man's offers, and sold his land.

Almost everywhere, the enclosing of open fields and the division of common land were followed by the sale of a great many properties. The enclosures and the engrossing of farms are two facts which eighteenth-century writers considered as inseparable, whether they wished to speak for or against them. The engrossing of farms was not always a consequence of the enclosure; sometimes, on the contrary, it took place before an enclosure. But whether it was the consequence or the purpose of the operation, we know for certain that the total number of farms had become very much smaller in the latter half of the century. One village in Dorsetshire where, in 1780, as many as thirty farms could be found, fifteen years later had the whole of its land divided between two holdings; in one parish in Hertfordshire, three landowners had together engrossed no less than twenty-four farms, with acreages averaging between 50 and 150 acres. An admirer of enclosures, little inclined to exaggerate their evil effects, put the number of small farms absorbed into larger ones between 1740 and 1788 as an average of four or five in each parish, which brings the total to forty or fifty thousand for the whole Kingdom. Here was the important fact, undoubtedly more important than the division of the commons, although it disturbed the public opinion of the time much less. It was carried out by means of private deeds, unobtrusively and without intervention either by Parliament or the local authorities; and it almost escaped notice. But it was the real end towards which efforts of the great landowners were ultimately directed; the enclosures and all their array of legal proceedings were chiefly the means of compelling the farmers to sell their land, or of improving estates that had been enlarged by recent purchases. The figure of forty to fifty thousand farms in less than fifty years, which does not seem exaggerated, shows how far-reaching were the changes wrought in landed property in the course of that half-century.

It is true that the disappearance of a farm did not necessarily mean that of a property. Engrossing often consisted in joining together several small holdings on an estate into one larger farm. But that very change amounted to a revolution, for it involved deep modifications in the method of cultivation and in the use of labour.

During the first two-thirds of the eighteenth century, the reduction in the number of small holdings was followed, as in the days of the Tudors, by the extension of pasture land. Arthur Young, in his *Farmer's Letters* (1767), wrote that a farm could make better profits by breeding than by tillage, and cost less labour. A number of counties where cultivation still held its ground, in spite of previous enclosures, now put on a new aspect. Towards the end of the century, Leicestershire, that had been famous for its crops, was almost entirely covered with artificial meadows; more than one-half of Derbyshire, three-quarters of Cheshire, three-quarters of Lancashire, had become grazing land. Since 1765 or so, the rise in prices stimulated corn-growing, and the movement for transforming tilled land into pasture slackened down. But even if the cultivation of oats or wheat required more labour than the rearing of sheep, the total number of farm-hands had, in any case, been reduced. Was it not one of the chief aims of the joining together of the plots formerly scattered over the open fields, to effect such a reduction?

The Bills of Enclosure met with little active opposition; nor is the reason far to seek. Those who had most to complain of dared scarcely lift their voices. If they ventured to put forth a claim or send a petition to Parliament, the only probable result for them was money spent fruitlessly—legal expenses, or the fees of experts, counsels and solicitors. Often they would merely refuse to sign the petition drafted by their neighbours, the great landowners: even then, they would at once declare that they did not mean to oppose that petition: an attitude showing that the villager, as the phrase goes, "knew his betters." Thus, formal protests were comparatively rare. Yet a few of them have reached us. Sometimes they attacked the very principle of the enclosure, as being "very injurious to the petitioners, and tending to the ruin of many, especially the poorer"; sometimes they denounced its operation as "partial and unjust . . . hurtful to the petitioners in particular and to the community in general." After 1760, such protests became more frequent and forceful. The suppressed anger of the villagers would break out suddenly. In some parishes, the announcement of the enclosure caused riots. Formal notices could not be posted on the church doors, because of the obstruction by riotous mobs, who forcibly prevented the sticking up of bills. The constable in charge of those bills was confronted by threatening crowds, armed with cudgels and pitchforks: in a Suffolk village, on three successive Sundays, his notices were torn out of his hands, he was thrown into a ditch, and stones were hurled at him.

This passionate opposition, in strong contrast with the villagers' habitual timorousness, may have had no other cause than an instinctive distrust of change. But we find it supported by a full array of documents and facts. According to these, the enclosures resulted in the buying up of the land by the wealthier class; they lay at the root of all the evils of the period—the high cost of necessaries, the demoralization of the lower classes and the aggravation of poverty. "It is no uncommon thing for four or five wealthy graziers to engross a large inclosed lordship, which was before in the hands of twenty or thirty farmers, and as many smaller tenants or proprietors. All these are thereby thrown out of their livings, and many other families, who were chiefly employed and supported by them, such as blacksmiths, carpenters, wheel-wrights and other artisans and tradesmen, besides their own labourers and servants." Not only had the small landowner to give up his land, and either to leave the district or fall to the condition of labourer, not only was the cottager evicted from the common, but as the large farms needed comparatively less labour, a number of journeymen were left unemployed.

The result was depopulation, if not everywhere, at least in a number of rural districts.

The enclosures also had admirers who dwelt upon their undeniable advantages, and strove to prove that most of the evil consequences imputed to them were purely imaginary. The most earnest among them were the writers on husbandry, in whose eyes the distribution of the land had far less importance than its capacity for production. For them the supreme argument was that large holdings offered the best conditions for the practical and theoretical progress of agriculture. Arthur Young compared big farms to big workshops, and, after quoting Adam Smith's famous passage on the manufacture of pins, he added: "Agriculture will not admit of this, for men cannot be employed their whole lives in sowing, others in ploughing, others in hedging, others in hoeing, and so on, but the nearer we approach to this the better: which can only be on a large farm. In a small one, the same man is shepherd, hogherd, cowherd, ploughman, and sower; he goes about ten different sorts of labour and attention in the same day, and consequently acquires no habitual skill peculiar to himself." Yeoman farms were ill-cultivated, and "generally the residence of poverty and misery." The great landowner had more intelligence and initiative, and above all he could afford to make experiments and undertake more or less expensive improvements. Wherever enclosure had taken place and large farms had been established, there had been a rise in rent. This was an unanswerable argument for those students of agriculture, who were at the same time economists, and to whom men were of little account when production and profit were at stake.

They could hardly dispute the fact that the consolidation of estates very often resulted in the absorption of small holdings, but they denied that the condition of labourers had become worse in consequence. We know what their opinion was concerning the division of common lands; arguments against it, they thought, were "grounded on mistaken principles of humanity." As for complaints about the reduced demand for agricultural labour and the depopulation of villages, they dismissed them as absurd stories. How could anyone believe that to let part of the land lie fallow and to cultivate the rest as badly as possible was the means to occupy and feed the greatest possible number of men? "This appears to my poor understanding a most extraordinary paradox. There is in my neighbourhood a fine heath, consisting of about a thousand acres. In its present uncultivated state, it does not support a single family, nor does almost anyone receive benefit from it, but some of the farmers around, who occasionally turn a few of their cattle upon it. Whereas, were it enclosed, well cultivated and improved, it would make six or eight good farms, from £70 to £100 a year each. These, besides the farmers and their several households, would require near thirty labourers, who, together with their wives and children, added to the tradesmen and mechanics that would be necessary to supply their respective wants, would raise the population on this single spot, in the course of a very few years, at least two hundred persons." To make such optimistic calculations more likely, carefully selected figures were brought forward, showing that the ill effects of engrossing were more than compensated by the cultivation of the waste lands. It was even maintained that cultivation on a large scale was the system that would give the rural population the best opportunities in respect of both work and wages. At the same time, those who represented the body of opinion hostile to enclosures were committing an error and supplying

their adversaries with a ready argument. They believed that, all over the Kingdom, the population was decreasing, and they represented the alarming fact as a consequence of the enclosures. The party of the agricultural experts had no difficulty in proving that this alleged depopulation of England was a mere fancy and whenever, on the contrary, they observed an increase in the population of any county, they did not fail to attribute it to the beneficial changes in the distribution of the land. Their triumph was easier still when, as disciples of Adam Smith, they adopted the economic point of view: a system that resulted in the production of the largest quantity of goods at the smallest cost must be the best system for the whole community. If this is not admitted, they said, the Turks rightly object to the introduction of the printing press, which might be prejudicial to the copying profession, "and all civilized Europe is in error." Would any one be so ill-advised as to maintain that the husbandman should lay by the plough and take up the spade to dig the earth, on the plea that this would afford labour for a larger number of men?

Yet they made some significant admissions. In spite of their optimism, they bore witness to the wrongs suffered by the poor under their very eyes. A commissioner of enclosures wrote: "I lament that I have been accessory to injuring two thousand poor people at the rate of twenty families per parish. Numbers, in the practice of feeding on the commons, cannot prove their right; and many, indeed most who have allotments, have not more than one acre, which being insufficient for the man's cow, both cow and land are usually sold to the opulent farmers." After an impartial inquiry, the Board of Agriculture acknowledged that in most cases the poor had been stripped of what little they owned. In some villages, they could not even get milk for their children. The available evidence is heartrending in its monotony. The Earl of Leicester, upon being congratulated on his newly-built castle at Holkham, answered with remorseful melancholy: "It is a sad thing for a man to be alone in the district of his residence: I look around, and can see no other house than mine. I am like the ogre in the tale, and have eaten up all my neighbours."

Does this mean that those neighbours had disappeared, that they had been wiped out like a nation overrun by barbarous hordes? No, indeed. But a section of the rural population, having been torn away from the land that nourished them, having lost their homes and seen their former ties broken, became unsettled and migratory; the small landowners and farmers on the one hand, the cottagers and journeymen on the other, were ready to leave the countryside if they could make a better, or indeed a plain, living elsewhere.

Let us consider these two classes of men in turn. One is no other than the smaller yeomanry, whose decline will now be comprehensible. There was no room for them in the system which had been framed by the apostles of the new agriculture and carried out by means of Acts of Enclosure: Arthur Young asked what would be the use to a modern State of having a whole province cultivated by peasant proprietors, as in the early days of Rome, "except for the mere purpose of breeding men, which of itself is a most useless purpose." On the large estates, the exploitation of which was methodically conducted by their wealthy owners, a new type of farmer made his appearance, who compares with the old-time farmer as a millowner compares with the master manufacturer. He paid a high rent and looked forward to high profits, and the sort of life he was able to lead would have been regarded as extravagant by a country squire of the previous generation. He fed well, and, when he had friends to dinner, offered them claret or port wine. His daughter was taught to play the harpsichord and dressed "like the daughter of a duke." There was nothing in common between him and the labourer in his employment, and he was very unlike the old yeoman whose place he had taken, although he often sprang from the yeomanry. But, for one small landowner who succeeded in exchanging his former independence for the position of a prosperous tenant, how many were driven either to work as hired labourers, or to leave their villages?

The temptation to go in search of work was still greater for unemployed labourers. In many localities the men in need of parochial relief were sent round from one farm to another for employment, part of their wages being paid from the poor rates. They formed thus a somewhat unsettled element, and were ready to go anywhere to find occupation, whenever they succeeded in evading the servitude imposed on them by the Poor Law, which bound the pauper to his parish. This, according to the supporters of the new system of agriculture, explained the seeming depopulation of the country, which was used as an argument against enclosures. "The men were not lost but, perhaps, with the ground, better employed." If there was less time and labour wasted on the land it was for the benefit of the towns and of their trades. Before 1760 a movement of population could already be observed "from rural parishes to market towns, and from both of them to the capital city: so that great multitudes of people who were born in rural parishes are continually acquiring settlements in cities or towns, particularly in those towns where considerable manufactures are carried on." Industry was in fact the only refuge for thousands of men who found themselves cut off from their traditional occupations. The manufacturers were to offer them the living they could no longer earn on the land.

On the movement of rural labour in search of work information is scanty and unreliable. But whenever such information can be obtained, it reveals the steady movement of land-workers to industrial towns. "About forty years ago (this was written in 1794) the southern and eastern parts of the country (Warwick) consisted mostly of open fields, which are now chiefly inclosed. . . . Upon all inclosures of open fields the farms have generally been made much larger. These lands being now grazed want much fewer hands to manage them than they did in their former open state: from these causes the hardy yeomanry in country villages have been driven for employment into Birmingham, Coventry and other manufacturing towns." A petition signed by the inhabitants of a rural parish of Northamptonshire described the local peasantry as "driven from necessity and want of employ, in vast crowds, into manufacturing towns, where the very nature of their employment, over the loom or the forge, may waste their strength, and in consequence debilitate their posterity."

Thus the enclosures and the engrossing of farms resulted in placing at the disposal of industry resources in labour and energy which made it possible for the factory system to develop. Industry was becoming, as it were, a new land in the midst of the country, another America attracting immigrants by the thousand—with this difference: that instead of being a discovery it was a creation, the very existence of this new world being conditioned by the increase of population. Each newcomer brought with him what he had been able to save before leaving the old country. Those among the yeomen who had suffered least from the redistribution of the land, and had succeeded in getting a fair price for their property, were in possession of a small capital. Having, more or less against their own will, given up their rooted traditions and habits, they were now ready to try their fortune in the new field by launching into ventures which on all sides attracted their enterprise. From their number were to rise many of the first generation of manufacturers, who started and led the industrial movement, and were soon to form a class of men rivalling in wealth and influence the great landowners now in possession of their land. But comparatively few, of course, attained that degree of success. Many of the small yeomen and farmers, reduced to the condition of wage-earners, shared the fate of the labourers who came to the towns in search of work. They possessed nothing, and could offer nothing, but their labour. They were to form the working population, the anonymous multitude in the factories—the army of the industrial revolution.

The changes in the conditions of rural life had a still more direct influence on the progress of industry. We know that one of the characteristic features of the domestic system of manufacture was the scattering of workshops in the villages, the very basis of that system consisting in a close alliance between cottage industry and the cultivation of small holdings. We have noticed how a weaver would eke out his earnings with the product of a plot of ground, and how a rural family would in the evening spin wool for the merchant manufacturer. The blow dealt to peasant property broke that time-honoured alliance of labour on the land and industrial work. The village artisan, when deprived of his field and of his rights of common, could not continue to work at home. He was forced to give up whatever independence he still seemed to have retained, and had to accept the wages offered to him in the employer's workshop. Thus labour was becoming more and more concentrated, even before the competition of machinery had finally destroyed the old village industries.

There is, therefore, an intimate connection between the movement by which English agriculture was transformed, and the rise of the factory system. The connection being of a less simple nature than a mere relation between cause and effect, the two events might at first sight appear to have sprung from entirely different sources, only influencing each other in the course of their respective developments. The disappearance of the yeomanry, for instance, was not caused by the industrial revolution, but the industrial revolution made it more rapid and complete. As for the movement of labour from country to town, it certainly assisted, though it could not have determined, the progress of industry. If one of the two factors had been lacking, would not the other have continued to develop, although most probably its progress would have taken a somewhat different course? Had the bulk of the rural population remained on the land, the triumph of the factory system might have come later, but it could not have been indefinitely postponed, as is shown conclusively by what took place in France. Might it not therefore be held that the relation between the transformation of agriculture and that of industry was limited to accidental influences —technical improvements based on entirely different methods accounting in both cases for separate and parallel developments?

But these improvements, independent though their progress may seem to be, were only part of a more general evolution, and their success was largely due to the support they received from each other. The growth of great industrial centres would have been impossible if agricultural production had not been so organized as to provide for the needs of a large industrial population, and agricultural production, on the other hand, could not have developed had not the industrial districts supplied adequate markets with growing numbers of consumers. This was one of the favourite arguments used by the advocates of enclosure: "By the produce being greater there will be a surplus for manufactures, and by this means manufactures, one of the mines of the nation, will increase in proportion to the quantity of corn pro-

duced." And, while the two movements were thus connected in their respective consequences, another and stronger connection was that between their causes. What accounts for the change in rural conditions, for the enclosures, the division of the common lands and the engrossing of farms, is the introduction of a business spirit into the management of agriculture, landowners thereafter considering the land as capital, from which a better income could be drawn by improved methods of exploitation. In agriculture, as in industry, the initiative of the capitalist proved both self-seeking and beneficial to the community, for it did away at the same time with obnoxious routine and with old institutions, to which the working men were still looking for protection. The conditions of all successful business are the reduction of cost and the increase of profit. The enclosures resulted in a reduction of labour and an increase of production. A comparison between their effect and that of the introduction of machinery was well justified, for their ultimate origin was one and the same.

Jonathan D. Chambers and Gordon E. Mingay

ENCLOSURES NOT GUILTY

Chambers' early career was spent in school-teaching and in adult education. His book *Nottinghamshire in the Eighteenth Century* (1932), and learned articles, established his scholarly reputation. He was Professor of Economic History at Nottingham, 1958–64. Mingay studied under him. His first book was *English Landed Society in the Eighteenth Century* (1963). He is now Professor of Agrarian History in the University of Kent, Canterbury.

QUOTING from a number of Acts and Awards the Hammonds certainly convey the impression that the system of parliamentary enclosure was in fact a gigantic swindle by which the wealthy owners gained land and wealth, and in which they rode roughshod over the rights of small men. Other writers who have carried out very extensive examinations of many hundreds of en-

From Jonathan D. Chambers and Gordon E. Mingay, *The Agricultural Revolution 1750–1880* (Batsford, London, 1966), pp. 86–99, 101–4. By permission of B. T. Batsford Ltd. and Schocken Books Inc.

closures have arrived, however, at very different conclusions. Professor Gonner, whose work on enclosure was outstanding for its care and detail, was impressed by the complexity of the task of enclosure and the fairness with which the commissioners generally carried it out. The commissioners had to take into account that some land possessed more common rights than did other land, and that some land had no common rights attached to it at all; that some unenclosed land was worth more than other, and in estimating values that small farmers were rented more highly than large ones. The commissioners had often to assess what quantity of land was a fair allotment in lieu of tithes; they had to put land aside for roads, and perhaps for a quarry or gravel pit to keep the roads in repair; and sometimes they reserved some land for the poor as cow pastures and vegetable gardens, and for the parish for a school or a poorhouse. "When the gravity and delicacy of the task undertaken by the commissioners is considered," wrote Gonner, "the existence of complaint against them is not astonishing. It is rather a matter for wonder that the complaints were not far louder and universal."

The conduct of enclosure was such a complex matter that in practice it became a professional occupation for the country gentlemen, land agents and large farmers who were experienced in it, and we find the same commissioners acting at a variety of different places. Gonner found that the commissioners did not take a strict view of the legal validity of claims but often gave favourable consideration to claims for compensation based on custom or equity rather than on legal right. Even the Hammonds conceded that the squatters who had settled on the waste and were suffered in the villages as "poor aliens" were sometimes treated fairly, some with more than 20 years standing as occupiers being allowed to keep their encroachments, and those of a lesser standing being allowed to purchase them. "Taken as a whole," said Gonner, "the work of division and apportionment appears to have been discharged conscientiously and fairly."

A more recent investigator, Mr. W. E. Tate, has endorsed Gonner's conclusion. A remarkable feature of eighteenth-century enclosure, he has said, was the "care with which it was carried out and the relatively small volume of organised protest which it aroused." On the basis of his evidence he found that the instances of enclosures deliberately rigged against the small man, which the Hammonds quoted, were "in the highest degree exceptional . . . ," and that it would be quite unfair to suppose them typical of the country in general. Ultimately, of course, the enclosure commissioners relied for their employment on the large proprietors, and were bound to satisfy them. But apparently this was not incompatible with the striking of a fair balance between the claims of both large and small men, and it is clear that small owners did not always fear the outcome. Together with other writers, Mr. Tate finds that it is untrue that small proprietors were invariably opposed to enclosure, that they refused to sign petitions or were afraid to oppose them. "The weight of propertied opinion was overwhelmingly in favour of enclosure in whatever units that weight was expressed."

The controversy continues. In a recent work Dr. Hoskins, a distinguished authority on Leicestershire, pointed out that at Wigston Magna the extinction of the tithes at the enclosure involved an appropriation of 380 acres, or one-seventh of the available land, and that the titheholder's allotment was fenced at the expense of the other proprietors, a very common provision. As a consequence the small farmers at Wigston came out of the business with a smaller acreage than before (although of course with land free of tithes), and some of their holdings were too small to be successfully worked. In a heavily populated and densely settled county like Leicestershire, where available waste land was small or non-existant, Dr. Hoskins comments, enclosure and engrossing were bound to have serious effects on the small farmers.

Other investigators have tended to support Mr. Tate by emphasising that it was sometimes the larger owners and the parsons (concerned with their allotment in lieu of tithes), rather than the small owners, who opposed enclosure. This was the case, for example, in the East Riding; and in the Vale of Pickering, as William Marshall the contemporary agricultural writer pointed out, it was the owners of houses with common rights attached to them, rather than the owners of farmland, who pressed for the enclosure of the commons.

The consequences of enclosure for the village population we must now discuss, but in regard to the procedure of obtaining parliamentary authority and the reallotment of the land we can say this: that in the opinion of most careful investigators it almost always worked fairly as between the various classes of proprietors; that it is not true that all small proprietors were opposed to it; and that in at least a proportion of cases the equitable claims of the squatters and the poor were taken into consideration. This was not perfect justice, but in an age of aristocratic government and exaggerated respect for the rights of property, it was not a bad approximation to it. Indeed, it may well be said that parliamentary enclosure represented a major advance in the recognition of the rights of the small man.

In the words of the Hammonds, "enclosure was fatal to three classes: the small farmer, the cottager, and the squatter."

Let us begin with the small farmer and see how he might be affected by the abolition of open fields and commons. It will simplify the discussion if we consider first the small farmers who owned their farms: the freeholders or owner-occupiers. (Strictly there was no clear division between owner-occupiers and tenant-farmers, for many small owner-occupiers rented some land, and they often rented more land than they owned; but we will ignore this complication for the moment.)

The main way in which the Hammonds supposed small owners to be adversely affected was through the burden of expenses involved in enclosure. Apart from mentioning some enclosures where the cost was unusually high, however, they produced no evidence that these expenses were in fact fatal to small owners. And when the matter is looked at closely it does not seem very probable that the cost of enclosure, by itself, forced very many small proprietors to sell out and decline to the status of labourers. It was only the really small farmers, with holdings too small to be described as farms, who were likely to have found the expenses too great for it to be worth keeping their land: they depended on some supplementary or alternative occupation in any case, and they may well have found the occasion of enclosure a good time to sell. Many of these, it must be remembered, were *absentee* owners who had let out their land, and not occupiers. Indeed, some of the sales of absentee owners must have consolidated the holdings of small farmers, and strengthened their position. In addition, many large landowners at this time were selling some land in order to raise money for enclosures and other improvements, or to clear up their debts. During the reign of George III private estate Acts sought by landowners in order to allow sales or freer use of land tied up in family settlements were nearly half as numerous as the enclosure Acts. No doubt a good deal of this land went into the hands of the gentry and smaller owners.

The true small farmer, with his 30 or 40 acres, may have been faced with a total bill of anything from £30 to £250, according to the circumstances. In general, however, unless the enclosure was unusually costly, he would not have to find more than about £50 to £100, with the payments spread over a period of time. If we suppose that his land was reasonably fertile and that much of it had been open before the enclosure, then its value would probably have at least doubled in the enclosed state, and would have a market value of £25 or £30 per acre, in total say £900 for the whole farm. It follows that for an expenditure of £50 to £100 on enclosure his land increased in value from about £450 to £900. Thus there would be little difficulty in mortgaging his land to meet the enclosure costs, or alternatively he might raise the sum by selling off a half-dozen acres and still show a capital gain on the transaction. Or again, he might prefer to sell his land at its improved value and use the capital to stock a really substantial farm as a tenant.

Of course, there is no doubt that some small owners who raised mortgages in order to meet enclosure costs, or to stock a farm newly converted from arable to pasture, in the end found themselves unable to pay off their debts and were forced to sell. Between 1760 and 1813, however, this seems unlikely to have affected large numbers of small owners for prices were rising and farmers were prosperous, and in any event there is little or no concrete evidence that enclosure did have the long-term effect of diminishing their numbers. A study of 70 Parliamentary enclosures in the Lindsey division of Lincolnshire found that 82 per cent of owners receiving allotments were owners of less than 50 acres. In nine villages there were some 70 or 80 sales of land before or after enclosure, and of course there may have been others that cannot be traced. These sales, however, did not mean a permanent decline in the number of small owners in total, for the land tax assessments show that they were more than made up by fresh purchases during the period of high prices at the end of the century. Where small owners eventually diminished after enclosure, as at Wigston Magna, it seems probable that other factors were also important, the rise in the burden of poor rates for instance, and the general long-run tendency towards larger and more efficient farms— a tendency which certainly did not begin with enclosure and did not end with it.

Many small owners, indeed, had been bought out before enclosure, as a necessary preliminary to it. There were obvious advantages in simplifying the reallotment of lands and making the farms larger and more compact if there were fewer owners to consider, and it was generally the case that the earlier enclosures occurred where the small owners were few or their lands had been gradually bought up by the larger owners over a period of years. It does not follow from this that small owners were always opposed to enclosure and were likely to try to prevent it. Detailed evidence shows that it was

frequently the case that enclosure proceeded smoothly in villages where there were enough small owners to have prevented it had they combined for the purpose. In discussing open-field cultivation we noticed that it was quite common for the farmers to cooperate in exchanges of lands, the stinting of commons, and the arrangement of small enclosures. There seems no reason why they would not have welcomed a complete enclosure and the abolition of inconvenient and inefficient open-field holdings. Sometimes, indeed, the initiative did come from the farmers. Thus we have a Gloucestershire farmer suggesting an enclosure to Lord Hardwicke's agent, "the generality of the Nation being so much Improv'd by Inclosures." At Somercotes in the Lincolnshire marshland the small common right owners were so eager for enclosure that they were prepared to indemnify the commissioner against his unwittingly committing legal irregularities. A preliminary survey of the number of acres held by each freeholder at Bromley in Kent in 1799, and the side he would probably take if an enclosure Bill were promoted, showed that 19 freeholders owning 2,177 acres would be in favour of the project, and 15 others owning 1,246 acres would be against it. But the "ayes" and "noes" fell into no definite pattern: some of the large freeholders were thought to be against the enclosure, and some of the small ones for it.

The individuals who stood in the way of enclosure were often the small *absentee* owners who had their land or common rights let out to the open-field farmers, and sometimes it was the larger owners of pasture land who opposed it because they benefited from a shortage of grazing in neighbouring parishes.

The evidence of the Land Tax Assessments shows that from the later eighteenth century up to probably about 1815 small owners were actually increasing in number and in acreage, even in some heavily enclosed counties. The complete accuracy of this source, however, must be considered as doubtful, and the figures for assessments tell us little about the size of farms or the total acreage, both owned and rented, in the hands of small men. The broad conclusions of the Land Tax Assessments, nevertheless, are valid and important. They show that enclosure was not a very important factor in the survival of owner-occupiers, at least when prices were good, and that there was an extremely numerous class of very small owners whose land could not have been sufficient for a full-time holding. The figures also reveal, incidentally, how very numerous were the small absentee owners of farmland; and that the fewest small farmers, both occupying and absentee, were to be found, as might be expected, in the villages enclosed earlier in the eighteenth century by agreement.

The increase in the numbers of small owners may have arisen in part from the recognition as freeholders, and taxpayers, of the owners of common rights, of copyholders, and even of squatters with encroachments on the waste. Small absentee owners found the high prices of the war period an inducement to sell, and we know too that large owners sometimes sold off part of their land to meet enclosure expenses. Tenant-farmers and existing owner-occupiers provided a ready market for small parcels of land at this prosperous period. The shrinkage in the number of small owners with the fall in prices at the end of the wars, and the fall in the area occupied by them, suggest that it was not enclosure but the level of prices in years of depression, and possibly the growth of alternative occupations outside farming, which were the important determinants of survival. According to Davies's figures for Cheshire, Derbyshire, Leicestershire, Lindsey, Northamptonshire, Nottinghamshire and Warwickshire, the decline in the early nineteenth century was not very marked: in 1832 there were about as many, or more, small owners as in 1780, although the totals had fallen from the wartime peak. It is possible that in areas of light soils, where the competitive advantage of large farms was greater, the decline may have been considerably greater than Davies's figures suggest. At all events, at the end of the nineteenth century only about 12 per cent of the cultivated land was worked by its owners (excluding the

land of larger proprietors currently in hand); and it is known that this figure was near 20 per cent about 1800, so that there was evidently a considerable decline in the land occupied by small owners in the nineteenth century after 1815, and probably even after the end of active enclosure of open fields and commons.

Turning to the more general question of the decline of small farmers as a whole, there was undoubtedly a long-term tendency in favour of the consolidation of farms into larger and more efficient units. This tendency was encouraged by enclosure, but in no sense depended on it. The move towards larger farms was marked even in open-field villages, and the most drastic changes in the size of farms sometimes occurred before enclosure. At Wigston Magna the size of farms grew steadily throughout the seventeenth century, and the enclosure of the village in the eighteenth century "did not directly create any greater inequality than had existed beforehand."

Farms grew in size for a whole variety of reasons: because except in certain specialised branches of farming large units were technically more efficient and more progressive; because the advances in husbandry involving the cultivation of roots and legumes generally demanded fairly large acreages; because large farmers had the resources to withstand occasional bad years and periods of low prices; and perhaps not least because landowners took great care in selecting the tenants for their large farms, and saw that they had the capital and knowledge to farm successfully. The long-term tendency was therefore in favour of larger farms, and enclosure usually served only to accelerate the effect of factors unfavourable to small men. The change was essentially a gradual one: there was no sudden or cataclysmic decline of small farms, and to speak of their "disappearance" in the eighteenth century is absurd. By 1851 the advance of large-scale farming had indeed gone so far that farms of 300 and more acres occupied over a third of the cultivated acreage, while small farms and holdings of under 100 acres occupied less than 22 per cent. But the number of small occupiers was still very large—over 134,000—as compared with 64,200 farmers of 100 to 299 acres, and only 16,671 farmers of 300 acres or more. The family farmer who employed no labour beyond that of his family was still very much in evidence. In 1831 of the 275,000 farming families in Britain, nearly half fell into the family-farmer category.

Of course, enclosure itself might have a considerable impact on small farmers if it led to large-scale engrossing or encouraged a considerable change in the nature of the farming. Enclosure provided landlords with an excellent opportunity of consolidating small farms into large ones which were easier to manage and meant less outlay on building and repairs. But on the other hand, as landlords well knew, small farmers paid a higher rent per acre than did large ones, and owing to the considerable capital required to stock large farms suitable tenants for them were not easy to come by. Indeed, to a considerable extent the pace of enclosure was determined by the availability of farmers able and willing to change their methods and pay the higher rents landlords expected from enclosed farms. Consequently, many landlords preferred (or were obliged) to leave their small tenants undisturbed, and there was in fact a powerful convention among reputable landlords that they did not disturb tenants who were competent and paid their rents regularly.

The fact that many small owners rented some land in addition to their own complicated the situation. The availability of additional land clearly improved the efficiency and flexibility of freeholders and made their post-enclosure survival more probable. But it was considered undesirable for landlords to have their land let in this way because of the tendency for freeholder-tenants to neglect the rented land in favour of their own. Consequently, some large owners no doubt saw enclosure as a good opportunity for reform, and consolidated their rented plots into substantial farms to be let to tenant-farmers only. Where this happened the acreage available to freeholders would fall and their post-enclosure prospects would diminish to that extent. How important this was in the survival of small freeholders it is impossible to say, but for many of them it may well have given rise to more intractable difficulties than did the more obvious but less serious problem of enclosure costs.

Quite often enclosure was undertaken in order to extend the practice of convertible husbandry, and where the farms were too small for this, or the occupiers could not afford to marl their land or pay the high rents demanded after enclosure, some of them might after a period of years give way to larger farmers. In the west and central Midlands especially—in Leicestershire, Warwickshire, Worcestershire, Northamptonshire, Huntingdonshire and Buckinghamshire—there was a strong tendency for enclosure to extend the area under grass. The low acreage of many of the post-enclosure farms, unsupported by common pasture, made it difficult or impossible for small men to succeed in convertible husbandry, and sometimes in fattening or dairying. In the Vales of Evesham and Berkeley corn growing and population were reduced by the conversion of deep-soiled arable ground to permanent pasture; in Lincolnshire the technical advantages of amalgamation of marshland with upland farms made the large farms larger, partly at the expense of smallholders; in chalkland areas, as in Wiltshire, Hampshire and Dorset, enclosure reinforced an old-established tendency towards expansion of arable cultivation at the expense of downland sheep pastures. In this development, too, the small men found conditions against them: reduced pasture made it difficult to graze their flocks, and they were obliged either to combine flocks for folding purposes, or to resort to artificial grasses and roots and all the capital and labour required in alternate husbandry in order to feed their flocks. Nevertheless, the post-enclosure changes did not always put small men at a disadvantage. Where the soils were sufficiently varied to allow mixed farming and specialisation to succeed the small man could prosper, and there is good evidence of stability in the farming population even in areas where arable was converted to permanent pasture, as in the north-eastern districts of Leicestershire and Rutland.

It is important to remember, however, that the impact of enclosure on husbandry practices was very much less than has often been supposed. Changes in agriculture rarely come about suddenly. The movement towards large arable farms in East Anglia, towards permanent pasture and ley farming in the Midlands, and towards the extension of arable at the expense of sheep in chalk areas of the south were all in train in the seventeenth century and earlier, and certainly long before the period of heavy enclosure after 1760. Enclosure certainly accelerated or intensified trends towards more productive farming, but it was not always the initiating force of these trends. Therefore it is not to be expected that changes in the size of farms or in their occupiers should necessarily proceed very much more rapidly after enclosure than before it. And in some areas, as in Cheshire, Wales and the northern counties where the enclosure was mainly of waste, there was an increase rather than a decline in the number of holdings.

Of course, the very changes brought about by enclosure, the opportunities which it might provide for adopting different and more productive methods of cultivation, could have a very stimulating effect on the farmers, changing their whole outlook. Dr. Thirsk found that in Lincolnshire enclosure "roused ambitions in the ordinary farmer for the first time, and that the fresh opportunities, suddenly opened up, brought into action stores of human energy never previously tapped. The psychological effects of change doubled and trebled the force of the original stimulus, with the result that people were willing to go beyond the economic limit in expending effort and money on their farms. The steward of the Duchy of Cornwall lands in the soke of Kirton-in-Lindsey twice commented on the large, almost foolhardy, outlay of tenants, who had no certainty of tenure of their holdings. An occupier of land at Heapham had carried manure

seven miles to cover his new enclosure, while the lessee of Kirton-in-Lindsey manor was enclosing and building in 1796 'with a spirit almost unequalled considering his term was a short one for an undertaking of such great magnitude'."

However, there is also a good deal of evidence that in many cases enclosure had little or no effect upon the character of the farming. This might be because even in the open fields the land might be cultivated "in severalty," i.e. without common rights, or because the surviving area of open fields was very small. An Enclosure Act might be invoked merely in order to incorporate waste land into the farms or to consolidate the existing holdings and closes for easier working. Enclosure did not necessarily lead to changed or better farming—and especially was this so if the soil did not lend itself to the cultivation of turnips or clover, or if the farmers were conservative. Marshall was one of a number of authorities who held summer-fallowing to be essential on heavy soils, and it is clear from the county *Reports* that bare fallows continued in many different areas. In Cambridgeshire Vancouver found enclosed parishes still following the rotation of open-field parishes, and Young noticed the same thing in Lord Chesterfield's new enclosures in Buckinghamshire. In Lincolnshire and Bedfordshire Stone and Batchelor saw only a few signs of improvement, and at Knapwell in Northamptonshire Young found the husbandry so bad that he was at a loss to know why the proprietors had troubled to enclose. And in Wiltshire Davis believed that enclosure had led to deterioration, because some farmers had extended their arable without adopting new rotations while at the same time allowing their sheep flocks to decline.

Finally, it may be argued that what really counted in the survival of small farmers were the levels of prices and costs. As we have remarked before, the rising prices between 1760 and 1813 must have made it possible for many small men to carry on who would have failed in the conditions prevailing before 1750, and who perhaps actually did fail in the depression after the Napoleonic Wars. It seems likely that their costs per unit of output were higher than those of large farmers, partly because they paid a higher rent per acre and bore a relatively heavier burden of poor rates, and partly because they lacked the economies of scale, the technical efficiency, capital resources and flexibility which helped the larger farmers. Thus, when prices fell their higher costs might prove fatal, as was the experience, for example, of the unfortunate farmers of the unimproved heavy clays.

We come last to the lowest level in rural society, the cottagers and squatters. "The effect on the cottager can best be described by saying that before enclosure the cottager was a labourer with land, after enclosure he was a labourer without land." Thus the Hammonds. There is indeed a great deal of truth in the Hammonds' brief summary, for access to commons and waste may have played an important part in the economy of many cottagers. Such access might make it possible for them to keep pigs, a cow or some geese, to gather fruit and firewood, and in the case of squatters to find a place for their dwelling, such as it was. The removal of this prop of the labourers' existence was undoubtedly a factor in the increasing poverty which characterised much of the countryside in the later eighteenth century and after.

However, we must be careful not to exaggerate the extent or the importance of the loss. There is some evidence to support those contemporaries who held that the commons were of little real advantage to labouring men, for when in some enclosures land was set aside for labourers' cow pastures or vegetable gardens it was sometimes difficult to find cottagers to take them. On the other hand, there is contrary evidence that such allotments were greatly appreciated by the labourers, and were instrumental in keeping them off the poor rates. Perhaps much depended on the local circumstances, the amount of employment available, the situation of the allotments and the nature of the soil, and so forth. In any case, it must be remembered that even before enclosure the majority of cottagers had no rights of common. Such rights did not belong to every villager but were attached to open-field holdings or certain cottages, and only their owners or occupiers were certainly entitled to make use of them.

The legal owners of common rights were always compensated by the commissioners with an allotment of land. (The *occupiers* of common right cottages, it should be noticed, who enjoyed common rights by virtue of their *tenancy* of the cottage, received no compensation because they were not, of course, the owners of the rights. This was a perfectly proper distinction between owner and tenant, and involved no fraud or disregard for cottagers on the part of the commissioners.) Unfortunately, the allotment of land given in exchange for common rights was often too small to be of much practical use, being generally far smaller than the three acres or so required to keep a cow. It might also be inconveniently distant from the cottage, and the cost of fencing (which was relatively heavier for small areas) might be too high to be worth while. Probably many cottagers sold such plots to the neighbouring farmers rather than go to the expense of fencing them, and thus peasant ownership at the lowest level declined.

Most labourers who made use of a common had access not by right but by custom. Customary rights to enjoyment of the common were sometimes recognised by the Commissioners, but quite often not. In any case, the common was usually a very limited benefit. In Clapham's opinion the right to keep a cow was probably rare, and Arthur Young's famous outburst contained much exaggeration: "by nineteen Enclosure Acts out of twenty, the poor are injured, in some grossly injured. . . . The poor in these parishes may say *Parliament may be tender of property; all I know is I had a cow, and an Act of Parliament has taken it from me.*" "These parishes," commented Clapham, "were not the nineteen out of twenty." In fact there were some places where the poor were left with cow pastures. At Sutton Cheney in Leicestershire, for instance, provision in the shape of "a sufficient quantity of land" (44 acres for 13 cow-keepers), was made "for all those who had cows before." In general, however, there is strong evidence that allotments and cottage gardens were scarcest in areas of recent enclosure, and particularly in corn country. Nevertheless, over England as a whole the majority of labourers, "probably the great majority," had either a garden or a patch of potato ground.

To some extent the loss of commons might be compensated, however, by an increase in the volume and regularity of employment after enclosure. Where the area of farmland was considerably expanded by the cultivation of commons and waste there would obviously be an increased demand for labour, and the work of the enclosure itself, in the making of fences and hedges, and in the laying down of new roads and the building of new farmhouses and barns, also created much employment. In the newly-cultivated fenlands of Lincolnshire, for instance, there was for many years an acute labour problem, and labourers had to be brought from old villages five or six miles away. Furthermore, the extension of alternate husbandry and leys required more labour for the work of drilling and hoeing roots and the management of the beasts fed on the legumes and artificial grasses. Heavier crops required more hands in harvesting and in the winter occupations of threshing and winnowing. The processing of agricultural produce, the milling of flour, the malting of barley, the drying of hops, the making of cheese, the curing of bacon and the tanning of leather, and all the rural trades and crafts serving the farmers were expanded as the cultivated area and agricultural output rose.

It should be emphasised that in the eighteenth century, with the exception of the late innovation (and only gradual adoption) of the threshing machine, the improved methods of farming were *not* labour-saving (although it is probable that the labour required per unit of output was reduced). And in so far as enclosure encouraged the rise of better farming and an expanded acreage

it must have greatly increased the supply of rural employment. Only where permanent pasture increased at the expense of arable was the labour requirement likely to fall off. In consequence there was in fact no general exodus of unemployed rural labour, pauperised by enclosure, to seek work in the industrial centres. The population of the numerous Nottinghamshire villages affected by enclosure rose only slightly less fast in the early nineteenth century than did the villages dominated by mining and textile manufactures. The census figures also confirm that agricultural employment was expanding, not declining: in 1831, for instance, 761,348 families were reported as employed in farming as compared with 697,353 families 20 years earlier.

In view of this evidence it is difficult to understand the attacks that contemporaries made on enclosure as the cause of unemployment and depopulation in the countryside. Before the censuses of the nineteenth century, however, there were no reliable statistics to be obtained; and enclosure, it seemed, was a subject on which few writers could avoid making statements completely unsupported by evidence, or on which they could eschew rancour and hyperbole. Dr. Price, one of the most bitter opponents of enclosure, claimed that its effects were visible in the half-empty and decayed churches, the ruined houses and unused roads of East Anglia. His remarks drew the fire of no less an enthusiast than Arthur Young. Rural improvement, answered Young, in the work of enclosing, marling, dunging, ploughing, turnip-hoeing, etc., had given more work than ever before, and particularly in Norfolk, the most improved county. The annual influx of Scots and Irish seeking harvest work, and the numerous wastes and heaths brought into production proved his point: "INCLOSURES alone have made these counties smile with culture which before were dreary as night." As for the half-empty churches, they had been built too large in the first place (which was true), while ruined houses were largely the result of the poor laws which induced landlords and farmers to pull down cottages and hire men from other parishes. This last contention also had some truth in it, for the Law of Settlement did lead to a growth of "closed parishes" where to keep down the poor rates newcomers were refused a settlement.

But whatever the merits of the controversy, both sides recognised that poverty was increasing in the countryside. Even the protagonists of enclosure were obliged to admit this unpalatable fact. Arthur Young, although he happily found a number of instances where enclosure had not been accompanied by rising poor rates, was dismayed to see that in general the poor rates in enclosed parishes, despite increased employment, had kept pace with those in other parishes. After a tour of villages in the south of England he arrived at the conclusion that the phenomenon arose from the failure of the commissioners in most enclosures to allot part of the commons or waste to the poor. Properly supervised allotments, he argued, had been shown greatly to benefit the poor and were effective in reducing the poor rates. Some landlords, the Duke of Bedford, the Earl of Egremont and Lord Hardwicke, for example, had done much good by providing cottage gardens and prizes for the best cultivation. But he found that in 25 of the 37 enclosures he examined the lot of the poor had deteriorated.

Young noticed that in many recently enclosed villages there were still areas of waste left uncultivated, and he believed that the cheapest way of providing for the poor would be to put labouring families on this land with a cottage and three acres apiece. They should be allowed to keep this allotment indefinitely so long as they never asked for relief from the parish. To do this, he estimated, and provide a cow, pig, seed and implements, would cost about £50 per family. This might seem a large capital outlay, but in the long run it would prove economical for it cost £60 to keep a family of five in a workhouse for a year, and £20 a year for the same family maintained on outdoor relief. Property, he always held, gave the poor the incentive to work hard, be frugal

and save, and was effective in keeping them off the parish. And for illustration he quoted 48 parishes in Lincolnshire and Rutland, where there were as many as 753 cottagers with cow pastures and nearly 1,200 cows between them. It had been found that these cottagers did not come to the parish for relief, and they were acknowledged by the farmers to be the most hard-working of labourers. Indeed, the poor rates in these parishes were less than half the average elsewhere.

There was the problem, however, that in many villages, and especially in those enclosed before the era of parliamentary enclosure, no waste land was now left. Here the poor could not even help themselves: they could not find land to build their own cottage (which could be done for a little over £20, paid back to the carpenter over 15 years); nor could they cultivate a vegetable patch, nor keep a pig. It was to this situation that his most famous quotation relates: "Go to an alehouse kitchen of an old-enclosed country, and there you will see the origin of poverty and the poor-rates. For whom are they to be sober? For whom are they to save? For the parish? If I am diligent, shall I have leave to build a cottage? If I am sober, shall I have land for a cow? If I am frugal, shall I have half an acre of potatoes? You offer no motives, you have nothing but a parish officer and a workhouse. Bring me another pot." It is important to notice that this was said in reference to *old-enclosed* villages, and not to enclosure in general.

Where no waste was left, and kind landowners willing to let land to the poor were lacking, Young suggested that the parish itself should buy some land, borrowing the money on the security of the rates, and should fence and stock it and let it out to the poor. Young's scheme was only a partial solution, of course. It might have prevented much misery and degradation, but it could not overcome the effects of rising numbers. He himself noted that families settled on allotments revealed an alarming tendency to propagate, "so that pigs and children fill every quarter," thus intensifying the very problem he sought to solve.

In practice it was not at all easy to distinguish the influence of enclosure among the various factors affecting poor-law expenditure. With the growth in the countryside of such industries as textiles, mining and iron manufacture, the level of employment was affected by booms and slumps in trade. In some areas, as in East Anglia, Sussex and the Forest of Dean, the decline of the obsolete textile, coal and iron industries gave rise to growing unemployment. Even in villages still entirely agricultural harvest failures or the growth of permanent pasture could have serious effects. Marshall held that "agriculture occasions very few poor, on the contrary it provides them almost constant labour. It is only the blind, the extreme old, the very young children and idiots which become chargeable in a parish purely agricultural." He was surprised to find that in some places this was not true.

We see now that the fundamental factor was the great upswing of population. Population increase, which became far more rapid in the late eighteenth century than hitherto, was expanding the labour force at a rate faster than agriculture could absorb it, and the growth of numbers, of landless and sometimes unemployable labourers, was observable both in enclosed and the still open villages. It was this natural phenomenon, the origins of which are still obscure, which lay at the bottom of unemployment and the rising poor rates. Of course, there had always been a good deal of rural poverty: in Leicestershire in 1670 there was already a large proportion of villagers too poor to pay the hearth tax. There was also at the end of the seventeenth century already a high proportion of landless labourers. The changes of the eighteenth and early nineteenth centuries added to this rural proletariat, but not to the extent that might be supposed: about 1690 there were nearly as many as two landless labourers to every occupier; and in 1831, after nearly a century and a half of enclosure and engrossing, there were still only five landless labourers to every two occupiers. More precisely, as Sir John Clapham pointed out long ago, the proportion of landless to occupiers rose only from 1.74:1 to 2.5:1. Much of this increase came from the growing numbers of surviving younger sons with no land to inherit; population growth was the main factor in the increase in the landless, as well as a partially workless, labour supply in the countryside.

The increase in population was spread fairly evenly over the country, but in areas of developing industries there was migration away from the agricultural villages, able-bodied workers attracted by better pay and wider opportunities of employment moving over distances of 20 or 30 miles to the industrial towns and villages. In consequence, the effects of population growth on rural unemployment and poverty were much more marked where alternative industrial occupations were not available. The statistics of poor relief bear this out, showing that the distribution of poverty was not related to the extent of recent enclosure but to the availability of work outside farming. The per capita expenditure on poor relief was higher in some counties virtually unaffected by eighteenth-century enclosure than in others exposed to the full flood of the movement. According to Gonner's figures, Kent and Sussex, for example, spent as much or more per head on relief as did the heavily-enclosed counties of Bedfordshire, Huntingdonshire, Leicestershire, Rutland and Northamptonshire; and much more was spent in heavily-enclosed counties that remained largely agricultural, like Berkshire, Wiltshire, Oxfordshire and Huntingdonshire, than in the heavily-enclosed but semi-industrialised Nottinghamshire and Leicestershire.

The same picture emerges if one looks not at poor law expenditure but at the proportion of population actually in receipt of relief. The counties little affected by enclosure, like Kent, Sussex and Hertfordshire, had as high a proportion of paupers as had the heavily-enclosed Northamptonshire, Leicestershire, Rutland and Nottinghamshire. And more detailed investigations within the heavily-enclosed counties have shown that whether the villages were enclosed recently by Act of Parliament, were old-enclosed by agreement, or still remained open, had little connection with the proportion of population receiving relief.

Returning to the importance of alternative employment in the distribution of poverty, it is very significant that it was not the heavily-enclosed Midlands but the old-enclosed, poverty-stricken counties of southern England, Kent, Sussex, Hampshire and Dorset, that were the scene of the last Labourers' Revolt of 1830. Undoubtedly low wages, unemployment and bad living conditions lay at the origin of the outbreaks of violence and destruction, but there was obviously no connection between the revolt and enclosure, as the Hammonds' references to it would suggest.

To sum up, the effects of enclosure were rarely great or immediate. In some instances enclosure came as the last act of a long-drawn-out drama of rural change, and merely put *finis* to the story. In others it sometimes introduced, but more often accelerated, a similar story of change. As the result of enclosure improved farming spread more rap-idly than would otherwise have been the case, larger and more efficient farms were more readily developed, and the long-run decline of the smallholder and cottager hastened and made more certain. Enclosure provides a leading example of the large gains in economic efficiency and output that could be achieved by reorganisation of existing resources rather than by invention or new techniques. Enclosure meant more food for the growing population, more land under cultivation and, on balance, more employment in the countryside; and enclosed farms provided the framework for the new advances of the nineteenth century. But in our period enclosure did not affect the whole country, and even the limited area that felt its influence was not suddenly transformed.

Enclosure remains an important and indeed vital phase in English agricultural development, but we should be careful not to ascribe to it developments that were the consequences of a much broader and more complex process of historical change.

John L. and Barbara Hammond

THE RULERS AND THE MASSES

> The Hammonds wrote all their books on social history as partners, principally between 1910 and 1925. Although heavily attacked by some scholars for the lack of balance inherent in their sympathy for victims of oppression and in their emphasis on cultural and moral factors, their interpretation still holds sway over the English general reader. In its content and tone the excerpt that follows is entirely typical.

ROME imported slaves to work in Italy: Englishmen counted it one of the advantages of the slave trade that it discouraged the competition of British colonists with British manufacturers. For the slaves were chiefly needed for industries like sugar planting, in which Englishmen at home were not engaged. Thus it might be argued that England had escaped the fate of Rome and that she so used the slave trade as to make it a stimulus rather than a dis-

From John L. and Barbara Hammond, *The Rise of Modern Industry* (Methuen, London, 1925), pp. 194–201, 203–8, 210–13, 217–20, 222–4, 226–32. By permission of Associated Book Publishers, Ltd.

couragement to native energy and skill.

Yet England did not escape the penalty. For it was under this shadow that the new industrial system took form and grew, and the immense power with which invention had armed mankind was exercised at first under conditions that reproduced the degradation of the slave trade. The factory system was not like war or revolution a deliberate attack on society: it was the effort of men to use will, energy, organization and intelligence for the service of man's needs. But in adapting this new power to the satisfaction of its wants England could not escape from the moral atmosphere of the slave trade: the atmosphere in which it was the fashion to think of men as things.

In the days of the guilds the workman was regarded as a person with some kind of property or status; the stages by which this character is restricted to a smaller and smaller part of the working classes, and more and more of the journeymen and apprentices fall into a permanently inferior class have been described by historians. In the early nineteenth century the workers, as a class, were looked upon as so much labour power to be used at the discretion of, and under conditions imposed by, their masters; not as men and women who are entitled to some voice in the arrangements of their life and work. The use of child labour on a vast scale had an important bearing on the growth of this temper.

The children of the poor were regarded as workers long before the Industrial Revolution. Locke suggested that they should begin work at three; Defoe rejoiced to see that in the busy homes of the Yorkshire clothiers "scarce anything above four years old, but its hands were sufficient for its own support." The new industrial system provided a great field for the employment of children, and Pitt himself, speaking in 1796, dwelt on this prospect with a satisfaction strange to modern minds, and disturbing even to some who heard him. One of the most elaborate of all Bentham's fantasies was his scheme for a great series of Industry Houses, 250 in number, each to hold 2,000 persons, for whose work, recreation, education and marriage most minute regulations were laid down. An advantage he claimed for his system was that it would enable the apprentices to marry at "the earliest period compatible with health," and this was made possible by the employment of children. "And to what would they be indebted for this gentlest of all revolutions? To what, but to economy? Which dreads no longer the multiplication of man, now that she has shown by what secure and unperishable means infant man, a drug at present so much worse than worthless, may be endowed with an indubitable and universal value." Infant man soon became in the new industrial system what he never was in the old, the basis of a complicated economy.

Most children under the old domestic system worked at home under their parents' eyes, but in addition to such children there were workhouse children, who were hired out by overseers to every kind of master or mistress. Little care was taken to see that they were taught a trade or treated with humanity by their employers, and though London magistrates like Fielding did what they could to protect this unhappy class, their state was often a kind of slavery. The number of children on the hands of the London parishes was largely increased in the latter part of the eighteenth century, because an Act of Parliament, passed in 1767 in consequence of the exertions of Jonas Hanway, compelled the London parishes to board out their young children, and to give a bonus to every nurse whose charge survived. Until this time very few parish pauper children grew up to trouble their betters.

The needs of the London workhouses on the one hand, and those of the factory on the other, created a situation painfully like the situation in the West Indies. The Spanish employers in America wanted outside labour, because the supply of native labour was deficient in quantity and quality. The new cotton mills placed on streams in solitary districts were in the same case. The inventions had found immense scope for child labour, and in these districts there were only scattered populations. In the workhouses of large towns there was a quantity of child labour available for employment, that was even more powerless and passive in the hands of a master than the stolen negro, brought from his burning home to the hold of a British slave ship. Of these children it could be said, as it was said of the negroes, that their life at best was a hard one, and that their choice was often the choice between one kind of slavery and another. So the new industry which was to give the English people such immense power in the world borrowed at its origin from the methods of the American settlements.

How closely the apologies for this child serf system followed the apologies for the slave trade can be seen from Romilly's description of a speech made in the House of Commons in 1811. "Mr. Wortley, who spoke on the same side, insisted that, although in the higher ranks of society it was true that to cultivate the affections of children for their family was the source of every virtue, yet that it was not so among the lower orders, and that it was a benefit to take them away from their miserable and depraved parents. He said too that it would be highly injurious to the public to put a stop to the binding of so many apprentices to the cotton manufacturers, as it must necessarily raise the price of labour and enhance the price of cotton manufactured goods."

It was not until 1816 that Parliament would consent to reform this system of transportation. In that year a Bill that had been repeatedly introduced by Mr. Wilbraham Bootle passed both Houses, and it was made illegal for London children to be apprenticed more than forty miles away from their parish. But by this time the problem had changed, for steam-power had superseded water-power and mills could be built in towns; in these towns there were parents who were driven by poverty to send their children to the mills. In the early days of the factory system there had been a prejudice against sending children to the mill, but the hand-loom weaver had been sinking steadily from the beginning of the century into deeper and deeper poverty, and he was no longer

able to maintain himself and his family. Sometimes too an adult worker was only given work on condition that he send his child to the mill. Thus the apprentice system was no longer needed. It had carried the factories over the first stage and at the second they could draw on the population of the neighbourhood.

These children who were commonly called "free-labour children," were employed from a very early age. Most of them were piecers: that is they had to join together or piece the threads broken in the several roving or spinning machines. But there were tasks less skilled than these, and Robert Owen said that many children who were four or five years old were set to pick up waste cotton on the floor. Their hours were those of the apprentice children. They entered the mill gates at five or six in the morning and left them again at seven or eight at night. They had half an hour for breakfast and an hour for dinner, but even during meal hours they were often at work cleaning a standing machine; Fielden calculated that a child following the spinning machine could walk twenty miles in the twelve hours. Oastler was once in the company of a West Indian slave-master and three Bradford spinners. When the slave-master heard what were the children's hours he declared: "I have always thought myself disgraced by being the owner of slaves, but we never in the West Indies thought it possible for any human being to be so cruel as to require a child of nine years old to work twelve and a half hours a day."

This terrible evil fastened itself on English life as the other fastened itself on the life of the Colonies. Reformers had an uphill struggle to get rid of its worst abuses. Throughout this long struggle the apologies for child labour were precisely the same as the apologies for the slave trade. Cobbett put it in 1833 that the opponents of the Ten Hours Bill had discovered that England's manufacturing supremacy depended on 30,000 little girls. This was no travesty of their argument. The champions of the slave trade pointed to the £70,000,000 invested in the sugar plantations, to the dependence of our navy on our commerce, and to the dependence of our commerce on the slave trade. This was the argument of Chatham in one generation and Rodney in another. When Fox destroyed the trade in 1806 even Sir Robert Peel complained that we were philosophizing when our looms were idle, and George Rose, that the Americans would take up the trade, and that Manchester, Stockport and Paisley would starve. They could point to Liverpool, which had been turned from a small hamlet into a flourishing port by the trade. For Liverpool was the centre of the commerce that throve on this trade. She shipped Manchester goods to Africa, took thence slave cargoes to the West Indies and brought back sugar and raw cotton. In the eleven years from 1783 to 1793 Liverpool slaving ships carried over 300,000 slaves from Africa to the West Indies and sold them for over £15,000,000. In 1793 this single port had secured three-sevenths of the slave trade of Europe. A Liverpool Member said that nobody would introduce the slave trade, but that so large a body of interests and property now depended on it that no equitable person would abolish it.

The argument for child labour followed the same line. In the one case the interests of Liverpool, in the other those of Lancashire, demanded of the nation that it should accept one evil in order to escape from another. Cardwell, afterwards the famous army reformer, talked of the great capital sunk in the cotton industry and the danger of the blind impulse of humanity. Sir James Graham thought that the Ten Hours Bill would ruin the cotton industry and with it the trade of the country. The cotton industry had taken the place in this argument that had been held by the navy in the earlier controversy. Our population, which had grown rapidly in the Industrial Revolution, was no longer able to feed itself; the food it bought was paid for by its manufactures: those manufactures depended on capital: capital depended on profits: profits depended on the labour of the boys and girls who enabled the manufacturer to work his mills long enough

at a time to repay the cost of the plant and to compete with foreign rivals. This was the circle in which the nation found its conscience entangled.

The life of man had been regulated before by the needs of a particular order or the pattern of a particular society: the government of king or church or lord had defined narrow limits within which a man was to run his course. The new master was a world force, for this economy could make its profits, so it was believed, where it chose, and when Englishmen rebelled against its rule it would seek its gains and bestow its blessings elsewhere. This way of looking at the new industrial system put man at the mercy of his machines, for if the new power was not made man's servant, it was found to become his master. If at every point the governing claim was not man's good but the needs of the machine, it was inevitable that man's life and the quality of his civilization should be subordinated to this great system of production.

Nobody could argue that the ordinary worker before the Industrial Revolution was a free man, whether he was a peasant in the country or a journeyman in the town, but the age which watched the change from domestic to factory industry in Lancashire and Yorkshire could see that a great many men and women lost what they had possessed of initiative and choice. For the Industrial Revolution gave a look of catastrophe to the final stages of a process that had been in train for centuries. Before this time there had been fierce quarrels between master and journeyman. Professor Unwin describes a scene at Chester in 1358 when the master weavers, shearmen and challoners and walkers attacked their journeymen with iron-pointed poles during the Corpus Christi procession. It is true, as he says, that from the middle of the fourteenth century there was to be found in every industrial centre of Western Europe a body of workmen in every craft who had no prospect before them but that of remaining journeymen all their lives, that there was constant friction between this class and the masters, and perpetual disputes over hours, wages and other conditions. The Industrial Revolution did not create the quarrels of class, nor did it create the wrongs and discontents that are inevitable in any relationship, where interests are sharply opposed and power is mismatched. But it made the disproportion of power much greater, and the immense extension of industrial life which followed came at a time when there was a general disposition to regard the working-class world as idle and profligate, and to regard industry as a system that served men by ruling them. Consequently the Industrial Revolution, if it did not introduce all the evils that were so acute in the new factories, gave them a far greater range and importance.

What happened at the Industrial Revolution was that all the restraints that the law imposed on workmen in particular industries, were standardized into a general law for the whole of the expanding world of industry, and all the regulations and laws that recognized him as a person with rights were withdrawn or became inoperative. The workman, as we have seen, lost one by one the several Acts of Parliament that gave him protection from his master in this or that industry. His personal liberty was circumscribed by a series of Acts, beginning with the Act of 1719, which made it a crime for him to take his wits and his skills into another country: a law that applied to the artisan but not to the inventor. At the end of the century the masters were given complete control of their workmen, by a Combination Act which went far beyond the Acts against combinations already on the Statute book. By the Combination Act of 1799 any workman who combined with any other workman to seek an improvement in his working conditions was liable to be brought before a single magistrate—it might be his own employer—and sent to prison for three months. This Act, the chief authors of which were Pitt and Wilberforce, was modified next year, when Parliament decided that two magistrates were necessary to form a court, and that a magistrate who was a master in the trade affected should not try offences, but these modifications did not affect in practice the power that the law gave to employers. Under cover of this Act it often happened that a master would threaten his workman with imprisonment or service in the fleet in order to compel him to accept the wages he chose to offer. In 1824 Place and Hume, taking advantage of the reaction from the worst of the panics produced by the French Revolution, managed to carry the repeal of the Combination Laws. Next year, after their repeal had been celebrated by an outburst of strikes, a less stringent law was put in their place. But the view of the new system as a beneficent mechanism which the mass of men must serve with a blind and unquestioning obedience was firmly rooted in the temper of the time, and thus anyone who tried to think of Englishmen in the spirit of Burke's description of a man, found himself strangely out of tune in a world where the workman was refused education, political rights and any voice in the conditions of employment.

"At Tyldesley," it was said in a pamphlet published during a strike, "they work fourteen hours per day, including the nominal hour for dinner; the door is locked in working hours, except half an hour at tea time; the workpeople are not allowed to send for water to drink, in the hot factory: and even the rain water is locked up, by the master's order, otherwise they would be happy to drink even that." In this mill a shilling fine was inflicted on a spinner found dirty, or found washing, heard whistling or found with his window open in a temperature of 84 degrees. The men who were thrust into this discipline, however hard and bare their lives, had been accustomed to work in their own homes at their own time. The sense of servitude that was impressed on the age by this discipline, by the methods of government, the look of the towns and the absence of choice or initiative in the lives of the mass of the workpeople, was strengthened by the spectacle of the new power. "While the engine runs," wrote an observer, "the people must work—men, women and children yoked together with iron and steam. The animal machine—breakable in the best case, subject to a thousand sources of suffering—is chained fast to the iron machine which knows no suffering and no weariness."

"Two centuries ago not one person in a thousand wore stockings; one century ago not one person in five hundred wore them, now not one person in a thousand is without them." This sentence from *The Results of Machinery* (1831), one of the publications of the Society for the Diffusion of Useful Knowledge, illustrates a feature of the Industrial Revolution that made a profound impression on the imagination of the time. When capital was applied to production on a large scale, it gained its profits by producing in bulk; producing, that is, for mass consumption. Energy and brains were now devoted to satisfying, not the luxurious taste of the classes that were served by the commerce of medieval Europe, but the needs of the poor consumer.

It was natural for the age that witnessed the first triumphs of the new system to worship production for profit. This great addition to the wealth of the world seemed to follow automatically when men were left to acquire at their pleasure. Swift success is a dazzling spectacle, and the new industrial system provided a new miracle every day. A visitor to a mill in Bolton or Preston watching the inventions of Crompton, Hargreaves, Arkwright and Watt, stood before a power that was conquering the world as no Caesar or Napoleon had ever conquered it. To the generation that saw on the one hand the small farmer carrying the wool he had woven on his hand-loom at home to Leeds or Halifax on the back of his horse, and on the other the great mills at Blackburn or Rochdale sending out thousands of bales of cotton to be transported by rail and ship to the other ends of the earth, it looked as if progress that had dawdled through so many centuries was, now that man had learnt its simple secret, to follow a rapid and unbroken course; as if the society that surrendered itself to the control of private profit released a force that would regenerate the world. Any people into whose hands this power had fallen would probably have been plunged into the state described by Boulton as "steam-mill mad,"

just as any people that had first grasped the new wealth of America in the fifteenth century would have been as frantic as the Spaniards for gold and silver.

The English people, from the whole tone and cast of its thought and politics, was specially liable to be swept off its balance by this revolution. The positive enthusiasms of the time were for science and progress: for material development and individual liberty. The restraints of custom, tradition and religion had never been so frail over the classes that held power. In the Middle Ages the Church had laid a controlling or checking hand on manners: the Guilds had hampered individual enterprise by a corporate discipline. But the Church of the eighteenth century was merely part of the civil order, without standards, authority or conscience of its own; the Guilds were dead, and their successors stood not for corporate spirit, but for property and nothing else. Thus neither Church nor Guild survived to offer any obstacle to the view that headlong wealth was the sovereign good for society and for the individual, for cities and for men.

This view was powerfully encouraged by the philosophy of confidence which the eighteenth century had substituted for a religion of awe. Medieval religion had watched man's instincts with anxious eyes, as instincts needing to be disciplined, coerced, held fast by Pope and priest; the Puritans, though they gave him different masters, were not less suspicious of the natural man. The new philosophy, on the other hand, regarded man's instincts as the best guide to conduct, and taught that left to himself man so acted as to serve rather than injure the society to which he belonged. Capital was a magical power; man was a benevolent creature. Thus so far as an age lives by a system of belief, this age drew its wisdom from a philosophy that found nothing but good in the new force to which it had submitted.

The state of politics was also congenial to this impulse. Neither Conservative nor Radical offered any distracting or competing motive, for while they disagreed about political and administrative reform, they did not disagree about the advantages of a system under which acquisition and profit-making were unimpeded. If it was the manufacturers who promoted the new system in industry, the landowners were equally active in promoting it on their estates. The most important force in making the English an industrial people was the destruction of the village. Nations that kept the peasant could never be completely absorbed in the new industrial system, and it was the landowner, often of course the new landowner, who had come from the world of finance and industry, who pushed the English peasant out.

England was on the eve of a great expansion of resources, numbers, wealth and power. What were the new towns to be like? What their schools, their pleasures, their houses, their standards of a good life, their plans for co-operation and fellowship? What the fate of the mass of people who did not feel or force their way through the doors thrown open to enterprise? To all these questions the Industrial Revolution gave the same answer: "Ask Capital." And neither Conservative nor Radical, the man defending or the man attacking bad laws and bad customs, thought that answer wrong. But that answer meant that the age had turned aside from making a society in order to make a system of production.

The effect of this concentration is seen in the towns of the age. They were left, like everything else, to the mercy and direction of the spirit of profit. Mankind did not admire wealth for the first time; but the rich merchant of Bruges, Genoa, or Norwich, like the rich Pope or the rich noble of the Middle Ages, or the rich Senator of the Roman Empire, had regarded the beauty and culture of his town as a sign of his own importance and success. Vespasian, frugal as he was, did not hesitate to begin the restoration of the Capitol, though he had inherited a debt of over three hundred million pounds. The private citizen who gave Bordeaux an aqueduct costing £160,000, or the benefactor who spent £80,000 on the walls of Marseilles, the soldier who provided

free baths for slave girls at Suessa Senonum, the civic dignitaries who gave temples and theatres, these typical figures of the early Roman Empire would have been astonished to learn that in the districts of South Wales, where men had risen in a few years to such wealth as would have rivalled the wealth of Atticus or Herodes, the poorer classes had to go a mile for water, waiting in a queue a great part of the night; that the chief town of this rich district had neither public lighting nor drainage.

Yet the Industrial Revolution which had given these men their fortunes had made it much easier to supply the needs of the towns that sprang up beside their great establishments. One of the products of that revolution was gas lighting; the Soho Works were lighted with gas in 1802 to celebrate the Peace of Amiens. Great factories at Manchester and Leeds soon followed the example of Boulton and Watt. Another product was the cheap water-pipe. At the end of the American War English ironmasters were exporting water-pipes to Paris and New York. The Romans had no cheap water-pipes made by the help of mechanical power, but they could supply their towns with clean water, whereas the people of Merthyr Tydfil, their streets echoing by day and night with the clamour of forge and furnace, had to drink whatever the river brought them.

The rage for production had swept England, as the rage for piety had swept the age of the monachists. And production had taken a form that was intensely isolating; the successful man kept his secrets, tried to find his neighbours' secrets, strove for personal gain, took personal risks, made his way by personal initiative and personal enterprise.

This concentration led to the complete neglect of the most urgent tasks of the age. In the first twenty years of the nineteenth century the population of Manchester increased from 94,000 to 160,000; of Bolton from 29,000 to 50,000; Leeds more than doubled its population between 1801 and 1831; Bradford, which had 23,000 inhabitants in 1831, grew grass in its streets at the end of the eighteenth century. Oldham, which had 38,000 inhabitants in 1821, had three or four hundred in 1760. In the twenty years from 1801 to 1821 the population of Lancashire grew from 672,000 to 1,052,000; in the next twenty years it grew to 1,701,000. The population of Merthyr increased from 7,700 to 35,000 between 1801 and 1841, and that of the two counties of Glamorgan and Monmouth from 126,000 to 305,000. Industry was accumulating dense masses of people into particular districts, where the workman was shut up in melancholy streets, without gardens or orchards. England was passing from a country to a town life, as she passed from a peasant to an industrial civilization. What this meant is clear if we compare the state of the towns as revealed in the health statistics, with that of the country districts. In 1757, Dr. Percival put the death-rate for Manchester at 1 in 25, for Liverpool at 1 in 27. In Monton, a few miles from Manchester the ratio was at that time 1 in 68, at Horwich, between Bolton and Chorley, 1 in 66, at Darwen, three miles from Blackburn, 1 in 56. The Industrial Revolution was to spread the conditions of town life over places like Monton, Horwich and Darwen.

The problem of arranging and controlling the expansion of the towns was thus the most urgent of the problems created by the Industrial Revolution. Its importance was illustrated by a picture of some cottages near Preston published by the Health of Towns Commission in 1844. These cottages stood in two rows, separated by little back yards, with an open sewer running the whole length. The picture was given as an example of dangerous and disgusting drainage. But this is not its chief significance. One would suppose that these huddled cottages, without gardens of any kind, were built in a crowded town, where not an inch of space was available for amenities. They were in fact in the open country. Clearly then there was more here than a problem of drainage, for if it was left to private enterprise to develop this district, under the guidance of an uncontrolled sense of profit, these rows would spring up all round, and Preston would have another slum

on her hands. This is what happened in the new industrial districts. When the Health of Towns Commission investigated towns like Manchester, they were told that the worst evils were not the evils of the past, for new Manchester was reproducing the slums and alleys of the old, and spreading them, of course, over a far wider surface. Of no other problem was it so true that neglect by one generation tied the hands and the mind of the next.

In 1840 a Committee of the House of Commons recommended a series of reforms of a drastic and far-reaching character, and the Government of the day, represented at the Home Office by Normanby, a minister who was in earnest, introduced Bills to give effect to its proposals. This Committee regretted that there was no general building law in force at the beginning of the century, "the fulfilment of one of the first duties of a humane government," and called for a general building law, a general sewage law, the setting up of a Board of Health in every town, with instructions to look after water supply, burial grounds, open spaces and slums. Cellar dwellings and back-to-back houses were to be forbidden. The importance of preserving amenities, footpaths, and something of the look of the country was impressed on Parliament. The most significant comment of the neglect of these proposals is to be found in the recurring complaint that runs through all the Reports on Health and Housing that were issued in the nineteenth century. Town planning never found its way into an Act of Parliament until the twentieth century, and back-to-back houses (made illegal in 1909) were built in great numbers two generations after Normanby's Bill had proposed to forbid them. The Commission which sat in 1867 found in existence the main evils that were revealed by the Committee of 1840; the Commission of 1884 found in existence the main evils that had been revealed by the Commission of 1867. In many towns the death-rate was higher in 1867 than in 1842, and Cross, speaking as Home Secretary in 1871, could match the terrible revelations by which Chadwick had tried to rouse the indignation and fear of the Parliaments of Melbourne and Peel.

Before each Commission the large towns disclosed the same difficulties. The law did not enable them to control expansion, or to prevent the creation on their circumference of the evils they were trying to suppress at the centre. The Committee of 1840 had pointed out that back-to-back houses were being introduced into towns that had been free from them. Town clerks told the Commission of 1867 that whole streets were still being built on "a foundation composed of old sweepings, refuse from factories, old buildings and other objectionable matter." Parliament passed Public Health Acts and set up authorities with sharply limited powers, but the fatal blindness to the character of the problem, as a problem in the organization and planning of town life, which marked the early phases of the Industrial Revolution, persisted. England learnt sooner than other countries how to cleanse her towns, but towns still continued to grow at the pleasure of the profit seeker. Each generation looked wistfully back to its predecessor as living in a time when the evil was still manageable, and over the reforms of the century could be inscribed the motto "the Clock that always loses." For the creed of the first age of the Industrial Revolution, that the needs of production must regulate the conditions of life, and that the incidence of profits must decide in what kind of town, in what kind of streets, and in what kind of houses a nation shall find its home, had cast its melancholy fatalism over the mind of the generations that followed. The trouble was not merely that the evil was greater when a town had a quarter of a million of inhabitants instead of a hundred thousand. It was that men still saw with the eyes of their grandfathers, and that they were busy polishing the life of the slum, when a race that was free and vigorous in its mind could have put an end to it. With the consequences and the traditions of this neglect industrial civilization is still fighting an up-hill battle.

The other task that became immensely more important with the Industrial Revolution was the task of education. Adam Smith had pointed out that the division of labour, though good for production, was bad for the mind of the labourer. Men, women and children lost range, diversity and incentive in their work, when that work was simplified to a single process or a monotonous routine. Life was more versatile and interesting when craftsmanship was combined with agriculture. Under the new system a boy or youth learnt one process and one process only; a great part of his mind was never exercised; many of his faculties remained idle and undeveloped. Moreover, apprenticeship was declining and thus an important method of education was passing out of fashion.

Nor were these the only reasons why popular education was needed more urgently in this than in previous ages. Men learn from their leisure as well as from their work. Now the common life of the time was singularly wanting in inspiration, comparing in this respect unfavourably with the life of the ancient or that of the medieval world. The Greeks and the Romans put a great deal of beauty into their public buildings; they made provision, in some cases barbarous provision, for public amusement; they did not isolate art and pleasure for the delight of small classes. Life in Manchester or Merthyr was very different. Mr. and Mrs. Webb, who have described the work of the several bodies of Improvement Commissioners at this time, remark that even the most energetic among them made no provision for parks, open spaces, libraries, picture galleries, museums, baths, or any kind of education. The workmen put it that their sports had been converted into crimes, and their holidays into fast days. Rich men in the Roman Empire spent their money on things that were for common enjoyment as rich men in the Middle Ages spent their money on things that were for common salvation. Pliny gave to his native Como, a library, a school endowment, a foundation for the nurture of poor children and a Temple of Ceres with spacious colonnades to shelter the traders who visited the great fair. The wealthy Herodes Atticus, tutor of Marcus Aurelius, gave a theatre to

Athens with a roof of cedar to hold 6,000 persons, another theatre to Corinth, and a race-course to Delphi. Such gifts were common in the days of the Antonines. But in the England of the Industrial Revolution all diversions were regarded as wrong, because it was believed that successful production demanded long hours, a bare life, a mind without temptation to think or to remember, to look before or behind. Some Lancashire magistrates used to refuse on this ground to license public-houses where concerts were held. Long hours did not begin with the Industrial Revolution, but in the Middle Ages the monotony of industrial work was broken for the journeyman by frequent holidays, saints' days and festivals; for medieval Europe, like Rome, gave some place in common life to the satisfaction of the imagination and the senses.

Perhaps nothing served so directly to embitter the relations of class in the Industrial Revolution as this fashionable view, that the less amusement the worker had, the better. The love of amusement has a place of special significance in the English character. If the English workman stints himself for his holiday week at Blackpool, as the Scottish peasant stints himself to send his son into the Ministry, or the Irish or French peasant stints himself to own a little property, it is not merely because he sets his holiday high among the enjoyments of life. The satisfaction of this desire is connected with his self-respect. The football field and the holiday resort represent a world in which the poor man feels himself the equal of the rich: a corner of life in which he has not bargained away any rights or liberties. It might be said of the early Radicals, that they sought to extend to his view of politics, and of the early Socialists, that they sought to extend to his views of property, the spirit that ruled the workman's outlook on his pleasures: that they sought to make him resent in those spheres the inequalities he was so quick to resent, when employer or magistrate tried to keep from him amusement that other classes enjoyed.

The need for popular education became in these circumstances specially urgent. The reading of print is one way of using and exercising the mind, and its value at any moment depends on circumstances. In the days of pageants and spectacles, when story-tellers went from village to village, when pedlars and pilgrims brought tales of adventure or war or the habits of foreign countries, a man might be unable to read or write, and yet take a share in the culture of the time. Buildings, plays, music, these may be greater influences on the mind than book or pamphlet or newspaper. But the youth of the early nineteenth century who found no scope for initiative or experiment or design in his work, found no stimulus or education for his fancy from the spectacles and amusements provided for his recreation. Science was improving the mechanical contrivances of life, but the arts of life were in decline. To take advantage of these improvements, the power to read and write was essential. In a world depending on newspapers, the man who cannot read lives in the darkest exile; when the factory was taking the place of the craft, the newspaper the place of the pageant, illiteracy was the worst disfranchisement a man could suffer.

Horner, reporting in 1839 that a population of over a hundred thousand persons in a district of Lancashire comprising Oldham and Ashton was without a single public day-school for poor scholars, the Commissioner who said of South Wales in 1842 that not one grown male in fifty could read, both spoke of an age in which the story-teller had left the village, and the apprenticeship system was leaving the town. Adam Smith had argued that as the division of labour deprived the worker of opportunities of training his mind, the State ought to provide opportunities by public education. The ruling class argued, on the contrary, that with the new methods of specialization, industry could not spare a single hour for the needs of the men who served it. In such a system education had no place. The great majority of the ruling class believed, as one of them put it, that the question to ask was not whether education would develop a child's faculties for happiness and citizenship, but whether it "would make him a good servant in agriculture and other laborious employments to which his rank in society had destined him."

Thus England asked for profits and received profits. Everything turned to profit. The towns had their profitable dirt, their profitable smoke, their profitable slums, their profitable disorder, their profitable ignorance, their profitable despair. The curse of Midas was on this society: on its corporate life, on its common mind, on the decisive and impatient step it had taken from the peasant to

the industrial age. For the new town was not a home where man could find beauty, happiness, leisure, learning, religion, the influences that civilize outlook and habit, but a bare and desolate place, without colour, air or laughter, where man, woman and child worked, ate and slept. This was to be the lot of the mass of mankind: this the sullen rhythm of their lives. The new factories and the new furnaces were like the Pyramids, telling of man's enslavement, rather than of his power, casting their long shadow over the society that took such pride in them.

Edward P. Thompson

VARIETY WITHIN THE WORKING CLASS—AND THE FACTS

OF POLITICAL INEQUALITY

Thompson has spent most of his working life in adult education, but is now Reader in Economic History in the University of Warwick. An earlier book was *William Morris: from Romantic to Revolutionary* (1955). The very long book from which this excerpt is taken deals with the economic life, the attitudes, and the political organisation of the English working class during the Industrial Revolution; and it insists that class-conflict and the rise of a working-class ideology were dominant features of that period.

THROUGHOUT this time there are three, and not two, great influences simultaneously at work. There is the tremendous increase in population (in Great Britain, from 10.5 millions in 1801 to 18.1 millions in 1841, with the greatest rate of increase between 1811–21). There is the Industrial Revolution, in its technological aspects. And there is the political *counter*-revolution, from 1792–1832.

In the end, it is the political context as much as the steam-engine, which had most influence upon the shaping consciousness and institutions of the working class. The forces making for politi-

cal reform in the late eighteenth century —Wilkes, the city merchants, the Middlesex small gentry, the "mob"—or Wyvill, and the small gentry and yeomen, clothiers, cutlers, and tradesmen—were on the eve of gaining at least some piecemeal victories in the 1790s: Pitt had been cast for the role of reforming Prime Minister. Had events taken their "natural" course we might expect there to have been some show-down long before 1832, between the oligarchy of land and commerce and the manufacturers and petty gentry, with working people in the tail of the middle-class agitation. And even in 1792, when manufacturers

From Edward P. Thompson, *The Making of the English Working Class* (Gollancz, London, 1963), pp. 197–9, 202–7, 234–41, 250–3, 255–62. By permission of Victor Gollancz, Ltd.

and professional men were prominent in the reform movement, this was still the balance of forces. But, after the success of the *Rights of Man*, the radicalisation and terror of the French Revolution, and the onset of Pitt's repression, it was the plebeian Corresponding Society which alone stood up against the counter-revolutionary wars. And these plebeian groups, small as they were in 1796, did nevertheless make up an "underground" tradition which ran through to the end of the Wars. Alarmed at the French example, and in the patriotic fervour of war, the aristocracy and the manufacturers made common cause. The English *ancien regime* received a new lease of life, not only in national affairs, but also in the perpetuation of the antique corporations which misgoverned the swelling industrial towns. In return, the manufacturers received important concessions: and notably the abrogation or repeal of "paternalist" legislation covering apprenticeship, wage-regulation, or conditions in industry. The aristocracy were interested in repressing the Jacobin "conspiracies" of the people, the manufacturers were interested in defeating their "conspiracies" to increase wages: the Combination Acts served both purposes.

Thus working people were forced into political and social *apartheid* during the Wars (which, incidentally, they also had to fight). It is true that this was not altogether new. What was new was that it was coincident with a French Revolution: with growing self-consciousness and wider aspirations (for the "liberty tree" had been planted from the Thames to the Tyne): with a rise in population, in which the sheer sense of numbers, in London and in the industrial districts, became more impressive from year to year (and as numbers grew, so deference to master, magistrate, or parson was likely to lessen): and with more intensive or more transparent forms of economic exploitation. More intensive in agriculture and in the old domestic industries: more transparent in the new factories and perhaps in mining. In agriculture the years between 1760 and 1820 are the years of wholesale enclosure, in which, in village after village, common rights are lost, and the landless and—in the south—pauperised labourer is left to support the tenant-farmer, the landowner, and the tithes of the Church. In the domestic industries, from 1800 onwards, the tendency is widespread for small masters to give way to larger employers (whether manufacturers or middlemen) and for the majority of weavers, stockingers, or nail-makers to become wage-earning outworkers with more or less precarious employment. In the mills and in many mining areas these are the years of the employment of children (and of women underground); and the large-scale enterprise, the factory-system with its new discipline, the mill communities—where the manufacturer not only made riches out of the labour of the "hands" but could be *seen* to make riches in one generation—all contributed to the transparency of the process of exploitation and to the social and cultural cohesion of the exploited.

We can now see something of the truly catastrophic nature of the Industrial Revolution; as well as some of the reasons why the English working class took form in these years. The people were subjected simultaneously to an intensification of two intolerable forms of relationship: those of economic exploitation and of political oppression. Relations between employer and labourer were becoming both harsher and less personal; and while it is true that this increased the potential freedom of the worker, since the hired farm servant or the journeyman in domestic industry was (in Toynbee's words) "halted half-way between the position of the serf and the position of the citizen," this "freedom" meant that he felt his *un*freedom more. But at each point where he sought to resist exploitation, he was met by the force of employer or State, and commonly of both.

For most working people the crucial experience of the Industrial Revolution was felt in terms of changes in the nature and intensity of exploitation. Nor is this some anachronistic notion, imposed upon the evidence. We may describe some parts of the exploitive process as they appeared to one remarkable cotton operative in 1818—the year in which Marx was born. The account—an Address to the public of strike-bound Manchester by "A Journeyman Cotton Spinner"—commences by describing the employers and workers as "two distinct classes of persons". . . . We need not concern ourselves with the soundness of all his judgments. What his address does is to itemise one after another the grievances felt by working people as to changes in the character of capitalist exploitation: the rise of a master-class without traditional authority or obligations: the growing distance between master and man: the transparency of the exploitation at the source of their new wealth and power: the loss of status and above all of independence for the worker, his reduction to total dependence on the master's instruments of production: the partiality of the law: the disruption of the traditional family economy: the discipline, monotony, hours and conditions of work: loss of leisure and amenities: the reduction of the man to the status of an "instrument."

That working people felt these grievances at all—and felt them passionately—is itself a sufficient fact to merit our attention. And it reminds us forcibly that some of the most bitter conflicts of these years turned on issues which are not encompassed by cost-of-living series. The issues which provoked the most intensity of feeling were very often ones in which such values as traditional customs, "justice," "independence," security, or family-economy were at stake, rather than straightforward "bread-and-butter" issues. The early years of the 1830s are aflame with agitations which turned on issues in which wages were of secondary importance; by the potters, against the Truck System; by the textile workers, for the 10-Hour Bill; by the building workers, for co-operative direct action; by all groups of workers, for the right to join trade unions. The great strike in the northeast coalfield in 1831 turned on security of employment, "tommy shops," child labour.

The exploitive relationship is more than the sum of grievances and mutual antagonisms. It is a relationship which can be seen to take distinct forms in different historical contexts, forms which are related to corresponding forms of ownership and State power. The classic exploitive relationship of the Industrial Revolution is depersonalised, in the sense that no lingering obligations of mutuality—of paternalism or deference, or of the interests of "the Trade"—are admitted. There is no whisper of the "just" price, or of a wage justified in relation to social or moral sanctions, as opposed to the operation of free market forces. Antagonism is accepted as intrinsic to the relations of production. Managerial or supervisory functions demand the repression of all attributes except those which further the expropriation of the maximum surplus value from labour. This is the political economy which Marx anatomised in *Das Kapital*. The worker has become an "instrument," or an entry among other items of cost.

In fact, no complex industrial enterprise could be conducted according to such a philosophy. The need for industrial peace, for a stable labour-force, and for a body of skilled and experienced workers, necessitated the modification of managerial techniques—and, indeed, the growth of new forms of paternalism—in the cotton-mills by the 1830s. But in the overstocked outwork industries, where there was always a sufficiency of unorganised "hands" competing for employment, these considerations did not operate. Here, as old customs were eroded, and old paternalism was set aside, the exploitive relationship emerged supreme.

This does not mean that we can lay all the "blame" for each hardship of the Industrial Revolution upon "the masters" or upon *laissez faire*. The process of industrialisation must, in any conceivable social context, entail suffering and the destruction of older and valued ways of life. Much recent research has thrown light upon the particular difficulties of the British experience; the hazards of markets; the manifold commercial and financial consequences of the Wars; the post-war deflation; movements in the terms of trade; and the exceptional stresses resulting from the population "explosion." Moreover, 20th-century preoccupations have made us aware of the overarching problems of economic growth. It can be argued that Britain in the Industrial Revolution was encountering the problems of "take-off"; heavy long-term investment—canals, mills, railways, foundries, mines, utilities—was at the expense of current consumption; the generations of workers between 1790 and 1840 sacrificed some, or all, of their prospects of increased consumption to the future.

These arguments all deserve close attention. For example, studies of the fluctuations in the demand of the South American market, or of the crisis in country banking, may tell us much about the reasons for the growth or retardation of particular industries. The objection to the reigning academic orthodoxy is not to empirical studies *per se*, but to the fragmentation of our comprehension of the full historical process. First, the empiricist segregates certain events from this process and examines them in isolation. Since the conditions which gave rise to these events are assumed, they appear not only as explicable in their own terms but as inevitable. The Wars had to be paid for out of heavy taxation; they accelerated growth in this way and retarded it in that. Since this can be shown, it is also implied that this was *necessarily* so. But thousands of Englishmen at the time agreed with Thomas Bewick's condemnation of "this superlatively wicked war." The unequal burden of taxation, fund-holders who profited from the National Debt, paper-money—these were not accepted as given data by many contemporaries, but were the staple of intensive Radical agitation.

But there is a second stage, where the empiricist may put these fragmentary studies back together again, constructing a model of the historical process made up from a multiplicity of interlocking inevitabilities, a piecemeal processional. In the scrutiny of credit facilities or of the terms of trade, where each event is explicable and appears also as a self-sufficient cause of other events, we arrive at a *post facto* deter-

minism. The dimension of human agency is lost, and the context of class relations is forgotten.

It is perfectly true that what the empiricist points to was there. The Orders in Council had in 1811 brought certain trades almost to a standstill; rising timber prices after the Wars inflated the costs of building; a passing change of fashion (lace for ribbon) might silence the looms of Coventry; the power-loom competed with the hand-loom. But even these open-faced facts, with their frank credentials, deserve to be questioned. Whose Council, why the Orders? Who profited most from corners in scarce timber? Why should looms remain idle when tens of thousands of country girls fancied ribbons but could not afford to buy? By what social alchemy did inventions for saving labour become engines of immiseration? The raw fact—a bad harvest—may seem to be beyond human election. But the way that fact worked its way out was in terms of a particular complex of human relationships: law, ownership, power. When we encounter some sonorous phrase such as "the strong ebb and flow of the trade cycle" we must be put on our guard. For behind this trade cycle there is a structure of social relationships, fostering some sorts of expropriation (rent, interest, and profit) and outlawing others (theft, feudal dues), legitimising some types of conflict (competition, armed warfare) and inhibiting others (trades unionism, bread riots, popular political organisation)—a structure which may appear, in the eyes of the future, to be both barbarous and ephemeral.

It might be unnecessary to raise these large questions, since the historian cannot always be questioning the credentials of the society which he studies. But all these questions were, in fact, raised by contemporaries; not only by men of the upper classes (Shelley, Cobbett, Owen, Peacock, Thompson, Hodgskin, Carlyle) but by thousands of articulate working men. Not the political institutions alone, but the social and economic structure of industrial capitalism, were brought into question by their spokesmen. To the facts of orthodox political economy they opposed their own facts and their own arithmetic. . . . If those in employment worked shorter hours, and if child labour were to be restricted, there would be more work for hand-workers and the unemployed could employ themselves and exchange the produce of their labour directly— short-circuiting the vagaries of the capitalist market—goods would be cheaper and labour better-rewarded. To the rhetoric of the free market they opposed the language of the "new moral order." It is because alternative and irreconcilable views of human order—one based on mutuality, the other on competition—confronted each other between 1815 and 1850 that the historian today still feels the need to take sides.

It is scarcely possible to write the history of popular agitation in these years unless we make at least the imaginative effort to understand how such a man as the ".Journeyman Cotton Spinner" read the evidence. He spoke of the "masters," not as an aggregate of individuals, but as a class. As such, "they" denied him political rights. If there were a trade recession, "they" cut his wages. If trade improved, he had to fight "them" and their state to obtain any share in the improvement. If food was plentiful, "they" profited from it. If it was scarce, some of "them" profited more. "They" conspired, not in this or that fact alone, but in the essential exploitive relationship within which all the facts were validated. Certainly there were market fluctuations, bad harvests, and the rest; but the experience of intensified exploitation was constant, whereas these other causes of hardship were variable. The latter bore upon working people, not directly, but through the refraction of a particular system of ownership and power which distributed the gains and losses with gross partiality.

The occupational tables of the Census of 1831 make no effort to differentiate between the master, the self-employed, and the labourer. After the agricultural labourers and . domestic servants (670,491 female domestic servants alone being listed for Great Britain in 1831), the building trades made up the next largest group, accounting per-

haps for 350,000 to 400,000 men and boys in 1831. Leaving aside the textile industries where outwork still predominated, the largest single artisan trade was that of shoemaking, with 133,000 adult male workers estimated for 1831, followed by tailoring, with 74,000. (Such figures include the employer, the country cobbler or tailor, the outworker, the shop-keeper, and the urban artisan proper.) In London, the greatest artisan centre in the world, where Dr. Dorothy George appears to lend her authority to a rough estimate of 100,000 journeymen of all types in the early 19th century, Sir John Clapham advises us:

the typical London skilled workman was neither the brewery hand, shipwright nor silk weaver, but either a member of the building trades; or a shoemaker, tailor, cabinet-maker, printer, clockmaker, jeweller, baker—to mention the chief trades each of which had over 2,500 adult members in 1831.

The wages of the skilled craftsman at the beginning of the nineteenth century were often determined less by "supply and demand" in the labour market than by notions of social prestige, or "custom." Customary wage-regulation may cover many things, from the status accorded by tradition to the rural craftsman to intricate institutional regulation in urban centres. Industry was still widely dispersed throughout the countryside. The tinker, knife-grinder, or pedlar would take his wares or skills from farm to farm and fair to fair. In the large villages there would be stone-masons, thatchers, carpenters, wheelwrights, shoemakers, the blacksmith's forge: in the small market town there would be saddlers and harness-makers, tanners, tailors, shoemakers, weavers, and very possibly some local speciality such as stirrup-making or pillow-lace, as well as all the business of the posting-inns, carriage of farm produce and of coal, milling, baking, and the like. Many of these rural craftsmen were better educated and more versatile and felt themselves to be a "cut above" the urban workers—weavers, stockingers or miners—with whom they came into contact when they came to the towns. They brought their own customs with them; and no doubt these influenced wage-fixing and differentials in those small-town crafts which grew into great urban industries—building, coach-making, even engineering.

Customary notions of craftsmanship normally went together with vestigial notions of a "fair" price and a "just" wage. Social and moral criteria—subsistence, self-respect, pride in certain standards of workmanship, customary rewards for different grades of skill—these are as prominent in early trade union disputes as strictly "economic" arguments.

It is sometimes supposed that the phenomenon of a "labour aristocracy" was coincident with the skilled trade unionism of the 1850s and 1860s—or was even the consequence of imperialism. But in fact there is both an old and a new elite of labour to be found in the years 1800–50. The old elite was made up of master-artisans who considered themselves as "good" as masters, shopkeepers, or professional men. (The *Book of English Trades* lists the apothecary, attorney, optician and statutory alongside the carpenter, currier, tailor and potter.) In some industries, the craftsman's privileged position survived into workshop or factory production, through the force of custom, or combination and apprenticeship restriction, or because the craft remained highly skilled and specialised—fine and "fancy" work in the luxury branches of the glass, wood and metal trades. The new elite arose with new skills in the iron, engineering and manufacturing industries. This is plain enough in engineering; but even in the cotton industry we must remember the warning, "we are not cotton spinners all." Overlookers, skilled "tenters" of various kinds who adjusted and repaired the machines, pattern-drawers in calico-printing, and scores of other skilled subsidiary crafts, at which exceptional wages might be earned, were among the 1,225 sub-divisions of heads of employment in cotton manufacture enumerated in the 1841 Census.

If a specially favoured aristocracy was to be found in the London luxury trades and on the border-line between skills and technical or managerial functions, there was also a lesser aristocracy of artisans or privileged workers in almost every skilled industry [On pp. 238–9 Thompson lists tailors, shoemakers, bookbinders, gold beaters, printers, bricklayers, coatmakers, hatters, curriers, masons, whitesmiths, coopers, shipwrights, wire-drawers, leather dressers, roemakers, clockmakers, etc.].

Similar important groups of privileged artisans or skilled workers will be found in the provinces, not only in the same trades, but in trades scarcely represented in London. This was true, in particular, of the Sheffield cutlery and Birmingham small-ware industries. In the latter, there persisted far into the nineteenth century the numerous petty workshops, which made Birmingham the metropolis of the small master. Boulton's Soho works bulks large in the story of economic growth. But the great majority of the city's population, at the close of the eighteenth century, were employed in very small shops, whether as labourers or as quasi-independent craftsmen. To enumerate some of the Birmingham products is to evoke the intricate constellation of skills: buckles, cutlery, spurs, candlesticks, toys, guns, buttons, whip handles, coffee pots, ink stands, bells, carriage-fittings, steam-engines, snuff-boxes, lead pipes, jewellery, lamps, kitchen implements. "Every man whom I meet," Southey wrote in 1807, "stinks of train-oil and emery."

Here, in the Black Country, the process of specialisation in the first three decades of the nineteenth century tended to take the simpler processes, such as nail and chain-making, to the surrounding villages of outworkers, while the more highly skilled operations remained in the metropolis of Birmingham itself. In such artisan trades the gulf between the small master and the skilled journeyman might, in psychological and sometimes in economic terms, be less than that between the journeyman and the common urban labourer. Entry to a whole trade might be limited to the sons of those already working in it, or might be bought only by a high apprenticeship premium. Restriction upon entry into the trade might be supported by corporate regulations (such as those of the Cutler's Company of Sheffield, not repealed until 1814), encouraged by masters, and maintained by trade unions under the aliases of friendly societies. Among such artisans at the commencement of the nineteenth century (the Webbs suggested) "we have industrial society still divided vertically trade by trade, instead of horizontally between employers and wage-earners." Equally, it might be that a privileged section only of the workers in a particular industry succeeded in restricting entry or in elevating their conditions. Thus, a recent study of the London porters has shown the fascinating intricacy of the history of a section of workers—including the Billingsgate porters—who might easily be supposed to be casual labourers but who in fact came under the particular surveillance of the City authorities, and who maintained a privileged position within the ocean of unskilled labour until the middle of the nineteenth century. More commonly, the distinction was between the skilled or apprenticed man and his labourer: the blacksmith and his striker, the bricklayer and his labourer, the calico pattern-drawer and his assistants, and so on.

The distinction between the artisan and the labourer—in terms of status, organisation, and economic reward—remained as great, if not greater, in Henry Mayhew's London of the late 1840s and 1850s as it was during the Napoleonic Wars. "In passing from the skilled operative of the west-end to the unskilled workman of the eastern quarter of London," Mayhew commented, "the moral and intellectual change is so great, that it seems as if we were in a new land, and among another race":

The artisans are almost to a man red-hot politicians. They are sufficiently educated and thoughtful to have a sense of their importance in the State. . . . The unskilled labourers are a different class of people. As yet they are as unpolitical as footmen, and instead of entertaining violent democratic opinions, they appear to have no political opinions whatever; or, if they do, . . . they rather lead towards the maintenance of "things as they are," than towards the ascendancy of the working people.

Mayhew was incomparably the greatest social investigator in the mid-century. Observant, ironic, detached yet compassionate, he had an eye for all the awkward peculiarities which escape statistical measurement. In a fact-finding age, he looked for the facts which the enumerators forgot: he wrote consciously against the grain of the orthodoxies of his day, discovering his own outrageous "laws" of political economy —"under-pay makes over-work" and "over-work makes under-pay." He knew that when a wind closed the Thames, 20,000 dock-side workers were at once unemployed. He knew the seasonal fluctuations of the timber trade, or of the bonnet-makers and pastry-cooks. He bothered to find out how many hours and how many months in the year scavengers or rubbish-carters were actually employed. If (as Professor Ashton has implied) the standard-of-living controversy really depends on a "guess" as to which group was increasing most— those "who were able to share in the benefits of economic progress" and "those who were shut out"—then Mayhew's guess is worth our attention.

Mayhew's guess is given in this form:

estimating the working classes as being between four and five million in number, I think we may safely assert—considering how many depend for their employment on particular times, seasons, fashions, and accidents, and the vast quantity of over-work and scamp-work in nearly all the cheap trades . . . the number of women and children who are being continually drafted into the different handicrafts with the view of reducing the earnings of the men, the displacement of human labour in some cases by machinery . . . all these things being considered I say I believe we may safely conclude that . . . there is barely sufficient work for the *regular* employment of half our labourers, so that only 1,500,000 are fully and constantly employed, while 1,500,000 more are employed only half their time, and the remaining 1,500,000 wholly unemployed, obtaining a day's work *occasionally* by the displacement of some of the others.

This remains no more than a guess, a grasping at the statistical expression of the complexities of London experience. But it arises from other findings; in particular, that "as a general rule . . . the society-men of every trade comprise about one-tenth of the whole." The wages of society men were those regulated by custom and trade union enforcement; those of the non-society men were "determined by competition." In London by the 1840s there was a clear demarcation between the "honourable" and "dishonourable" parts of the same trades; and trades in which this division was notorious included those of cabinet-makers, carpenters and joiners, boot- and shoemakers, tailors and all clothing workers, and the building industry. The honourable part comprised the luxury and quality branches: the dishonourable comprised the whole range of "cheap and nasty"—ready-made clothing, gim-crack or plain furniture, veneered work-boxes and cheap looking-glasses, sub-contract work (by "lumpers") in the building of churches, contract work for the Army or Government.

The history of each trade is different. But it is possible to suggest the outlines of a general pattern. Whereas it is generally assumed that living standards declined during the price-rises of the war years (and this is certainly true of the labourers, weavers, and wholly unorganised workers), nevertheless the war stimulated many industries and (except during the Orders in Council) made for fuller employment. In London the arsenal, the shipyards, and the docks were busy, and there were large Government contracts for clothing and equipment for the services. Birmingham prospered similarly until the years of the continental blockade. The later years of the war saw a general erosion of apprenticeship restrictions, both in practice and at law, culminating in the repeal of the apprenticeship clauses of the Elizabethan Statute of Artificers in 1814. According to their position, the artisans reacted vigorously to this threat. We must remember that this was a time when there was little schooling, and neither Mechanics' Institutes nor Technical Colleges, and that almost the entire skill or "mystery" of the trade was conveyed by precept and example in the workshop, by the journeyman to his apprentice. The artisans regarded this "mystery" as their *property,* and asserted their unquestionable right to "the quiet and exclusive use and enjoyment of their . . . arts and trades." Consequently, not only was repeal resisted, a "nascent trades council" being formed in London, and 60,000 signatures being collected nationally to a petition to *strengthen* the apprenticeship laws; but as a result there is evidence that the trades clubs were actually strengthened, so that many London artisans emerged from the Wars in a comparatively strong position.

But at this point the histories of different trades begin to diverge. The pressure of the unskilled tide, beating against the doors, broke through in different ways and with different degrees of violence.

The bitterness of the shoemakers' struggle may be gauged by the extreme radicalism of many of their members throughout the post-war years. The ladies' men clung on to their position in the boom years, 1820–5; but the recession of 1826 at once exposed their weakness. The organised men were surrounded by scores of small "dishonourable" workshops, where shoes were made up by "snobs" or "translators" at 8d. or 1s. a pair. In the autumn of 1826 several of their members were tried for riot and assault arising from a strike extending over seven or more weeks; a unionist is alleged to have told a "scab" that he "ought to have his liver cut out for working under price." But the boot and shoe workers notwithstanding maintained some national organisation, and in the great union wave of 1832–4 the Northamptonshire and Staffordshire outworkers came into the same struggle for "equalisation." It was only the destruction of general unionism in 1834 which finally deprived them of artisan status.

The tailors maintained their artisan status rather longer. We can take their union as a model of the quasi-legal trades union of the artisan. In 1818 Francis Place published the fullest account which we have of their operation. By effective combination the London tailors had succeeded in pressing up their wages throughout the war, although probably lagging slightly behind the advance in the cost-of-living. The figures run (in Place's average), 1795, 25s.; 1801, 27s.; 1807, 30s.; 1810, 33s.; 1813, 36s. With each advance the resistance of the masters became firmer: "Not a single shilling was obtained at any one of these periods but by compulsion." At the many "houses of call" of the aristocratic "Flint" tailors books of the members' names were kept, and the masters used the houses virtually as employment agencies. "No man is allowed to ask for employment"—the masters must apply to the union. The work was allocated by rota, and the union disciplined "unworkmanlike" men. The tailors had a dual subscription, the larger contribution being reserved for benefits, the smaller for the needs of the union itself. A twelve-hour day was enforced, except in times of full employment. There were levies for unemployed members, and special levies might be made, in preparation for a strike, as to which the members asked no question even if the purpose was not explained. The actual leadership of the union was carefully shielded from prosecution under the Combination Acts. Each house of call had a deputy,

chosen by a kind of tacit consent, frequently without its being known to a very large majority who is chosen. The deputies form a committee, and they again chose in a somewhat similar way a very small committee, in whom, on very particular occasions, all power resides.

"No law could put it down," Place wrote: "nothing but want of confidence among the men themselves could prevent it." And in fact the "Knights of the Needle" look extremely strong, at least until the recession of 1826. Their organisation could be fairly described as "all but a military system." But concealed within Place's own account there was a premonition of weakness:

They are divided into two classes, called Flints and Dungs—the Flints have upwards of thirty houses of call, and the Dungs about nine or ten; the Flints work by day,

the Dungs by day or piece. Great animosity formerly existed between them, the Dungs generally working for less wages, but of late years there has not been much difference in the wages . . . and at some of the latest strikes both parties have usually made common cause.

This may be seen as an impressive attempt to keep the dishonourable trade in some organisational association with the status-conscious "Flints." In 1824 Place estimated a proportion of one "Dung" to three "Flints"; but the "Dungs" "work a great many hours, and their families assist them." By the early 1830s the tide of the cheap and ready-made trade could be held back no longer. In 1834 the "Knights" were finally degraded only after a tremendous conflict, when 20,000 were said to be on strike under the slogan of "equalisation."

John Wade was still able to speak of the London tailors of 1833 as "enjoying a much higher remuneration than is received by the generality of workpeople in the metropolis." Indeed, he cited them as an example of artisans who by the strength of their combination had "fortified their own interests against the interests of the public and other workpeople." But when Mayhew commenced his enquiry for the *Morning Chronicle* in 1849 he cited the tailors as one of the worst examples of "cheap and shoddy" sweated industry. Of 23,517 London tailors in 1849, Mayhew estimated that 2,748 were independent master-tailors. Of the remainder, 3,000 were society men in the honourable trade (as compared to 5,000 or 6,000 in 1821), and 18,000 in the dishonourable trade were wholly dependent upon large middlemen for their earnings in the "slop" or ready-made business.

London conditions should not be seen as exceptional, although London was the Athens of the artisan. And it is important to notice that there is a pattern of exploitation here which runs counter to the evidence of wage-series compiled from the rates of organised men in the honourable trade. This takes the form both of a break-up of customary conditions and restraints, and of trade union defences. It is generally true that the "artisan" trades go through two critical periods of conflict. The first was in 1812–14, when apprenticeship regulations were repealed. Those trades, such as the shoemakers and tailors, which were already strongly organised in unions or trade clubs, were able in some degree to defend their position after repeal by strikes and other forms of direct action, although the same years saw greater organisation among the *masters*. But consolidation in closed "society" shops between 1815 and 1830 was at a price. "Illegal men" were kept out of the better parts of the trade only to swell the numbers in the unorganised "dishonourable" trade outside. The second critical period is 1833–5, when on the crest of the great trade union wave attempts were made to "equalise" conditions, shorten working hours in the honourable trade and suppress dishonourable work. These attempts (notably that of the London tailors) not only failed in the face of the combined forces of the employers and the Government; they also led to at least a temporary deterioration in the position of the "society" men. The economic historian should see the cases of the Tolpuddle Martyrs and the great lock-outs of 1834 as being as consequential for all grades of labour as the radicals and trade unionists of the time held them to be.

But this conflict between the artisans and the large employers was only part of a more general exploitive pattern. The dishonourable part of the trade grew, with the displacement of small masters (employing a few journeymen and apprentices) by large "manufactories" and middlemen (employing domestic outworkers or sub-contracting): with the collapse of all meaningful apprenticeship safeguards (except in the honourable island) and the influx of unskilled, women and children: with the extension of hours and of Sunday work: and with the beating down of wages, piece-rates and wholesale prices. The form and extent of the deterioration relates directly to the material conditions of the industry—the cost of raw materials—tools—the skill involved—conditions favouring or discouraging trade union organisation—the nature of the market. Thus, woodworkers and shoemakers could obtain their own materials cheaply and owned their own tools, so that the unemployed artisan set up as an independent "garret-master" or "chamber-master" working his whole family—and perhaps other juveniles—round a seven-day week and hawking the products on his own account. Carpenters requiring a more costly outlay were reduced to "strapping-shops" where a sickening pace of gimcrack work was kept up under the foreman's patrol and where each man who fell behind was sacked. Tailoring workers, who could rarely purchase their own cloth, became wholly dependent upon the middlemen who farmed out work at sweated prices. Dressmaking— a notoriously "sweated" trade—was largely done by needlewomen (often country or small-town immigrants) in shops connected with large establishments. The building worker, who could neither buy his bricks nor hawk a part of a cathedral round the streets, was at the mercy of the sub-contractor; even the skilled "society" men expected to be laid off in the winter months; and both classes of worker frequently attempted to escape from their predicament by direct speculative building—"the land," as Clapham says, "rented in hope, materials secured on credit, a mortgage raised on the half-built house before it is sold or leased, and a high risk of bankruptcy." On the other hand, the coach-builder, the shipwright, or engineer, who did not own all his tools nor purchase his own materials, was nevertheless better situated, by reason of the character of his work and the scarcity of his skill, to maintain or extend trade union defences.

A similar collapse in the status of the artisan took place in older provincial centres. There are many complexities and qualifications. On one hand, the boot and shoe industry of Stafford and of Northamptonshire had long lost its artisan character and was conducted on an outwork basis when the London shoemakers were still trying to hold back the dishonourable trade. On the other hand, the extreme specialisation of the Sheffield cutlery industry—together with the exceptionally strong political and trade union traditions of the workers who had been the most steadfast Jacobins—had led to the maintenance of the skilled workers' status in a twilight world of semi-independence, where he worked for a merchant (and, sometimes, for more than one), hired his motive-power at a "public wheel," and adhered to strict price-lists. Despite the Sheffield Cutlers Bill (1814) which repealed the restrictions which had limited the trade to freemen and which left a situation in which "any person may work at the corporated trades without being a freeman, and may take any number of apprentices for any term," the unions were strong enough—sometimes with the aid of "rattening" and other forms of intimidation—to hold back the unskilled tide, although there was a continual threat from "little masters," sometimes "illegal" men or self-employed journeymen, who sought to undercut the legal trade. In the Birmingham industries, every kind of variant is to be found, from the large workshop through innumerable mazes of small shops and self-employed workmen, honourable and dishonourable, to the half-naked and degraded outworkers of the nail-making villages. An account from Wolverhampton in 1819, shows how the "garret-master" appeared at a time of depression:

The order of things . . . is completely inverted. Now, the last resource of the starving journeyman is to set up master; his employer cannot find him work, on which there is any possible profit, and is therefore obliged to discharge him; the poor wretch then sells his bed, and buys an anvil, procures a little iron, and having manufactured a few articles, hawks them about . . . for what he can get . . . He might have previously received 10s. a week as a servant; but now he is lucky if he gets 7s. as a master manufacturer.

In the Coventry ribbon-weaving industry there was another twilight, half-outworker, half-artisan situation: the "first-hand weavers" maintained a poor artisan status, owning their own costly looms, and sometimes employing a "journeyman's journeyman," while other weavers in the city were employed in workshops or factories at comparable wages: but in the weaving villages to the north there was a large reserve pool of semi-unemployed weavers, working at debased rates as casual outworkers.

From one point of view, the true outworker industry can be seen as one which has wholly lost its artisan status and in which no "honourable" part of the trade remains:

Capitalistic outwork may be said to be fully established only when the material belongs to the trading employer, and is returned to him after the process for which the outworker's skill is required has been completed—the wool given out to be spun, the yarn given out to be woven, the shirt given out for "seam and gusset and band," the nail-rod to be returned as nails, the limbs to be returned as dolls, the leather coming back as boots.

This, Clapham estimates, was the "predominant form" of industrial organisation in the reign of George IV; and if we add to the true outworkers (hand-loom weavers, nail-makers, most wool-combers, chain-makers, some boot and shoe workers, framework-knitters, fustian-cutters, glove-makers, some potters, pillow-lace-makers, and many others) the workers in the "dishonourable" parts of the London and urban artisan trades, it probably remained predominant until 1840.

We shall look at the weaver, as an example of the outworker, later. But there are some general points which relate both to the outworker and to the artisans. First, it will not do to explain away the plight of weavers or of "slop" workers as "instances of the decline of old crafts which were displaced by a mechanical process"; nor can we even accept the statement, in its pejorative context, that "it was not among the factory employees but among the domestic workers, whose traditions and methods were those of the eighteenth century, that earnings were at their lowest." The suggestion to which these statements lead us is that these conditions can somehow be segregated in our minds from the true improving impulse of the Industrial Revolution—they belong to an "older," pre-industrial order, whereas

the authentic features of the new capitalist order may be seen where there
are steam, factory operatives, and meat-
eating engineers. But the numbers employed in the outwork industries multiplied enormously between 1780–1830;
and very often *steam and factory were
the multipliers*. It was the mills which
spun the yarn and the foundries which
made the nail-rod upon which the outworkers were employed. Ideology may
wish to exalt one and decry the other,
but facts must lead us to say that each
was a complementary component of a
single process. This process first multiplied hand-workers (hand calico-
printers, weavers, fustian-cutters, wool-
combers) and then extinguished their
livelihood with new machinery. Moreover, the degradation of the outworkers
was very rarely as simple as the phrase
"displaced by a mechanical process" suggests; it was accomplished by methods
of exploitation similar to those in the
dishonourable trades and it often preceded machine competition. Nor is it
true that the "traditions and methods"
of the domestic workers "were those of
the eighteenth century." The only large
group of domestic workers in that century whose conditions anticipate those
of the semi-employed proletarian outworkers of the nineteenth century are
the Spitalfields silk-weavers; and this
is because the "industrial revolution" in
silk preceded that in cotton and in wool.
Indeed, we may say that large-scale
sweated outwork was as intrinsic to this
revolution as was factory production
and steam. As for the "traditions and
methods" of the "slop" workers in the
dishonourable trade, these, of course,
have been endemic for centuries wherever cheap labour has been abundant.
They would, nevertheless, appear to con-
stitute a serious reversal of the conditions of late eighteenth-century London
artisans.

What we can say with confidence is
that the artisan *felt* that his status and
standard-of-living were under threat or
were deteriorating between 1815 and
1840. Technical innovation and the su-
perabundance of cheap labour weakened his position. He had no political

rights and the power of the State was
used, if only fitfully, to destroy his trade
unions. As Mayhew clearly showed, not
only did under-pay (in the dishonourable trades) make for overwork; it
also made for *less* work all round. It was
this experience which underlay the political radicalisation of the artisans and,
more drastically, of the outworkers.
Ideal and real grievances combined to
shape their anger—lost prestige, direct
economic degradation, loss of pride as
craftsmanship was debased, lost aspirations to rise to being masters (as men
in Hardy's and Place's generation could
still do). The "society" men, though
more fortunate, were not the least radical—many London and provincial working-class leaders came, like William
Lovett, from this stratum. They had
been able to hold their status only by an
accession of trade union militancy; and
their livelihood provided them with a
running education in the vices of competition and the virtues of collective
action. They witnessed less fortunate
neighbours or shopmates (an accident,
a weakness for drink) fall into the lower
depths. Those who were in these depths
had most need, but least time, for political reflection.

If the agricultural labourers pined
for land, the artisans aspired to an "independence." This aspiration colours
much of the history of early working-
class Radicalism. But in London the
dream of becoming a small master (still
strong in the 1790s—and still strong in
Birmingham in the 1830s) could not
stand up, in the 1820s and 1830s, in
face of the experiences of "chamber" or
"garret" masters—an "independence"
which meant week-long slavery to warehouses or slop shops. This helps to explain the sudden surge of support towards Owenism at the end of the 1820s
—trade union traditions and the yearn-
ing for independence were twisted together in the idea of social control
over the means of livelihood; a *collective* independence. When most of the
Owenite ventures failed, the London
artisan still fought for his independence
to the last: when leather, wood or cloth
ran out, he swelled the throng of street-

sellers, hawking bootlaces, oranges or nuts. In the main they were rural workers who entered the "strapping-shops."

The London artisan could rarely stand the pace; nor did he wish to become a proletarian.

R. S. Neale

THE LABOURERS OF BATH

Educated at Leicester, R. S. Neale taught for several years in the City of Bath Technical College. He is now teaching British and Japanese Economic History, as Senior Lecturer, in the University of New England, New South Wales, Australia. He has published several articles on social class in the Victorian period, and others are likely to appear soon. The excerpt that follows is included as a valuable example of the way in which detailed local study can throw light on wider economic problems.

I

THE re-opening of the debate on the standard of living, 1780–1850, has provided an opportunity for much extravagant writing, the introduction of more sophisticated economic and sociological terminology into the discussion, a growing recognition that economic advance does not preclude working-class discontent, and a plea for more industrial and regional research. Writing in 1949, T. S. Ashton said, "It is important to distinguish between the period of the war, the period of deflation and re-adjustment, and the succeeding period of economic expansion. . . . We require not a single index, but many, each derived from retail prices, each confined to a short run of years, each relating to a single area, perhaps to a single social or occupational group within an area." The last sixteen years has brought forth little of this kind of evidence. Instead, fashions have changed. There has been a move away from price and wage indices, relating to specific regions and groups, through indirect indicators of less specific applicability, like unemployment, mortality-rates, and *per capita* consumption, to the current belief in the usefulness of the macro-economic approach based on estimates of population, national income, national product and price deflators. Such a development, however, leaves the economic historian hovering on the brink of repeating the sociological error, made by Marx, that is, viewing labour, during the period 1780–1850, as "Labour," an homogeneous class experiencing and participating in the process of industrialisation as a whole. The present paper is an attempt to avoid this error and to meet some of the requirements set out by Professor Ashton.

Before doing so, however, it is advisable to look at two considerations of a general nature influencing the conclusion, which rarely receive sufficient attention. One is whether the post-war period should be compared with the years immediately before the war or with the war-time period. The other is whether one should study the experience of particular generations, or age cohorts of labourers, instead of "Labour."

The choice of the base year with which comparisons are to be made is crucial. Those who argue strongly for

From R. S. Neale, "The Standard of Living, 1780–1844: a Regional and Class Study," *Economic History Review*, Second Series, XIX (1966), 590–604. By permission of the author and of the Editor, *Economic History Review*.

improvement in living standards argue from 1800. Those who employ other years, as the base year for comparison, generally observe that the admittedly uneven post-war recovery to the mid-1840s, was barely sufficient to restore the position in existence before the war. Indeed, the choice of 1800 as a base has no deep rationale. It is true that the beginning of the century coincided roughly with the first fairly reliable estimates of national income, and with the first census, and thereby permits a rough calculation of income per head, yet it marks neither the end nor beginning of any trend, cyclic period or stage of growth conventionally adopted. In the area with which the main body of this paper is concerned, the city of Bath, the year 1800 and the winter of 1800–1801 were disastrous. The harvest month of September 1799 had 8.8 inches of rain, and the price of wheat at Warminster rose from 82s. per quarter in January to 160s. by the end of June 1800. In Bath, in the same six months, the penny loaf of best wheaten bread fell in weight from 5 to 2½ ounces. Rents were stable, but other prices were high. Coal was 10d. per cwt., and meat 8d. or 9d. per lb. The earnings of labourers remained unchanged until May 1801. During July imports from abroad—wheat from Europe, flour and rice from America—helped to reduce wheat to a low point of 86s. and to increase the weight of the penny loaf to 4.4 ounces. But, from then on, in spite of the increase in marketable corn from the home harvest, the price of wheat rose steadily to 144s. in December 1800, and the penny loaf finished the year a third lighter than when the year started. Prices remained high throughout the first months of 1801 and by February wheat reached 184s. per quarter. In March, the quartern loaf, at 1s.11d., was one halfpenny dearer than in London and was five-pence more than a day's pay for an unskilled labourer.

The resultant famine conditions precipitated violent rioting and arson. To alleviate the worst consequences rice was bought and rationed out at reduced prices to half the city's population of 33,000, a woollen manufacturer baked bread to sell at a 24 percent reduction in price to his workmen, poor relief expenditure rose by 50 percent and a minimum of £13,000 was publicly spent on relief and charity in one year. Thus it would not be difficult to show that real incomes for most classes were higher in every other year between 1780 and 1850 or, indeed, during the rest of the century. A *fortiori* the choice of almost any other year between 1780 and 1800 as a base year makes it doubtful whether real incomes did remain stationary during the war years and whether the immediate post-war improvement in real incomes was sufficient to make good the wartime deterioration. On the other hand, the decade 1780–1790, before the house and canal building locally associated with the early 1790s got under way, and before the Napoleonic Wars, was a period of stability in wage-rates, earnings and prices. Thus for a broader perspective the year, against which comparisons will be made, will be 1780.

The importance of the age-cohort approach to the experience of members of the labour-force can best be appreciated, given the following: the working life of an adult male was about thirty years, the bulk of working men, in the early nineteenth century, reached their maximum earnings early in life and could expect their earnings to decline during the final third of the working life, the rise in real wages between 1780 and 1850, or between 1800 and 1850, was interrupted by periods of stagnation and deterioration. Then, leaving aside the problems of regional and industrial deviations from the average, and redistribution of income, and looking at the labour-force as a succession of cohorts moving through employment from different starting points and at different relative rates of change in money incomes, it becomes possible to argue that large groups of workers could pass through working lives of thirty years, within a period of 50 or 60 years, the terminal point of which indicates a rise in average real income, experiencing a below-average rise or no rise at all. That is, there is no reason to suppose that the evidence of a general rise in *per capita* income, between 1800 and 1850, based on national estimates for discontinuous years, rules out the existence of real economic distress, caused by a fall in real wages for many workers, particularly if this age-cohort approach is linked with the social consequences of structural changes in the economy. Only detailed work on lines suggested by Ashton can help to resolve this problem for individual regions, industries and classes.

II THE EXPERIENCE OF BATH

Traditionally the city of Bath is held to be outside the main stream of eighteenth century and early nineteenth century development. The appeal of its history—literary, architectural, genteelly erotic—has diverted the attention of historians away from its essential economic substructure. And few recognise that, as the Miami of the eighteenth century, its creation, construction and operation depended on widespread entrepreneurial activity and considerable investment; that the multiplier effect stimulated the building industry, the development of extensive stone quarries, the growth of industrial villages, the construction of tramways and the canalisation of the river Avon, all before the middle of the eighteenth century. Thereafter continued building, rebuilding and a high level of expenditure on high-quality consumer goods attracted a heavy concentration of craftsmen, tradesmen and non-agricultural labourers. By the beginning of the nineteenth century the city, with a resident popula-

tion of 33,000, was one of the largest in the country. It continued to increase in population, during the first two decades, at a rate comparable with that of the country as a whole and by 1831 had a population of 50,000.

Between 1800 and 1830 there was incipient industrialisation with the establishment of steam-powered manufactories in brewing, glass and soap making. Stothert's ironmongery developed into ironfoundry, woollen mills were established on the Avon at Twerton, coal-mining was attempted at Batheaston and a railway company projected to connect Bath with Bristol. Thus in one sense the city of Bath is an example of an isolated region with a leading sector—a quality entertainment industry having some backward linkages—brought into existence by concentrated and sustained aristocratic expenditure. This luxury expenditure, however, made little contribution to the development of the surrounding complex of industrial villages whose course and decline was determined by the main current of economic development. Consequently, and as fashion changed, the city failed to "take off" and after a period of readjustment replaced its highly profitable growth industry with one which continued to use the existing stock of social overhead capital but produced little stimulus to further investment.

Table 1 shows the occupational distribution of the adult male population in 1831 and the extent to which employment depended on manufacturing, building and the retail trade.

TABLE 1.   OCCUPATIONAL DISTRIBUTION OF MALES IN THE CITY OF BATH, 1831

Occupation	No. of males over 20 years of age
Capitalists, bankers and other educated men	1,196
Building trades	1,074
Labouring (non-agricultural)	1,480
Retail (including some craftsmen)	2,797
Domestic service	670
Shoemaking	529
Furniture and coachmaking	351
Tailoring	349
Labouring	110
Total	8,556

Census of Population, 1831

The growth of the city also placed concentrations of population under local administration by parish officers, and stimulated the newspaper industry: two developments important for this article. The first led to attempts to systematise the administration of the parish of Walcot, which had a population of 26,000 in 1831. This resulted in a good series of wage-accounts kept by the Overseers of Highways from 1780–1851. The second provided the opportunity for the weekly publication of a series of retail prices in Bath market.

III   EARNINGS

The first point to be emphasised in this section is that unlike all other wage-series for the late eighteenth and early nineteenth centuries the Bath series is compiled entirely from records of actual weekly earnings. The Highway Accounts record the number of men employed each week, their weekly earnings, the number of days or half days worked and the daily rate. The index, based on 1780=100=8s. per week for a six-day week, shows the average earnings of all men employed on the Walcot highways for the first week in January, May and September each year. Unfortunately the numbers employed in the earlier years

are smaller than in the later period, consequently the average is probably more meaningful for the period 1832–1851. Where possible the annual earnings or wage experience of individual labourers has been traced over several years, and all figures are supplemented by wage-rates. The data for the index is tabulated in the statistical appendix and, in Table 2, is simplified into an annual index.

It is probable that the movement of wages for this group of highway labourers indicates the direction and magnitude of wage movements for the whole group of 1,480 non-agricultural labourers who, in 1831, constituted approximately 20 per cent of the adult male work-force in the city. These were men who earned 8s. per week in the 1780s, between 7s. and 9s. in the 1830s, and 10s. to 12s.6d. in the 1850s. There is some evidence for 1865 to show that about 42 percent of 600 outpatients at the United Hospital then earned less than 12s. per week, and to suggest that the size of this class did not decline after 1830 even though the census returns for 1851 record only 10 percent of males as labourers [see Table 2].

1780–1809. Wage-rates and earnings remained fairly constant from year to

TABLE 2.   AVERAGE WEEKLY EARNINGS OF NON-AGRICULTURAL LABOURERS IN THE CITY OF BATH, 1780–1851 (1780=100)

(a) 1780–1809

	Rate	Earnings		Rate	Earnings		Rate	Earnings
1780	100	100	1789	100	96	1801	113	119
1781	100	92	1790	100	95	1802	150	120
1782	100	102	1791	100	108	1803	113	113
1783	100	83	1792	113	114	1804	113	119
			1793	113	101			
1786	100	101	1794	113	102	1807	125	120
1787	100	100	1795	113	114	1808	125	125
1788	100	96	1796	113	118	1809	125	117

(b) 1832–1851

		Earnings		Rate	Earnings		Rate	Earnings
1832		96	1839	141	103	1846	141	138
1833		97	1840	141	128	1847	141	132
1834		86	1841	141	127	1848	141	136
1835		95	1842	141	134	1849	141	142
1836		98	1843	141	134	1850	141	137
1837	100*	95	1844	141	137	1851	141	141
1838	100	98	1845	141	134			

*After 1837 rates varied between 1s.4d and 1s.5d. per day. After 1839 between 1s.5d. and 2s. The index averages maximum and minimum rates.
Source: Highway Accounts, Walcot.

year from 1780 to May 1792, when wage-rates were increased 13 percent to 1s.6d. per day. Earnings, however, had begun to increase in 1791, and in the early part of 1792, through much overtime working of six and a half and seven-day weeks. Subsequently, in 1793 and 1794, earnings fell to only one or two points above the 1780 level. After 1795 earnings began to rise again and received a boost from a rise in rates of 33 percent from 1s.6d. to 2s., during the period from May 1801 to May 1803. Consequently, average earnings, 1801–1804, were 18 percent higher than in 1780. In May 1803 rates fell again to 1s.6d., the level prevailing from 1792–1801. There was a further rise to 1s.8d. in 1807, but in 1809 earnings were only 17 percent higher than in 1780.

Overall rates rose more than earnings. In eleven years they rose, on average, ten points more, in four years both indices moved to the same extent and in the same direction, and in seven years earnings rose, on average, three points more than rates. Where it is possible to compare rates, weekly earnings and yearly earnings, the evidence suggests that rates rose more than weekly earnings while yearly earnings fluctuated more and tended to rise less, over a long period, than weekly earnings. This point is illustrated in Table 3, which, although by no means conclusive, serves as a reminder of the problems of determining actual income, and ultimately real wages, from evidence of rates of pay or even average weekly earnings.

TABLE 3.   WAGE RATES, AVERAGE WEEKLY AND AVERAGE YEARLY EARNINGS
1803–1809 (1780=100)

	Rate	Weekly earnings	Yearly earnings*	No. of weeks worked†
1803	113	113	116	51
1804	113	119	130	52
1807	125	120	103	47
1809	125	117	113	50

*Based on the earnings of one labourer employed from 1803–1809 and compared with a full year's earnings of a different labourer in 1780.
†Refers to the number of weeks worked by the labourer whose yearly earnings are recorded in col. 3.
Source: Highway Accounts, Walcot.

1832–1851. It is difficult to establish an index of rates for these years, since rates were not recorded from 1832 to 1837. Thereafter they varied from employee to employee. Between 1837 and 1839 the range, from 1s.4d. to 1s.5d., was much the same as for the period 1780–1792. After 1839 the range was from 1s. 5d. to 2s.

Apart from the high earnings in September 1832, average earnings 1832–1839 fluctuated at a level 5 to 10 per cent below the base year 1780. This could have resulted from the employment of large numbers of unemployed skilled workmen on road construction and it could be supposed that earnings were depressed in consequence. However, it has been argued above that numbers of labourers and craftsmen earned less than those employed by the parish. Consequently the figures for the 1830s

probably minimise the decline in the earnings of non-agricultural labourers after 1809. Rates were increased in May 1839 and average earnings increased 20 per cent. Thereafter earnings rose more slowly until by 1843 they were between 30 and 40 per cent higher than for the early 1830s. The wage experience of two long-serving men illustrates most clearly the course of earnings between 1836 and 1851 [see Table 4 on page 90].

One point is clear, both from the index of average earnings and from the table, it is that earnings rose rapidly between 1839 and 1843. Such a rise, which appears to be unequalled elsewhere and in other industries merits explanation. It may well have been the intention of the Assistant Surveyor of Highways to pursue a policy of high or higher wages in order to build up a permanent and re-

TABLE 4.   AVERAGE WEEKLY EARNINGS OF TWO LABOURERS, 1836–1851

Year	1836	'37	'38	'39	'40	'41	'42	'43	'44	'45	'46	'47	'48	'49	'50	'51
Rose	← 7s. ──→			← 8s.──→			←		9s.6d.			──→	←		10s.──	→
Slade	←8s. to→ 9s.	← 9s.6d. →	←11s.→	←12s.──			→ ←		12s.6d.				──→			

liable labour-force able to work well without supervision, or at least with less supervision than was required with the hundred or so men employed in the early 1830s. There is some evidence that this might have been so. The status of the foreman was reduced by reducing the differential between his salary and the weekly earnings of labourers, men were rewarded with higher wages for particular jobs and dismissals for bad work or drunkenness were recorded. Yet it is difficult to believe that a public body, open to popular criticism from year to year, could pursue for long a policy of paying wages greatly in excess of those paid for similar work elsewhere in the parish and the city, particularly since it is possible to suggest an alternative explanation of the initial rise in 1839 and 1840.

In the early part of 1839 work on the construction of the G.W.R. railroad in the neighbourhood was begun. By midsummer work was under way on a viaduct, alterations to the approach road from Wells and on the permanent way. By the end of the year the Kennet and Avon canal was turned from its original course, and the construction of tunnels, cuttings, the skew bridge and the station were begun with the result that "The contractors appeared to put an embargo upon all the disposable labour of the city and its suburbs." It is also possible to suggest that wages in Bath were unduly depressed throughout the

1830s, even when compared with agricultural wages in neighbouring counties, and that the lift given to wages in 1839–1840, by railroad construction, restored the early urban advantage which remained to the end of the period.

Prices

Only three budgets were discovered for the period 1800–1850. One was for a Bristol artisan in 1842, one was a minimum estimate for a labourer's family in 1831, the third was a pauper dietary for 1836. They largely support each other as indicators of the proportion of income spent on different commodities. The budget for 1831 shows the following [see table below]. The pauper dietary in 1837 suggests that a weekly subsistence diet, i.e. the item "subsistence" to which 65 per cent of expenditure was allocated in 1831, for a family of four, would have consisted of: 33½ lbs. of bread, 1 lb. 11 ozs. of meat, 1 lb. 1 oz of bacon, 4¼ lbs. of cheese and 6 lbs. of potatoes. The cost of this basket of goods in Bath market at the lowest retail prices in 1837 was 8s. 10¾d. Prices were slightly higher in 1831, consequently the 7s.9d. then allocated to subsistence, would have purchased considerably less.

Labourers' wages seldom rose above 8s. per week throughout the 1830s and only reached 12s. in a few cases in the 1840s, consequently it was decided that

"The Charge Per Week for Keeping a Poor Man, Wife and Two Children, with Nothing Superior to Gaol Allowance"

	s. d.	Percentage.
Subsistence for man, wife and two children	7. 9.	64.5
Beer	8.	5.5
Clothing and shoes	1. 4.	11.1
Washing, soap and candles	3. }	6.2
Fuel	6. }	
Rent	1. 6.	12.5
	12. 0.	99.8

an index, weighted very much in favour of food, is to be preferred to a more general index incorporating a wide range of manufactured products. Thus the price index is based on six items: the retail prices of bread, potatoes, mutton, pork and coal, and the rent of housing. Prices for potatoes, mutton and pork are minimum quotations. Those for bread are for the best quality wheaten loaf and, as for coal, are either the only or maximum quotations. Bread prices are continuous from 1800 to 1844, all others from 1812 to 1844 with exception of potatoes which run to 1832 after which cheese is substituted in 1834. The disadvantage in using maximum prices for bread and coal is that the price may not reflect the absolute cost to this group of workers. There is, however, some reason to suppose that the cheaper brown household loaf was held to be greatly inferior to white bread and that all classes considered it better value to pay an extra 1d. or 2d. for a quartern of white bread rather than save on an inferior brown bread. In addition all bread prices moved in the same direction whilst remaining in a constant relationship with each other. In Bath the difference between the wheaten and the standard loaf was always 1d. on a quartern. The difference between the wheaten and the household loaf was always 2d. Thus the movement of maximum bread prices indicates the movement of all bread prices. The advantage in using maximum prices is that other prices were frequently not quoted at all. In the case of coal the maximum is often quoted as including the cost of transport from the weighing engine to the city outskirts. Since working-class areas, with one exception, were on the outskirts of the city the maximum price can be regarded as representing the retail price of coal plus transport costs.

Rents were estimated for 81 working-class houses in Avon Street, at five-yearly intervals, from the poor and highway rate books. Of the rate assessments four were based on rent, the remainder on annual value. In 1841 and 1845 the rate was based on estimates of rent and annual value. In both cases the rent es-

timates were generally more than those for annual value. Thus annual value probably underestimates the level of rent. There is also some scatter of evidence to suggest that the poundage of the rate assessments reflected the level of rents actually paid for whole houses. Rate assessments, however, do not reveal the extent of sub-letting, the cost of a single room or part of a house, or the degree of bed sharing. Nevertheless, it seems likely that the movement of rate assessments is a reasonable indication of the movement of rents.

In order to attempt the construction of an index of real wages for non-agricultural labourers it was decided to use 1838 as the base year for prices and to allocate the following weights: bread 12, potatoes 3, pork 2, mutton 1, coal 2, rent 3. For the period 1832–1844 it is possible to construct an index of real wages entirely from local material. The lack of price data prevents this for the earlier period. Nevertheless, Table 5 includes an index of real wages for the period 1780–1812 compiled with the aid of the Schumpeter-Gilboy Consumer Goods(a) Index. Unfortunately it is not possible to bridge the crucial twenty-three-year gap between 1809 and 1832 for although local price data exist after 1812 there is no local wage data of any kind for non-agricultural labourers [see Table 5 on page 92].

Real Wages
1780–1812 After 1780 real wages fluctuated at a level slightly lower than in the base year and it was only in 1792 that they rose above the level of 1780 as a result of much overtime working and a 13 per cent increase in wage-rates in the middle of the year. From then on, in spite of the rise in rates, real wages fell to 1801, improved slightly in 1804–5 then fell again to 1812 to a level 50 per cent lower than in 1780.

1812–1832 In order to provide what can only be a tenuous link between the earlier period and 1832–1844 it is assumed that the average wage for 1807–1809 equals the wage for 1812. This appears legitimate on two grounds. One, the accounts for the years 1810–1811, although confused and unsuitable for

TABLE 5.   EARNINGS AND REAL WAGES, NON-AGRICULTURAL LABOURERS, IN THE CITY
OF BATH, 1780–1812 (1780=100)

Year	Average weekly earnings	Schumpeter-Gilboy consumer goods (a)	Price of quartern loaf	Real wage	Annual real wage
1780	100	100	100	100	100
1781	92	105	—	88	—
1782	102	105	—	97	—
1783	83	117	—	71	—
1786	101	108	—	94	—
1787	100	106	—	94	—
1788	96	100	—	86	—
1789	96	106	—	91	—
1790	95	112	—	85	—
1791	108	110	100	98	90
1792	114	110	—	104	—
1793	101	117	—	86	—
1794	102	123	—	83	—
1795	114	133	—	86	—
1796	118	140	—	84	—
1800	—	192	360	—	—
1801	119	207	278	55	—
1802	120	158	154	76	—
1803	113	142	141	80	81
1804	119	146	146	82	89
1807	120	169	175	72	61
1808	125	185	191	67	—
1809	117	192	229	61	58
1812	117	215	303	53	—

Source: Highway Accounts, Walcot. Elizabeth Boody Schumpeter, "English Prices and Public
Finance, 1660–1822," *Review of Economic Statistics,* XX (1938).

inclusion in the index, do not show any
increase in earnings. Two, it is certain,
from literary evidence, that the years
1809 to 1813 in Bath were marked by
stagnation, unemployment and special
measures of relief similar in extent to
those of 1800. Thus the 1807–1809
average is more likely to over- than
under-estimate the actual level of earnings in 1812. Given this assumption it
is possible to derive two estimates of
real wages for 1812. The first, using the
Schumpeter-Gilboy Index (1780=100),
gives a figure of 53 and indicates a decline in real wages of nearly 50 per cent
from 1780. The second, using the Bath
Index (1838=100) and a different basket of goods, results in a figure of 64
(67 including rent). This second index
indicates a rise of over 60 per cent in
real wages by 1832 (index of 106 or
103 including rent). This can only serve
as the roughest of guides to the movement of real wages over a very long
period and, of course, indicates nothing

about the movement of real wages during the period 1812–1832.

All that local data can show for this
period is the movement of retail prices.
In spite of a rise between 1815–1817,
retail prices fell after 1812 from 182
(173 including rent) to 95 in 1822–23
(119 including rent in 1820). Thereafter prices fluctuated between 14 and
34 points above this level—except for
1827–28—until 1832 when a further
downward drift of prices brought them,
in 1837–1842, to the low level prevailing in the early 1820s. Calculations of
the mean monthly deviation from the
average annual price of the quartern
loaf for five-year periods between 1800
and 1844 also suggests that this low
level of prices, after 1832, was accompanied by a reduction in the sharp price
fluctuations which were characteristic
of the years of high prices earlier in the
century. Consequently, labourers' experience of a rapid decline in real wages
within a short period of months, or

sometimes weeks, became less common. This might well be a factor easing the impact of the downward drift of real wages between 1835 and 1838 noted in the following section. Widespread unemployment, however, continued to bring the shock of a rapid fall in real income to many.

1832–1844. In the years 1832–1835 real wages averaged 112 and were about 70 per cent higher than in 1812. Between this and the subsequent period, 1836–1839, they fell by 12 per cent to 100 so that real wages were approximately 60 per cent higher than in 1812. A renewed rise began in 1839 and by 1840 real wages were approximately double the level of 1812. The wage experience of two regularly employed labourers shows that their rise in real wages was below that of the average, which was calculated by including the earnings of men less regularly employed. Nevertheless they too had increased their real wages 50 per cent between the mid-1830s and the mid-1840s [see Table 6].

Although these calculations for the two periods, 1780–1812 and 1832–1844, based as they are on different baskets of goods, do not permit a direct comparison between the levels of real wages

they do suggest: (a) real wages declined between 1790 and 1812, (b) a rise in real wages between 1812 and 1832 which probably more than restored the labourer to the position reached in the 1790s, (c) real wages fell throughout the 1830s and only remained above the pre-war level in the 1840s. Table 7, however, includes a third calculation of real wages for the whole period 1780–1850 using the Bath index of labourers' earnings and Silberling's cost-of-living index. The index of real wages thus calculated moves in much the same way as the Bath-Schumpeter/Gilboy Index, 1780–1812 and the Bath Index, 1832–1844. In doing so it confirms the impression that the rise in real wages after the Napoleonic Wars did not permanently restore the labourer to the real wage obtaining between 1780 and 1790 until the early 1840s even though the real wage was then double what it had been in 1812 [see Table 7 on page 94].

The application of the age-cohort approach would then suggest that very few labourers entering the labour market in the 1780s could have received a higher real wage at the end of a thirty-year working life. On the other hand, men starting work in the 1790s would probably have experienced a rise in real

TABLE 6. EARNINGS AND REAL WAGES, NON-AGRICULTURAL LABOURERS, IN THE CITY OF BATH, 1832–1844 (1838=100)

Year	Average weekly earnings (1780 = 100 = Sept. 1838)	Bath retail prices	Price of quartern loaf	Real wage	Real wage of Rose	Real wage of Slade
1812	117	182	191	64		
1832	96	90	94	106		
1833	97	85	84	114		
1834	86	82	84	105		
1835	95	78	73	122		
1836	95	90	84	109	91	
1837	95	102	94	93	86	92
1838	98	100	100	98	100	100
1839	103	101	105	102	99	115
1840	128	105	105	92	112	110
1841	127	103	100	123	114	113
1842	134	97	94	138	123	130
1843	134	83	78	161	142	152
1844	137	84	84	163	140	150

Source: Highway Accounts, Walcot; *Bath and Cheltenham Gazette.*

TABLE 7.   REAL WAGES OF NON-AGRICULTURAL LABOURERS IN THE CITY OF BATH, 1780–1850

	Bath-Schumpeter/ Gilboy (a) (1780 = 100)	Bath (a) excluding rent, (b) including rent (1838 = 100)		Bath-Silberling (1838 = 100)
1780–1783	89			118
1786–1790	90			123
1791–1796	90			115
1801–1804	73			94
1807–1809	66	(a)	(b)	90
1812	53	64	67	77
1832–1835	—	112	111	106
1836–1839	—	100	—	100
1840–1844	—	141	(Av. of 1840 + 1844, 144)	150
1845–1848	—	—	—	156
1849–1850	—	—	—	194

wages during the 1820s while others, starting in the first decade of the nineteenth century, would almost certainly have benefited from an early and rapid improvement in real wages only to have their experience of falling real wages and unemployment deepened by the fact of advancing age during the 1830s. By 1821 about one-third of the city's male population was aged between 20 and 40 years of age, and labourers in this age-group, as they moved into the 1830s ten years later, approaching 40 or 50 years of age, would certainly have been able to contrast their middle and old age with a more prosperous youth, whilst only men aged about 20 in 1821 would have benefited from the steep rise in real wages of the early 1840s when they would have been 40 years of age. Younger men starting work in the 1820s, in relatively favourable circumstances, would also have experienced unemployment and a cut in real wages in the 1830s and then, in the last third of life, particularly as labourers, would have shared in the general improvement to a lesser extent than those ten or twenty years younger whose first work experience began in the middle 1830s.

IV.   SUMMARY AND CONCLUSION

It has been argued that, in the discussion on the standard of living during the Industrial Revolution, wage and price data should relate to specific classes and regions and enable comparisons to be made with the pre-Napoleonic period. A further suggestion was that the real im-

pact and meaning of movements in real wages, for those classes and regions studied, could be clarified further if, to the consequences of differences between the experience of workers in different regions and industries, and to the consequences of possible shifts in income distribution and of development in technology, is added an awareness of the role of the age-cohort approach in focusing attention on the wage and life experience of people. This was followed by an attempt to explore the experience of non-agricultural labourers in Bath. The approach was made through the construction of an index of weekly earnings and an index of retail prices, both of which were new and firmly based on local wage, retail price, rent and budgetary data relevant to the real experience of these non-agricultural labourers. The general conclusion was: a decline in real wages from 1790 to 1812 followed by a rise to 1832, which restored the labourer to the real-wage position of the same class of labourers in 1780–90. This was followed, in the 1830s, by a decline in real wages which was made worse by unemployment although partially offset by a reduction in price fluctuations. Rising earnings and falling prices after 1839–40 meant that by 1850 real wages were about double what they had been in the period 1801–1804 and 50–60 per cent higher than in the pre-war period.

Although lack of data on the relationship of earnings to unemployment, age-structure and family size prevented a more rigorous discussion of the age-cohort approach, it was suggested that the experience of different generations or age-cohorts of labourers, within the seventy-year period, varied according to the way in which the phasing of the movement in real wages was imposed on the rhythm of their earning experience.

Thus it is held that at least some of the requirements set out by T. S. Ashton have been fulfilled in a way which sheds much light on the experience of one group of the lowest class of urban workers, and in a way which offers a further possibility of reconciling the fact of a rise in real wages over a long-term with the short-term experience of men.

Sidney G. Checkland

IMPROVEMENTS STILL UNACHIEVED IN THE

LATER NINETEENTH CENTURY

After early teaching at Liverpool and Cambridge, Checkland has been Professor of Economic History at Glasgow since 1957. He has written learned articles, but this is his only book. Although it appears in a series "Social and Economic History of England" it is far from a conventional text. On the contrary, it is a highly original account of English development, which places special emphasis upon the scientists, engineers, businessmen, and farmers who contributed initiative; upon the social classes and their way of life; and on the varied politics of protest and reform.

THE industrial cities of England came into being almost by inadvertence: they were merely the places where factories, offices, depots, and warehouses were built and to which the new industrial population was attracted. The long tradition of town planning and regulation going back to the middle ages had largely passed into abeyance. In the newer cities it had never been operative. The urban revolution was so great in scope and scale as to obliterate the older sense of responsibility.

Problems accumulated steadily. Down to the forties no real attempt at solution was made. Learning about cities had to be imposed by experience; deterioration had to be well advanced before the necessary response could be evoked, for the immensity of the effort required to

regulate an industrial city was so great that it was only forthcoming as an inescapable imperative. Moreover, the form and content of the new kind of city represented the attempts of its myriad of members to find the formula that allowed of the implementation of their individual plans, either as masters or men. Until the nature of the resulting complex could be perceived it was impossible to plan to control it. There was thus a paradox: for the morbid aspect of urban growth to be treated it had to be allowed to develop until it carried irresistible conviction.

By the forties a state of affairs had been reached in which three great dangers threatened. There had long been fear of the great mysterious masses accumulating in the areas that were

From Sidney G. Checkland, *The Rise of Industrial Society in England, 1815–1885* (Longmans, London, 1964), pp. 251–9, 262–3. By permission of Longmans, Green & Co., Ltd. and St. Martin's Press, Incorporated.

unknown and unpenetrated by the middle class. This could lead to a politically explosive situation. Even more imminent was the danger of epidemic. The cholera outbreak of 1832 and subsequent visits in the forties brought terror to the towns. Every middle-class family relied upon its servants; they constituted an almost instantaneous channel along which disease travelled from slums to residential squares. In the fifties it was discovered that the Royal apartments at Buckingham Palace were ventilated through the common sewer. Outbreaks of disease were predicted by the opponents of the Great Exhibition; before 1851 it was thought unreasonable that the Queen should visit Liverpool and Manchester, and when she did so in that year it was "almost a matter of wonder." Finally, the growth and deterioration of the cities was very damaging to efficiency and therefore an obstacle to the lowering of production costs. British industry and trade were doing well in the third quarter of the century, but it was becoming apparent that the conditions of living of the workers would soon become a seriously limiting factor.

The dangers of dirt were the first to provoke thought and action. The system of natural liberty could provide the food and raw materials required to maintain the population of vast cities; indeed the philosophically minded marvelled how the grand design of the Deity was thus demonstrated. But it could not purge its wastes. It was as though the organs of sustenance were efficient but the organisation of elimination were defective.

Men, women and children, in varying degree, were wearing, breathing and drinking refuse. Old garments moved down the social scale and passed from peer to pauper at its nether end. The air was defiled with industrial and human effluvia. Water-courses became open sewers. Tipping and dumping were uncontrolled; there was a lack of depots for night soil. The sewage system was largely on the surface, courts were unpaved, the movement of air was blocked by crowded buildings. The builder might

place the primitive privy where he wished, inside or outside the houses: when indoors the smells in winter were dreadful in houses tightly closed to keep them warm, when outdoors women and children, unwilling to visit them in exposed places, became habitually constipated. Cemeteries gave off noxious smells and polluted the water supplies; tanneries, breweries, dyeing works, chemical plants, slaughter houses, and manure driers were uncontrolled in their disposal of waste matter, as gas, liquid, or solid. The cesspool, "that magazine of all the contagions" as Farr described it, was still general. The children were the heaviest casualties. In the sixties about twenty-six of every hundred died under the age of five; in the best districts the number was eighteen, in the worst it was thirty-six. The first great task of the urban improvers was to deal with the toxic refuse of urban life.

Chadwick and his disciples began their attack in the forties. They encountered a confusion of authorities, sometimes ludicrous, sometimes tragic. Delay, confusion, waste, and omission were everywhere, presided over by a welter of Town Councils, Highway Boards, Health Committees, Commissioners of Sewers, Water and Gas Authorities, Improvement Commissioners, Watch Committees, Poor Law Unions, Turnpike Trusts. These bodies, laudable in themselves, relics of the tentativeness of the first decades of industrialisation, were now archaic.

At the death of William IV in 1837 the Statute Book contained no general sanitary law, in spite of the fact that for two years, from the autumn of 1831, England, in common with Europe, had passed through its first taste of Asiatic cholera. But the cholera did call attention to the depths to which much of urban life had sunk. At last the reformers could make progress against the inter-epidemical indifference. Edwin Chadwick, installed after 1834 as the Secretary of the new Poor Law Board, was placed in a position to begin systematic inquiry into sanitation. He and other devoted men, including Sir J. P.

Kay-Shuttleworth and Dr. Thomas Southwood Smith provoked committees of inquiry, culminating in 1842, with the *General Report on the Sanitary Condition of the Labouring Population of Great Britain.* But the scale of the political and administrative implications could not be accepted immediately: a Royal Commission was appointed in 1843, reporting in 1845. The Health of Towns Association and other such voluntary bodies helped the agitation.

At long last came the Public Health Act of 1848. A General Board of Health was established; and its inspectors of nuisances did good work under Chadwick, but the zest of Chadwick as its chief working member added to the animosity of hostile interests. The Board was reduced in effectiveness in 1854, wound up in 1858, its attenuated functions passing to the Privy Council. It had done much to deal with epidemics, improve water supplies, clear up the awful cemetery problem, and provide for sewage disposal, all against the powerful resistance of those who fought against additional charges on the rates and the enforcement of improvement from the centre. Fortunately Sir John Simon, the new Medical Officer of the Privy Council, appointed in 1855, was another dedicated man, under whom further progress was made. But he had to struggle with a situation with which Parliament was not really prepared to deal; in the absence of considered policy and without effective powers Simon's task was heartbreaking. An assortment of miscellaneous Acts were passed, affecting common lodging houses, powers to deal with epidemics, burials, various aspects of sanitation, food defilement and adulteration, and venereal diseases.

Between the fifties and the seventies England made substantial progress against the zymotic diseases: fevers, smallpox, cholera, diarrhoea—all due to filth. Deaths from such causes fell by some 23 per cent. But this was not enough. The shamefully high mortality of soldiers in barracks had been much reduced, inspiring contemporaries with the hope that more could be done in the towns. Southwood Smith, Edwin Chadwick, and Florence Nightingale were the driving forces of this second campaign.

By 1869 the confusion of authorities was so conspicuous that a new Royal Commission was appointed; its report of 1871 revealed the extent of the frustration. It called for a national sanitation and health policy. At long last prompt action was forthcoming; the Local Government Act of 1871 divided the country into sanitary districts and made obligatory the appointment in each of a Medical Officer and an Inspector of Nuisances. The Public Health Act of 1875 provided a code of principles and responsibilities. The real attack on urban filth could begin. But there were immense arrears to be overtaken.

More positively, there were new challenges in the provision of two great articles of public consumption: water and gas. A vast leap was required to move from the well and the water cart to a piped supply. For when taps appeared in houses, it was no longer a question of supplying the same quantity more conveniently; the consumption of water shot up at an extraordinary rate. Gas, too, was in ever-increasing demand. Private companies for the provision of both gas and water had come into existence, and were highly profitable, not least because their extension of supply lagged behind what was needed. Demonstrations that they had increased output and reduced prices could not dispose of the fact that by the fifties they were a serious clog on urban improvement. Rival companies, with their high overheads, were unwilling to invest more, because each was fearful that the other might cut prices. In the absence of water meters the companies imposed complex and troublesome regulations about installations and use. The worst sufferers were, of course, the workers and the poor. Only a fully planned and efficient service could bring an adequate supply of water and gas within their means. So great was the commitment to the competitive idea, and so little developed was the alternative, that effective resistance was prolonged. But advocacy was powerful also; by 1855 more than a dozen towns in the north were empowered to set up water undertakings. The gas companies held out a good deal longer, in spite of spokesmanship in the Lords in favour of consumers. But before 1870 some thirty-three towns had their own gas undertakings. In 1875 Birmingham bought out the private companies and through municipal enterprise showed what could be done with the economies of scale. The Public Health Act of the same year gave powers to urban authorities to supply gas where no private company existed. No powers of compulsory purchase of either water or gas companies were ever given. But ideas were changing. Municipal transport, especially in the form of tramway systems, was coming into being in the seventies. Though its actions were equivocal, Parliament sought to prevent a recurrence of the situation that had arisen over water and gas. In the case of electricity, Parliament, as early as 1878, regarded civic management as the best formula.

The new and better water supply aggravated the sewage problem—there was now so much more liquid waste to dispose of. Sir Joseph Bazalgette, servant of the Metropolitan Water Board, provided a mighty but invisible monument to himself by constructing the sewers of London. Other cities tackled the sewage problem: Birmingham's great drainage scheme was begun in 1845. Too often, however, the sewers served to pollute rivers and estuaries.

All the other challenges of a society that was both expanding its numbers and concentrating them in cities were accumulating. The widening of streets and the provision of bridges became pressing needs as the number of people and the volume of goods moving about increased. But each such improvement was an *ad hoc* affair, to be fought through confused jurisdictions and embattled resistance, paying as it went toll to those in possession of lands or rights affected. Not infrequently the town, in order to bear such costs, sold its own patrimony of land, making the problem of municipal improvement so much greater for the following genera-

tions. Not until the seventies did the idea of area planning make any converts and these were few. The provision of port facilities was something of an exception: from 1857 Liverpool's greatest collection of equipment was placed in the hands of the Mersey Docks and Harbours Board, a non-profit-making monopoly. By this time the railways had slashed their way into the centre of most cities. Parks sometimes came into the possession of the town through gifts or, occasionally, by purchase. Hospitals were built, and police and fire services, each with its many problems.

Public education received no financial support from the state until 1833; in that year the reformed Parliament voted the sum of £20,000 for buildings for elementary schools. There had been a good deal of voluntary activity which played a large part in causing this tardy and inadequate recognition of responsibility. The religious revival brought about by Methodism in the later eighteenth century had produced the Sunday School movement; the desire to encourage habits of industry had inspired "schools of industry," to teach children simple crafts; there were newly endowed parish schools combining religious instruction and the "three Rs." The development of educational theory had been accelerated by the discussions of the eighteenth century and by the experiments of Owen at New Lanark and of a few other factory masters. The most vigorous controversy was between Andrew Bell (1753–1832) and Joseph Lancaster (1778–1838) and their respective protagonists. But though they had their differences on implementation, they shared the same basic principle, that of the "mutual" or "monitorial" system, under which a single master taught monitors only, these, in turn, being responsible for the instruction of their school fellows. The economy of this system was very attractive to the education enthusiasts. By 1858 the government support amounted to about two-thirds of a million.

In that year the Newcastle Commission began its inquiries into the provision of education for the masses. Religious debate, bedevilling the matter from the outset, assumed a new virulence; many people came to favour a purely secular system in order to get on with the task of conveying knowledge and making possible the growth of mind. The effect of the religious controversy on the Commission, however, was quite otherwise—their reaction was to reject the principle of general compulsory education. The Educational Code of 1862 was intended to ensure "efficient" schooling, with money grants dependent upon satisfactory examination performances by the children. The education grant accordingly fell, as insufficient pupils qualified. The Education Act of 1870, presented by W. E. Forster, provided for elected School Boards to be set up where schools were inadequate.

A dual system was thus made explicit, composed of voluntary and Board Schools. The supporters of religious education, chiefly members and clergy of the Church of England, exerted themselves to increase the voluntary element, in order to preclude the necessity for Board Schools. The dissenters worked through the latter, in which an undenominational protestantism was taught. A further Act of 1876 brought compulsory education to the age of twelve. Though fees were payable until 1891, now for the first time universal literacy became possible. The state, having imposed educational duties on local governments, virtually withdrew, leaving the field to the church and the Boards. In many places the Boards, the object of great working-class interest, responded with vigour, causing a remarkable extension. Participation in such work was one of the first effective opportunities afforded to men of working origin to work for the improvement of their fellows.

Secondary education for the sons of farmers, traders, and manufacturers, and for the brighter and more fortunate sons of the workers, had enjoyed private endowments for a long time, though these were inadequate and unsystematic. Civic responsibility for endowed schools was very ancient, but the new conditions revolutionised the situation. The Taunton Commission reviewed the national provision in 1867–68. It found that those schools having connections with the universities were sufficiently bad, the others were in chaos. But the Endowed Schools Act of 1869 did not carry through the comprehensive reform called for by the Report, failing to treat English secondary education as a whole.

With the struggle for such rudimentary provisions as sanitation and education so long and so greatly resisted, it is hardly surprising that the positive idea of making the cities places of beauty and pleasure was scarcely broached. There were some who thought as planners, including the Owenite socialists, and James Silk Buckingham and Robert Pemberton, and later on, General Booth. Some of these men revived ideas from the great European tradition of town planning. But they were utopians: they thought and wrote in terms of new beginnings on an unencumbered site. They constructed ideal solutions which, in obviating all ugliness and conflict, ignored the essential dynamic character of cities in continuous response to changing conditions. The result was a formalism that looked slightly ludicrous in the light of actuality.

Moreover the utopians confined their thinking to a scale that ignored much of the problem. The great extension in the size of cities gave rise to changes that were qualitative as well as quantitative. For to add successive new blocks to the city was to cause the centre itself to change and with it the relationship of the components. Some parts of the city became enormously more valuable, others decayed and were rejected as growth assumed a new direction. Some parts were paradoxical: site values rose with scarcity, but there was no dramatic redevelopment to economise and make efficient use of the ground. Instead there was an intensification of the old use, with very high density slums as the result. Thus appeared the baffling situation, that in the case of landlords the market system could cause the highest level of gain to be associated with the lowest level of human degradation. If the deterioration went on long enough the basic shape of the city might be affected, for the new growth took place in areas chosen so as to avoid the area of dereliction, so that eventually the possibility of redevelopment passed away and the slum was further confirmed. The only hope then for its removal was public intervention. But this called for a great effort of communal will that was not forthcoming.

In the newly forming suburbs developers bought parcels of land as they became available. Usually these were arbitrary in shape, defined by existing main roads, farm access roads, and even field boundaries; the layout of the houses was made to conform to the fragments so created. The city thus became a jig-saw of components, its coherence depending to a great degree upon luck. Those who lived in this ever-extending perimeter had homes divorced both from their place of work and from their places of urban entertainment. This dormitory kind of life was made possible by new transport facilities, in the fifties the omnibus, in the sixties the railways, and in the seventies the beginning of the tramways.

The architect could do little to improve the cities, proliferating without centres and without form. He could exercise himself on single buildings, or at best on a range of terraces. But he had little or no control of the use of space or of the relationship between buildings. Older towns in the south of England had their great churches, market places, castles, and guildhalls upon which to focus; the new cities of the north had little around which to synthesise their meaning. Leeds, Sheffield, Bradford, and Birmingham, the creations of the new age of independence of water travel, had paid the price of this freedom in being denied that greatest of urban amenities, a noble river. Even a monumental town hall was no substitute for a true focus. In London a traditional glory had been defiled; by the forties the Thames had become so noisome that the city turned its back upon its river; it was in Belgravia to the north that wealth went to dwell, and not on the South Bank. It was only in the sixties that the northern side of the Thames was embanked.

Cities, in short, as well as houses, were constructed on the cheap, with virtually no restraints upon the builders except such as were archaic, arising from a cumbersome system of law and land tenure. The conditions of urban living, like the conditions of working, made their contribution to the great task of capital formation, for both were catered for on a minimal scale. Not only were costs kept down; flexibility was maximised in both cases, for both builder and entrepreneur could delimit their problems, excluding from their risk calculations difficult considerations arising from the social interest, especially as it would develop in the longer run, and could thus produce startling growth. In both cases a point was reached at which cheapness and flexibility ceased to be economic because of the impairment of efficiency.

The conditions of work were improved first, beginning in the thirties; the conditions of living were redeemed much more slowly, for in spite of the heroic efforts of the pioneers, the effective national attack upon dirt really dated from the seventies, and positive thinking about the urban environment had not made much progress even by the end of the century. But it had made its entry into the political arena.

Phyllis Deane

AN ATTEMPTED SUMMING-UP

Fellow of Newnham College, and Lecturer in Economics, at Cambridge, Miss Deane has published, with W. A. Cole, *British Economic Growth, 1688–1959: Trends and Structure,* and, with B. R. Mitchell, *Abstract of British Historical Statistics,* both in 1962. Although the excerpt I have chosen has the character of a summing-up of the present controversy, the book from which it is taken has a far wider scope. It is an exceptionally intelligent summary of the economic facts and relationships of the Industrial Revolution, with brief but up-to-date bibliographies.

THE net result of the galaxy of revolutions in the way men organised their economic life was that continuous economic change came to be part of the natural order of things and that the scale of the economy began to expand perceptibly and without limit. It was within the century 1750–1850 that the crucial transformation took place that led eventually to a sustained growth in incomes per head. It is difficult at this distance in time and with the sketchy statistical data at our disposal to calculate precisely when this sustained growth began, how much it amounted to and how rapidly it developed. But analysis and interpretation of the existing statistical series suggests a certain pattern, and this pattern is probably reliable enough even if the precise figures are questionable.

Somewhere about the middle of the eighteenth century there is evidence that total national output began to grow —perhaps not faster than it had ever done before in earlier decades, but certainly faster than it had over most of the preceding century. At this stage, however, population had also begun to grow, and it is doubtful whether output was growing any faster than population at the beginning of the period, and hence whether incomes per head were growing at all. In the last quarter of the century, however, the evidence for an improvement in incomes per head becomes much stronger, though it is still not conclusive. We know that population and prices, and certain kinds of production and incomes, and overseas trade, were growing much more strongly than ever before in the fourth quarter of the century. Our problem is to decide whether prices were growing so fast that they outweighed any improvement in incomes, or whether population was growing so fast that it outweighed any improvement in production.

If we take money-income statistics as our starting-point in trying to assess this growth and then adjust them for changes in the value of money with the aid of the existing price indices, we find little evidence of growth in real incomes per head in the last quarter of the eighteenth century and the first decade of the nineteenth century. Indeed when we apply price indices to national income or to wage data the results suggest a decline in the standard of living over this period. But the problem is that the rising price indices cannot be regarded as a reliable reflection of the fall in the value of money because they are incomplete, and moreover they are incomplete in a biased way. In particular they are heavily weighted with commodities which rose sharply in price (these of course were the prices which contemporaries were most concerned to

From Phyllis Deane, *The First Industrial Revolution* (Cambridge University Press, Cambridge, 1965), pp. 220–4, 241–53. By permission of Cambridge University Press.

record) and exclude many commodities whose prices fell (especially manufactured products which being non-homogeneous commodities are not in any case easily included in a price series). Hence the price indices tend to exaggerate the fall in the purchasing power of incomes at this period.

If however we take output and trade statistics as our starting-point in trying to assess the national rate of economic growth and make the assumption that foreign trade (which provides us with our best continuous statistical series for the eighteenth century) was of considerable importance to the economy, we find convincing evidence not only of growth in total national product but also in national productivity and standards of living; that is, a growth in real incomes per head. In this approach we avoid having to depend on biased price statistics but, since we do not have enough production and trade statistics to cover the whole economy, we have to make certain assumptions about the relative importance in the total national output of the production and trade sectors whose growth we *can* measure. Clearly we cannot get an accurate measure of the rate of economic growth from these rough calculations but it is reasonable to suppose that we can get answers of the right order of magnitude.

The results, then, are as follows. After a period of stagnation in output, prices, population, incomes and standards of living in the first part of the eighteenth century, there was a noticeable upward trend in total national output dating from somewhere about or just before 1750. At this stage, however, population was growing fast enough to outweigh the improvement in total national product and it is doubtful whether the improvement in standards of living was appreciable enough to be obvious to contemporaries. A considerably sharper upward trend appears in the 1780s and 1790s when total national output may have been growing at a rate of 1.8 per cent per annum (approximately twice the rate of growth in the middle of the century) and output per head at a rate of about 0.9 per cent per annum. In sum, when Adam Smith was writing he

was looking back on a period in which the rate of growth in the total national product would imply its doubling in 70–80 years. This is not a fast rate of growth but it should have been obvious to contemporaries that the economy was in fact growing, and it is not surprising that Adam Smith was conscious of national growth. On the other hand, it is doubtful whether the improvement in standards of living—which was proceeding at a rate implying the doubling of the standard in about a century and a half—*was* very obvious to contemporaries except in those sectors which were growing fastest. But by the beginning of the nineteenth century the growth in national output was proceeding at a rate which implied its doubling in not much more than forty years and the growth in incomes per head at a rate which implied its doubling in 70–80 years. A significant feature of this end-of-century acceleration in the rate of growth of incomes per head is that it was accompanied by an acceleration in the rate of growth of population. This is the justification for the importance which economic historians have attached to the last two decades of the eighteenth century. It seems to have been the period during which the rate of growth in national product effectively outstripped the rate of growth in population and the spectre of Malthusian stagnation was finally exorcised.

It seems likely that the national rate of growth was retarded, though not actually checked, by the French wars, and that it accelerated again in the 1820s and 1830s. So that as between the first and fifth decades of the nineteenth century total national product seems to have been growing at a rate of about 2.9 per cent per annum (this implies a doubling in not much more than a quarter of a century) and incomes per head at about 1½ per cent (which implies a doubling in about half a century). This was not yet the peak rate of growth achieved by the British economy —that came in the second half of the nineteenth century—but it represented sustained growth on a scale which was beyond the wildest dreams of earlier generations. The middle and upper classes certainly got a good deal more out of this improvement than the working classes; capital got a bigger share than labour; some groups in the community came near to starvation levels. But, when all allowance has been made for changes in the distribution of income which accompanied economic growth, it can hardly be doubted that by the middle of the nineteenth century the majority of the population were beginning to experience, though not yet to expect, a slow rise in their ordinary standard of living.

To say this is not to deny that the 1830s and 1840s were periods of widespread social and economic distress or that the condition of large sections of the population was at times as bad—perhaps worse—than it had ever been before. The "hungry forties" did not owe their name simply to the accident of the Irish famine. Engels' passionate denunciation of the industrial system was based on a biased selection of information, but it was not without substance. The deplorable cases of poverty and degradation that he cites were by no means uncommon. The fact is that economic growth was not a process of steady improvement in standards of living for the mass of the population. It was a process of economic and social change which often left certain sections of the population very much poorer in every sense than they had been in pre-industrial times, and which made larger and larger sections of the population acutely vulnerable to depressions in trade or industry or to variations in the state of the harvest. Even those whose standards of living were, on balance, improving, were subject to unpredictable periods of unemployment or short-time which would bring them face to face with destitution again. Engels recognised this clearly enough. After citing three horrible cases of London poverty he wrote:

It is not, of course, suggested that all London workers are so poverty-stricken as these three families. There can be no doubt that for every worker who is rendered utterly destitute by society there are ten who are better off. On the other hand it can be confidently asserted that thousands of decent and industrious families . . . live under truly deplorable conditions which are an affront to human dignity. It is equally incontestable that every working man without exception may well suffer a similar fate through no fault of his own and despite all his efforts to keep his head above water.

This was one of the penalties of industrialisation. At the pre-industrial stage, where manufacturing was generally organised on a domestic basis, a trade depression would mean that the average manufacturer had less money to spend, but not that he would starve, for he could still work as an agricultural labourer or cultivate his own plot of land. Similarly, when harvests fell short of the normal the agricultural family could often add to its income and so meet the higher food prices, by working harder at the spinning wheel or the loom. By contrast, in an industrial economy any state of depression, however slight, is liable to involve unemployment for some workers and hence complete destitution for them. Moreover in an integrated industrialised economy where there is a high degree of specialisation, there is inevitably a high degree of interdependence between the different sectors of the community. A depression in one branch of trade is liable to be communicated at once to the ancillary and related occupations. Whereas in a traditional economy, in which each region or family is accustomed to produce a large proportion of its subsistence requirements, a depression in one sector has only limited effects on other sectors, the reverse is true for an industrial economy. There a loss of trade or a reduction in output in one industry affects the prospect of a wide range of other industries and the chain of bankruptcies and redundancies spreads rapidly, and often with cumulative force, throughout the economy.

On the face of it, then, we might say that since the evidence points on the whole to an increase in national output per head of the population, beginning probably in the 1780s, muted by the French and Napoleonic Wars and resuming strongly at the end of the second decade of the nineteenth century, it implies a rising standard of living on the average. Actually, whether it does or not depends on whether there were significant changes in the distribution of the national income. It may be that all the value of the increase in national output accrued to the upper income groups—to the mill-owners and the iron-masters, for example, rather than to the workers. Or it may be that the growth in marketed output of corn or meat, say, due to the enclosures, accrued to a small group of owner-farmers, while the cottagers were evicted from their food plots and deprived of the common pasture for cow or pig to become a distressed agricultural proletariat. It is possible for national output to rise faster than population and for the standard of living of the majority of people to fall because a few people are monopolising the results of the increase or because the new goods are not consumption goods but capital goods.

One might also say, of course, as many holders of the "optimistic" view have said, that the evidence for a sharp decrease in mortality at the end of the eighteenth century points to a rise in the standard of living. If people were becoming more resistant to disease this could have been either because medical skills were improving or because they were living better. The medical historians, however, have discounted the evidence for striking medical advances which could have had this result and they fall back on the view that "there was a general advance in the standard of living in consequence of the economic development of the period." Here again there is a problem of distribution to be taken into account, though in this case it is a question of distribution through time. As Hobsbawm has pointed out:

It should be remembered that the decrease in mortality which is probably primarily responsible for the sharp rise in population need be due not to an *increase* in per capita consumption per year but to a greater *regularity of supply*: that is, to the abolition of the periodic shortages and famines which plagued pre-industrial economies and decimated their populations. It is quite possible for the industrial citizen to be worse fed in

a normal year than his predecessor, so long as he is more regularly fed.

To this improvement in the temporal flow of incomes, investment in communications (better roads, canals, etc.) and regular marketing of foodstuffs may have contributed more than increased productivity in industry or increase in output per acre.

However, the most striking feature of the mortality figures, if we try to use them as an index of standards of living, is that they show the decline in the death rate to have been arrested, probably even reversed, in the period when the industrial revolution was in full swing and began notably to affect the way of life of the majority of the population. Death rates estimated from burial figures reached an average of 35.8 per 1,000 in the 1730s and then fell steadily (with an interruption in the 1770s, when there was a slight rise) to reach an average of 21.1 per 1,000 in the decade 1811–20. This was an impressive achievement. Then, however, they began to rise again to reach 23.4 in the decade 1831–40 and remained more or less constant at over 22 per 1,000 (these are the official figures based on registration) in the 1840s, 1850s, and 1860s.

The main reason for the rise in the national death rate in the early nineteenth century was the influx of people into the towns which had a high, and in some cases a rising, death rate. The average death rate of the five largest towns outside London (Birmingham, Bristol, Leeds, Liverpool and Manchester) rose from 20.7 in 1831 to 30.8 in 1841. For Liverpool parish the death rate for the decade 1841–50 averaged 39.2 per 1,000 and in Manchester it was 33.1. The fact is that the towns had been outgrowing the existing technology of urban living. "Over half the deaths were caused by infectious diseases alone. . . . Infant diseases, product of dirt, ignorance, bad feeding and overcrowding swept one in two of all the children born in towns out of life before the age of five." As the towns expanded over the countryside and the population living in their centres multiplied, the existing sanitation systems became so inadequate as to be a growing menace to health. "Street sewers were immense brick caverns, flat bottomed and flat sided, washed only by a feeble trickle of water," and cleared by excavation of the streets every 5–10 years. In some cases town sewage was allowed to flow into the rivers from which the water companies were taking their water supply. It took a series of cholera epidemics and some alarming sanitary inquiries to persuade central and local authorities to take positive action to clean filth from the streets and courts, to adopt piped sanitation, and to make the private water-companies chlorinate their water supplies. Meanwhile it is fair to say that in most urban areas the human environment was deteriorating perceptibly through the first half of the nineteenth century and that it probably did not begin to improve generally until the 1870s and 1880s.

To probe more directly the question whether the standard of living of the working classes rose or fell in the course of the Industrial Revolution we need to look at the data on wages. What can we deduce from the way the real incomes of the workers moved over the period of early industrialisation? Here the problem of interpreting the incomplete record is twofold—whose wages should we consider and how are we to allow for changes in the value of money?

First of all then, whose wages? For the data do not permit us to compile a national wage bill which might give a measure of overall average earnings from employment. All that is available is a somewhat heterogeneous mass of wage quotations for particular industries, occupations and regions which economists and economic historians may or may not have been able to combine into meaningful aggregates. In general, of course, the wages of workers in industry were higher than those in agriculture, so that as the proportion in industrial employment rose, the average money-wage probably grew. In the expanding industries wages sometimes rose spectacularly. Take cotton, for example. Manchester cotton weavers were earning 7s. to 10s. a week

when Arthur Young toured the north of England in 1769—*before* the spinning-jenny provided them with enough yarn to keep their looms going constantly. By 1792, made scarce by the enormous quantities of yarn which the spinning-machines made available, they were earning 15s. to 20s. a week. But these boom wages did not last long. The supply of weavers proved highly elastic and the labour market was soon flooded with them. Their bargaining-power fell steeply. By 1800 a "good workman working 14 hours a day was hardly able to earn 5s. or 6s. between one Sunday and the next."

Clearly the wage data for specific occupations or industries may shed little or no light on the movement of wages over wide areas of the economy. And as far as the eighteenth-century wage data are concerned there is the additional problem that there was no really integrated national market for labour until the very end of the century. In effect, the outstanding characteristic of eighteenth-century wage history was the existence of wide regional variations in both levels and trends. In Lancashire, for example, the money wages of builders' labourers almost doubled between the 1750s and early 1790s. In London they seem to have risen by less than 5 per cent; and in Oxfordshire the increase was of the order of 15 per cent. Actually there was a marked narrowing of the regional wage differentials before the end of the eighteenth century, and by the late 1780s Lancashire building labourers whose earnings had been two-thirds of the London average in the 1750s were earning about 9s. a week compared with about 8s.6d. in London and about 9s. 6d. in Oxfordshire.

Of course the typical wage-earner in the late eighteenth century was not the labourer in industry but the labourer in agriculture. Bowley's figures for agricultural earnings suggest that the average agricultural wage increased by something like 25 per cent between the late 1760s and 1795. The rise was most marked in the Yorkshire Ridings, Lancashire, Northumberland and Staffordshire where the increase exceeded 50 per cent; but over a very large part of eastern, middle and southern England in the second half of the eighteenth century agricultural wages seem to have been in a state of relative stagnation similar to that which characterised the London building-trades for this period. When war with France broke out in the early 1790s, however, the economy rapidly moved into a state of relatively full employment and money wages in agriculture soared. Before the end of the Napoleonic Wars a "national" index of money wages, calculated by combining Wood's index of average money wages in towns with Bowley's index of money wages in agriculture, showed an increase of about 75 per cent.

On the other hand if money wages rose steeply over this war period 1792–1815, prices rose even more. For this was a period of galloping wartime inflation. Which brings us to our second major problem of interpretation, the problem of allowing for changes in the value of money. In order to get some measure of the change in the standard of living we must form some view of the movement of *real* wages; that is, to adjust money wages so as to eliminate the effect of the upward movement in prices.

What I have said about regional variations in the price of eighteenth-century labour applies also to the price of commodities at this period—sometimes to an even greater extent. For eighteenth-century England in which it took 10–12 days to travel from London to Edinburgh (that was in the 1750s), when the price of coal could vary from 15s. a chaldron to over £3 a chaldron according to distance from the pits (this was true even in the 1790s), and when the wages of a building craftsman could vary from 2s. to 3s. a day according to the region in which he operated, there is no satisfactory way of constructing a general price index which could reflect changes in the value of money for the economy as a whole. Each region had its own price history and its own set of price relationships. Even if we knew enough about the prices of each region to construct a true national average it is doubtful what meaning we could attribute to the result.

On the other hand it is certain that there were important changes in the value of money during the latter part of the eighteenth century and these changes must have had their effect on prices. By the 1790s (probably by the 1760s) the majority of prices had developed an upward trend. Until after the Napoleonic Wars, however—possibly until the beginning of the railway age—the movements of individual prices are so divergent and so variable that the attempt to measure the changes in the form of a general price index is a dubious procedure. Moreover in a period of violent inflation—such as that which developed in the last decade of the eighteenth century when the cumulative effects of a rapidly rising population, a succession of poor harvests and an expensive war drove up the price of many foodstuffs—price indices based on weights relevant to a less disturbed period do not adequately reflect changes in the value of money. This is because they do not take account of the fact that consumers look for substitutes for goods whose prices have soared. They substitute goods which are less vulnerable to harvest and war crises and their standard of living does not fall to the extent that it would have done if they had obstinately persisted in their old pattern of consumption.

So far I have been considering the conceptual difficulties of constructing price indices that might enable one to allow for changes in the purchasing power of money and so to convert money wages to "real" wages. But it goes without saying that there are formidable data problems too. We don't have all the price data we need for this purpose. Most of the prices that are regularly available for the period of the industrial revolution relate to commodities which tended to be particularly vulnerable to trade dislocations and harvest crises. In particular they seldom cover the prices of manufactured goods (many of which were reduced by the falling costs associated with industrialisation) or of rent, which is generally a fairly steady price even in inflation. And they are rich in the prices of foodstuffs and imported goods, which tended to rise sharply when harvest failure or war made them temporarily scarce. To some extent this bias is inevitable, for it was the vulnerable prices which contemporaries chose to collect and publish regularly and which are accordingly still on record. But it means, of course, that indices based on these selective quotations tend to exaggerate the movements in the general price level and become difficult to use as indications of changes in the value of money during periods of inflation.

The result is that when we try to take out from the wage data the effects of the price rises due to harvest crises and war shortages we completely wipe out any improvement in money wages and it then looks as though average real wages were declining over the period 1782 to 1815. Perhaps indeed they were. When we also bear in mind the burdens of war—the British people paid heavy subsidies to their continental allies, one in ten of the labour force was absorbed in the unproductive employment of the armed forces and the growth of industries producing for peacetime markets slackened perceptibly—it is not difficult to believe that consumption standards were actually falling. On the other hand when one takes into account the fact that total war involved full employment for adult males, while the spread of the factory system and the expansion of agricultural acreages widened the employment opportunities for women and children, it seems likely that the decline in the standard of living of the typical working-class family—if decline there was—was less drastic than the wage-price data might lead one to believe.

After the war, however, inflation turned to deflation and the picture changes. Average money-wages declined and so did prices. Within ten years (i.e. 1816 and 1824, again using the Bowley-Wood indices of agricultural and urban earnings combined into a national average) money wages had fallen by more than 10 per cent: by the 1840s the fall was 15 per cent. Prices, however, fell faster and at first glance we might deduce that the purchasing power of the worker's wage rose. For the longer period, up to about mid-nineteenth cen-

tury, this certainly seems to be the most plausible interpretation of the data. But for the distressed years of the immediate post-war aftermath when the demobilised soldiers and seamen flooded the labour market and the industries which had thrived in war were facing a slump in demand, it is likely that higher real wages earned by those who were lucky enough to be in regular employment were insufficient to compensate for the loss of earnings experienced by the unemployed or the under-employed. In the tense years between Waterloo in 1815 and the massacre of Peterloo in 1819 it has been said that England was nearer to social revolution than at any other time in her history. It seems probable that the real earnings of the average working-class family were lower in these years than they had been in the 1780s.

Thereafter the evidence for a rise in the average real wage becomes more convincing. It does not become absolutely conclusive because we do not know the incidence of unemployment. In years, in regions or in sectors of the economy where there was trade depression the evidence of acute poverty is overwhelming. But there are three plausible presumptions in favour of a rising standard of living, on the whole, after the end of the war: (1) that as industrialisation gathered momentum in the 1820s employment became more rather than less regular than it had been in pre-war years; (2) that the goods that tended to be omitted from the price indices, being largely manufactured goods, were more likely to be falling in price than the goods (largely raw materials) that were included—and hence of course that the price indices understated the post-war price fall; and (3) that the falling weight of taxation would, in a period when most taxes were indirect and therefore regressive, give perceptible relief to the working classes.

Actually the conviction of the "optimists" grows stronger for years towards the end of the controversial period than for the periods towards the beginning. Professor Ashton for example is more confident about the period after 1820. "Let me confess, therefore, at the start," he says, "that I am one of those who believe that all in all, conditions of labour were becoming better, *at least after 1820,* and that the spread of the factory played a not inconsiderable part in the improvement." Most observers agree that the 1790s, with war, harvest failures and a rapidly increasing population, was a tragic period for English labour. Clapham, another of the optimists, calls 1795, the year when the Speenhamland system was introduced to augment men's wages out of the rates, "the blackest year," and goes on to conclude that,

whereas on the average the potential standard of comfort of an English . . . rural labouring family in 1824 was probably a trifle better than it had been in 1794, assuming equal regularity of work, there were important areas in which it was definitely worse, others in which it was probably worse, and many in which the change either way was imperceptible. In the bad areas the rates were drawn upon for the deficit.

Not even the most convinced "optimists" have claimed that working-class standards of life improved perceptibly during the French wars or their immediate aftermath, though full employment financed by income-tax may well have involved some transfer of incomes from rich to poor. On the other hand even the pessimists will allow that perceptible improvements in working-class standards of living set in in the 1840s.

In effect then we can narrow down the area of fiercest controversy to the 1820s and 1830s. Here the data on wage-rates and prices suggest a rising real wage, though not a very great improvement. Between 1820 and 1840, for example, the Bowley-Wood wage data suggest a fall of about 10 per cent in money wages: and the Gayer-Rostow-Schwartz price index suggests a fall of about 12 per cent in prices. Professor Phelps Brown's index of builders' wage rates, expressed in terms of the basket of consumers' goods they might buy, suggests an improvement of about 5 per cent over the same period. Now if we assume, as the pessimists do, that "the period 1811–42 saw abnormal problems and abnormal unemployment," then the irregularity of work could easily have outweighed these rather feeble improvements in real incomes suggested by the wage/price data. On the other hand if we assume, as the optimists do, that the price indices understate the price fall (and hence the rise in purchasing power of wages) because they omit the commodities whose prices were influenced most strongly by the cost reductions of the industrial revolution, then we would argue that the wage/price data are only a pale reflection of the true rise in the standard of living. Without a great deal more research in the areas of doubt—the incidence of unemployment for example and the rise in the value of money—it is impossible to resolve this problem, though on the whole the evidence for an improvement in standards seems stronger than the evidence for a fall at this period.

Nor indeed can we say much about standards of consumption more directly. Figures of imports of tea, sugar and tobacco for example show very little rise (in some cases there are declines) over the controversial period, and the current pessimists' case rests a good deal on this negative evidence. Unfortunately these imported commodities were not consumed in large quantities by the average family and were subject to import duties which made important differences to the rate of consumption. For sugar there is evidence of a stagnant, even a falling consumption: from 29½ lb. per head in 1811 to 15 lb. per head in 1840. For tea there is evidence of a rise from about 1 lb. per head in 1811 (when, however, the duty paid was 4s. per head) to about 1½ lb. per head in 1841 (when the duty had fallen to under 3s. per head). Consumption of tobacco, on the other hand, went down from about 19 oz. per head in 1811 to about 14½ in 1841, but the duty had gone up and no one knows how much tobacco was smuggled in. These consumption figures are inconclusive in their implications therefore, and we have no reliable estimates of the consumption of more important items of working-class expenditure, of bread for example, of milk or meat or butter or eggs. True there are figures of beasts slaughtered at Smithfield market but these are for numbers only, they make no allowance for changes in average weight and they are incomplete even as an index of London consumption, for we have no information on the trade in other London meat-markets.

To sum up, then, what conclusions can we draw from all this? The first is that there is no firm evidence for an overall improvement in working-class standards of living between about 1780 and about 1820. Indeed, when we take into account the harvest failures, growing population, the privations of a major war and the distress of the post-war economic dislocation, we may reasonably conclude that on balance average standards of living tended to fall rather than to rise.

For the period from about 1820 to about 1840 it is difficult to be as definite. Certainly there is no evidence for a substantial rise in real incomes and what we can deduce from the statistics is not strong enough to compensate for the wide margin of error in the data. On the other hand the evidence for a fall in standards of living rests *either* on presumptions that we cannot empirically check with the information now accessible to us—like the incidence of unemployment, for example—*or* on data of actual consumption per head of certain not very important commodities whose consumption could as well be attributed to changes in taste or the weight of duties as to a fall in real incomes. Perhaps on balance the optimists can make out a more convincing case for an improvement in the standard of living than the pessimists can for a fall. But either case is based largely on circumstantial evidence and there is one thing that we can take as reasonably certain—and that is that whichever way it went, the net change was relatively slight.

Finally, beginning in the 1840s we find much stronger evidence of an improvement in the average real incomes of the working class, evidence that has been strong enough to convince even some of the remaining pessimists. It does not rest however on a perceptible increase in real wage rates. Habakkuk, for example, observes that "The inconclusive nature of the current debate about living standards in this period is perhaps a warrant for supposing that a substantial and general and demonstrable rise in the real wages of industrial workers did not occur until the 1850s and 1860s: and it was not until about 1870 that real wages in agriculture began to rise and a steady rise was apparent only in the 1880s." The argument for an improvement in the average standard of living in the middle of the century rests largely on a change in the composition of the labour force. To quote Hobsbawm, the most recent of the advocates of the pessimistic interpretation of the industrial revolution:

Little as we know about the period before the middle forties, most students would agree that the real sense of improvement among the labouring classes thereafter was due less to a rise in wage-rates, which often remained surprisingly stable for years, or to an improvement in social conditions, but to the upgrading of labourers from very poorly paid to less poorly paid jobs, and above all to a decline in unemployment or to a greater regularity of employment.

This shift in the distribution of the labour force from the traditional highly seasonal occupations characteristic of a pre-industrial economy to the modern sector with its mechanical aids to labour, its disciplined working habits and its continuous intensive use of capital equipment in day and night shifts is the true spirit and essence of the industrial revolution. Agricultural labourers, for example, normally earn less per week than factory workers of equivalent skill; handloom weavers earn less than power-loom weavers; canal bargemen less than locomotive drivers. Thus a shift in the composition of the labour force—a fall in the *proportion* of workers engaged in the low earning categories and a corresponding rise in the proportion of those in the high earning categories—would raise the average level of earnings per worker even if wage-rates in each occupation remained unchanged. This is the process that seems to have gathered momentum in the 1840s and to have brought with it perceptible improvements in material standards of life for the working classes. It may indeed have begun earlier, but it is not until the 1840s that we can be reasonably certain of its positive effects.

So much for the wage data. What about the national-income estimates? These suggest that between 1801 and 1851 national product per head at constant prices almost doubled. As between the pre-war period (say 1791) and 1851 the improvement was probably somewhat less, for 1801 was already a year of heavy inflation. In the controversial period between 1821 and 1841, however, there was an improvement, it seems, of over a third. Whether this meant a corresponding increase in the average real incomes of the working classes, however, would have depended on the way the increase in the national product was distributed. If the increase in incomes was entirely absorbed by the property-owning classes in the form of profits and rent, and if the increased output of foods and services took the form either of capital goods or of goods and services that were outside the normal budget of the wage-earners, then it is fair to presume that the employed population gained nothing from the process of early industrialisation.

To some extent it is undoubtedly true that there was a shift in the distribution of incomes in favour of profits and rent and a change in the composition of output in favour of capital goods, exports and goods and services for upper-class consumption. But it is manifest that this is not the whole story. The new factories were not producing entirely for the export or the luxury trade or for producers, and the fact that prices of manufactured consumer-goods fell substantially meant that the working classes gained as consumers where they did not gain as wage-earners. So that while on balance the evidence is strongly in favour of the view that working-class standards of living improved by less than the increase in national income per head would suggest over the first half of the nineteenth century; and while there is no doubt that certain sectors of the labouring poor suffered a serious deterioration in their earning-power because they were made redundant by technical progress, nevertheless it would be difficult to credit an overall decline in real incomes per wage-earning family in a period when aggregate real incomes for the nation as a whole were growing appreciably faster than population. In effect, the sustained growth of national product to which industrialisation gave rise tended to exert an upward pressure on working-class standards of living in three main ways, none of which implied a rise in the price of labour: (1) by creating more regular employment opportunities for all members of the family—this meant high earnings per year and per family even without a rise in wages per man-hour worked; (2) by creating more opportunities for labour specialisation and hence for the higher earnings that semi-skilled or skilled labour can command: here again the average earnings can rise without an increase in the wage rate because the composition of the labour force changes in favour of the higher earning group; and (3) the upward pressure on the workers' standard of living also operated through the reductions in the prices of consumer goods and the widening of the range of commodities which come within the budget of the working classes. Finally, of course, to the extent that it raised real purchasing power for the masses, industrialisation expanded the market for manufactured goods and so justified further increases in investment and output.

SUGGESTIONS FOR ADDITIONAL READING

Apart from the books and articles from which excerpts have been taken, there are several significant contributions to the argument about industrial living standards. The Hammonds' principal works are *The Town Labourer, 1760–1832* (1918); *The Skilled Labourer, 1760–1832* (1919); and *The Age of the Chartists* (1930).* The most relevant parts of John H. Clapham, *An Economic History of Modern Britain* (3 vols., Cambridge, 1926–38) are chapters i, ii, iv, v, vi, viii, xi, and, especially, xiv, in Volume I. Thomas S. Ashton's *The Industrial Revolution, 1760–1830* was published in 1948. Hobsbawm and Hartwell continued their argument in *Economic History Review*, XVI (1963), 119–46. Other articles of interest are W. Woodruff, "Capitalism and the Historians," *Journal of Economic History*, XVI (1956), 1–17; A. J. Taylor, "Progress and Poverty in Britain, 1780–1850: a Reappraisal," *History*, XLV (1960), 16–31; the mainly hostile review of Thompson's *Making of the English Working Class*, by R. Currie and R. M. Hartwell, in *Economic History Review*, XVIII (1965), 633–43; and the more sympathetic, though still critical, review of the same book, by J. D. Chambers, in *History*, LI (1966), 183–8.

On conditions among the rural classes, the following are of interest: John L. and Barbara Hammond, *The Village Labourer, 1760–1830* (1911); Edmund C. K. Gonner, *Common Land and Inclosure* (1912); Jonathan D. Chambers, *The Vale of Trent* (Cambridge, 1957); William G. Hoskins, *The Midland Peasant* (1957); and two articles by Chambers in *Economic History Review*, "Enclosure and the Small Landowner," First Series, X (1940), 118–27, and "Enclosures and Labour Supply in the Industrial Revolution," V (1953), 319–43.

A few other nineteenth-century observers call for mention: Michael W. Flinn, ed., *Report on the Sanitary Conditions of the Labouring Population of Great Britain by Edwin Chadwick, 1842* (Edinburgh, 1965); William Cobbett, *Rural Rides* (ed. G. D. H. and Margaret Cole, 3 vols., 1930); Friedrich Engels, *The Condition of the Working Class in England* (the most recent edition has been prepared by W. O. Henderson and W. H. Chaloner, Oxford, 1958; it has been criticised by Hobsbawm in *Labouring Men*, 1964, pp. 105–19); while Henry Mayhew's *London Labour and the London Poor* (1864, after earlier versions in serial and book form) has been abridged by Peter Quennell as *Mayhew's London* (1951). There is an anthology of contemporary accounts, very one-sided in the "pessimistic" direction, by E. Royston Pike, *Human Documents of the Industrial Revolution in Britain* (1966).

There are many general studies of social conditions during our period. David V. Glass and D. C. Eversley, *Population in History* (1965) contains essays by Marshall, Habbakuk, McKeown and Brown, Chambers, and the editors, all bearing upon Britain. On industrial conditions, the following throw light: Arthur Redford, *Labour Migration in England, 1800–50* (1926, revised edn. Manchester, 1964); Ivy Pinchbeck, *Women Workers and the Industrial Revolution* (1930); Frances Collier, *The Family Economy of the Working Classes in the Cotton Industry, 1784–1833* (Manchester, 1965, but based on work done forty years earlier); Neil J. Smelser, *Social Change in the Industrial Revolution* (1959), also on the cotton workers; and, more popular in style, Terry Coleman, *The Railway Navvies* (1965). Much of the substance of Sidney Pollard's two articles, "Factory Discipline in the Industrial Revolution, *Economic History Review*, XVI (1963),

---

*Unless otherwise stated, the place of publication of all books is London, and references to *Economic History Review* are to volumes in the Second Series.

254–71, and "The Factory Village in the Industrial Revolution," *English Historical Review*, LXXIX (1964), 513–31, is incorporated in his book *The Genesis of Modern Management* (1965), a striking study of industrialists' problems and of changing conditions for workers. See also Edward P. Thompson, "Time, Work-Discipline and Industrial Capitalism," *Past and Present*, XXXVIII (1967), 56–97. On rural conditions, additional material may be found in Edward W. Bovill, *English Country Life, 1780–1830* (Oxford, 1962); in Alfred J. Peacock, *Bread or Blood: a study of the agrarian riots in East Anglia, 1816* (1965); and, on the disturbances of 1830, Eric J. Hobsbawm and George Rudé, *Captain Swing* (1969). An interesting study, spanning rural as well as urban conditions, and demonstrating both the regional variety of diet and the extraordinarily limited range of food among the poorer workers, is John Burnett, *Plenty and Want: a social history of diet in England from 1815 to the present* (1966). See also Theodore C. Barker, J. C. McKenzie and John Yudkin, *Our Changing Fare* (1966). Other aspects of working-class life are covered by Asa Briggs, ed., *Chartist Studies* (1959); by his other collection, with John Saville, *Essays in Labour History* (1960); by John F. C. Harrison, *Learning and Living, 1790–1960: a study in the history of the English adult education movement* (1961); and by Mabel Tylecote, *The Mechanics' Institutes of Lancashire and Yorkshire before 1851* (Manchester, 1957). Something, too, can be seen through the eyes of two prominent social reformers: Richard A. Lewis, *Edwin Chadwick and the Public Health Movement, 1832–1854* (1952) and Royston Lambert, *Sir John Simon, 1816–1904, and English Social Administration* (1963).

For comparison with the earlier part of the eighteenth century, see Thomas S. Ashton, *Economic Fluctuations in England, 1700–1800* (Oxford, 1959); M. Dorothy George, *London Life in the Eighteenth Century* (1926); Dorothy Marshall, *English People in the Eighteenth Century* (1956); and Gordon E. Mingay, *English Landed Society in the Eighteenth Century* (1963). For similar comparison with the later years of the nineteenth century, see, apart from Checkland's book, Francis M. L. Thompson, *English Landed Society in the Nineteenth Century* (1963) and some of the essays in Hobsbawm's *Labouring Men* (1964).

General studies of the Industrial Revolution include: William H. B. Court, *A Concise Economic History of Britain from 1750 to Recent Times* (Cambridge, 1954); Thomas S. Ashton, *An Economic History of England: the Eighteenth Century* (1955); and the superb chapter by David S. Landes, who deals also with France and Germany, in Part I of *The Cambridge Economic History of Europe*, Vol. VI, *The Industrial Revolutions and After* (edited M. M. Postan and H. J. Habbakuk, Cambridge, 1965). Two interesting articles by R. M. Hartwell are "The Causes of the Industrial Revolution: an essay in methodology," *Economic History Review*, XVIII (1965), 164–82, and "Interpretations of the Industrial Revolution in England," *Journal of Economic History*, XIX (1959), 229–49.

Much used by other writers, especially for statistics, are Norman J. Silberling, "British Prices and Business Cycles, 1779–1850," *Review of Economic Statistics*, 1923; Elizabeth W. Gilboy, "The Cost of Living and Real Wages in Eighteenth Century England," *Review of Economic Statistics*, 1936; Rufus S. Tucker, "Real Wages of Artisans in London, 1729–1935," *Journal of American Statistical Association*, XXXI (1936); Werner Schlote, *British Overseas Trade from 1700 to the 1930s* (Translated W. H. Chaloner and W. O. Henderson, Oxford, 1952); Arthur D. Gayer, W. W. Rostow and A. J. Schwartz, *The Growth and Fluctuations of the British Economy, 1790–1850* (2 vols., Oxford, 1953); Walther G. Hoffmann, *British Industry, 1700–1950* (translated W. H. Chaloner and W. O. Henderson, Oxford, 1955); Ernest H. Phelps-Brown and S. V. Hopkins, "Seven Centuries of the Price of Consumables, compared with Builders' Wage Rates," *Economica*, XXIII (1956); and Brian R. Mitchell and Phyllis Deane, *Abstract of British*

Historical Statistics (1962). There is valuable pioneer work in George Wood, "The Course of Average Wages between 1790 and 1860," *Economic Journal*, 1899, and in Arthur L. Bowley, *Wages in the United Kingdom in the Nineteenth Century* (1900).

Studies of single regions or single industries are often helpful. Among the best are: William H. B. Court, *The Rise of the Midland Industries, 1600–1838* (1938); Conrad Gill and Asa Briggs, *History of Birmingham* (2 vols., 1952); Jonathan D. Chambers, *Nottinghamshire in the Eighteenth Century* (1932); William J. Rowe, *Cornwall in the Age of the Industrial Revolution* (Liverpool, 1953); Theodore C. Barker and J. R. Harris, *A Merseyside Town in the Industrial Revolution: St. Helens* (1954); Arthur H. Dodd, *The Industrial Revolution in North Wales* (1933); Arthur H. John, *Industrial Development in South Wales 1750–1850* (1950); Henry Hamilton, *The Industrial Revolution in Scotland* (1932); Thomas S. Ashton, *Iron and Steel in the Industrial Revolution* (1924); T. S. Ashton and J. Sykes, *The English Coal Industry of the Eighteenth Century* (Manchester, 1929); John P. Addis, *The Crawshay Dynasty* (Cardiff, 1957); T. S. Ashton, *An Eighteenth Century Industrialist: Peter Stubs of Warrington* (Manchester, 1939); Erich Roll, *An Early Experiment in Industrial Organisation . . . The Firm of Boulton and Watt, 1775–1805* (1930); William B. Crump, *The Leeds Woollen Industry, 1780–1820* (Leeds, 1931); and George Unwin, *Samuel Oldknow and the Arkwrights* (Manchester, 1924).

Relevant articles are likely to appear in the following journals: *Economic History Review, Journal of Economic History, Past and Present*, and perhaps in *Agricultural History Review, Journal of Transport History*, and *Victorian Studies*.

Two series of modern reprints should be mentioned, as being valuable for libraries even though far beyond the means of an average student. One is published by Frank Cass, and includes Ure, Kay and Mayhew. The other, which comes from Irish Universities Press, is a selection of Parliamentary Papers, which will include some of the great inquiries into social conditions. Although many of them exist, I make no mention of paperback editions; for it is hard to guarantee that copyright laws will permit any particular edition to be sold both in Britain and the United States.

Finally, five masterly books provide a broader historical background: David Thomson, *Europe since Napoleon* (1957), Eric J. Hobsbawm, *The Age of Revolution* (1962), and, on Britain alone, Hobsbawm, *Industry and Empire: an economic history of Britain since 1750* (1968), Asa Briggs, *The Age of Improvement* (1959), and George Kitson Clark, *The Making of Victorian England* (1962).